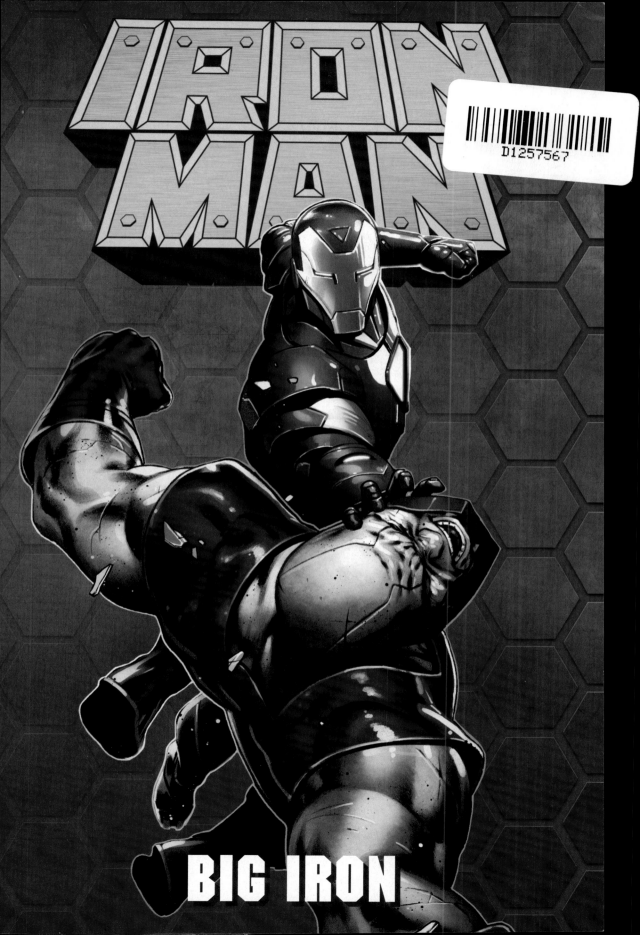

IRON MAN

BIG IRON

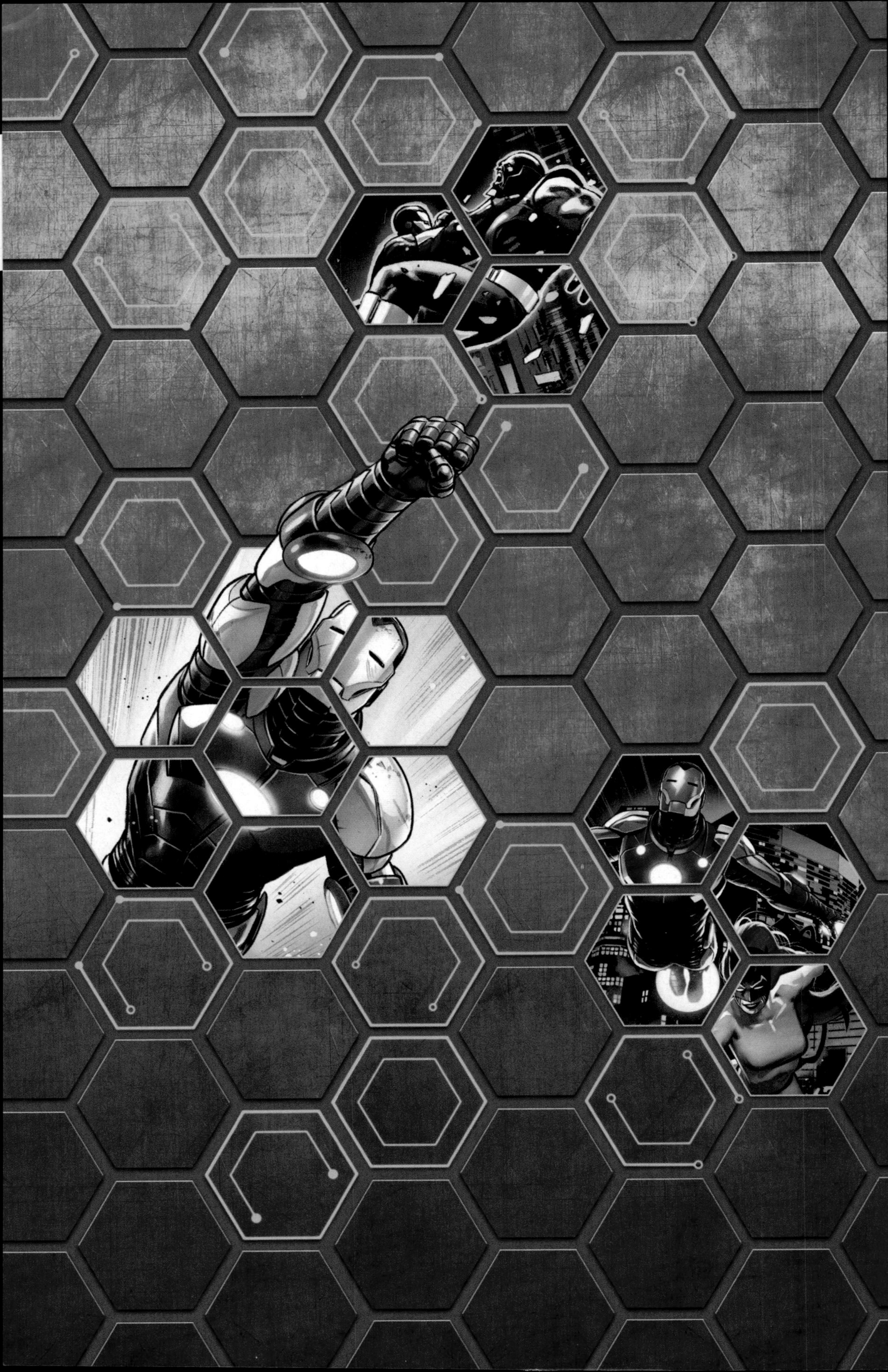

IRON MAN

BIG IRON

CHRISTOPHER CANTWELL
WRITER

CAFU
ARTIST

FRANK D'ARMATA
COLOR ARTIST

VC's JOE CARAMAGNA
LETTERER

ALEX ROSS
COVER ART

ALEX ROSS
IRON MAN ARMOR DESIGN

MARTIN BIRO
ASSISTANT EDITOR

ALANNA SMITH
ASSOCIATE EDITOR

TOM BREVOORT
EDITOR

IRON MAN CREATED BY STAN LEE, LARRY LIEBER, DON HECK & JACK KIRBY

COLLECTION EDITOR **JENNIFER GRÜNWALD**
ASSISTANT EDITOR **DANIEL KIRCHHOFFER**
ASSISTANT MANAGING EDITOR **MAIA LOY**
ASSISTANT MANAGING EDITOR **LISA MONTALBANO**
VP PRODUCTION & SPECIAL PROJECTS **JEFF YOUNGQUIST**
BOOK DESIGNER **STACIE ZUCKER**
SVP PRINT, SALES & MARKETING **DAVID GABRIEL**
EDITOR IN CHIEF **C.B. CEBULSKI**

ON MAN VOL. 1: BIG IRON. Contains material originally published in magazine form as IRON MAN (2020) #1-5. First printing 2021. ISBN 978-1-302-92551-2. Published by MARVEL WORLDWIDE, INC., a subsidiary of MARVEL TERTAINMENT, LLC. OFFICE OF PUBLICATION: 1290 Avenue of the Americas, New York, NY 10104. © 2021 MARVEL No similarity between any of the names, characters, persons, and/or institutions in this magazine with those any living or dead person or institution is intended, and any such similarity which may exist is purely coincidental. **Printed in Canada.** KEVIN FEIGE, Chief Creative Officer; DAN BUCKLEY, President, Marvel Entertainment; JOE JESADA, EVP & Creative Director; DAVID BOGART, Associate Publisher & SVP of Talent Affairs; TOM BREVOORT, VP, Executive Editor; NICK LOWE, Executive Editor, VP of Content, Digital Publishing; DAVID GABRIEL, VP of Print & gital Publishing; JEFF YOUNGQUIST, VP of Production & Special Projects; ALEX MORALES, Director of Publishing Operations; DAN EDINGTON, Managing Editor; RICKEY PURDIN, Director of Talent Relations; JENNIFER GRÜNWALD, nior Editor, Special Projects; SUSAN CRESPI, Production Manager; STAN LEE, Chairman Emeritus. For information regarding advertising in Marvel Comics or on Marvel.com, please contact Vit DeBellis, Custom Solutions & egrated Advertising Manager, at vdebellis@marvel.com. For Marvel subscription inquiries, please call 888-511-5480. **Manufactured between 1/22/2021 and 2/23/2021 by SOLISCO PRINTERS, SCOTT, QC, CANADA.**

987654321

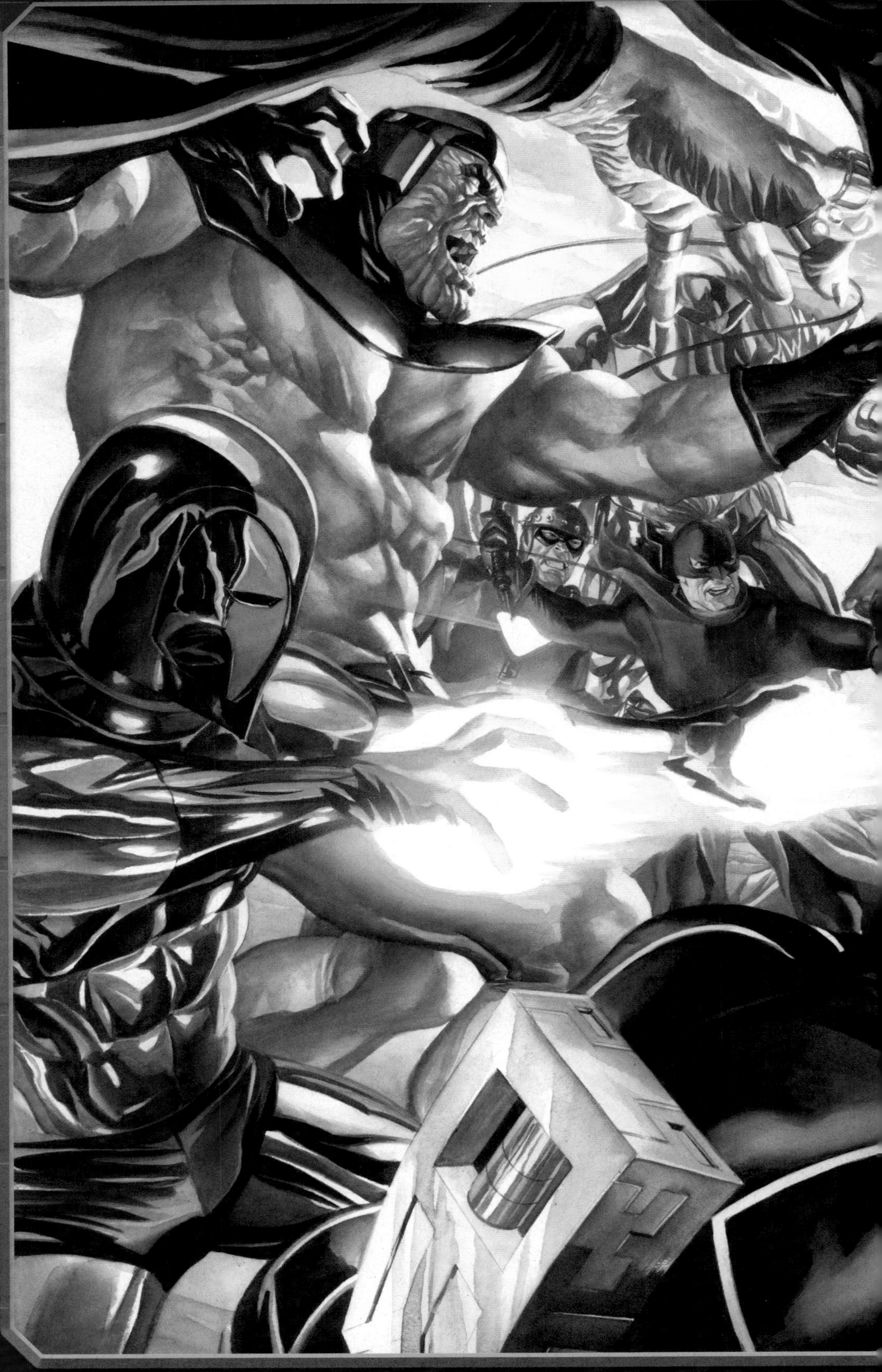

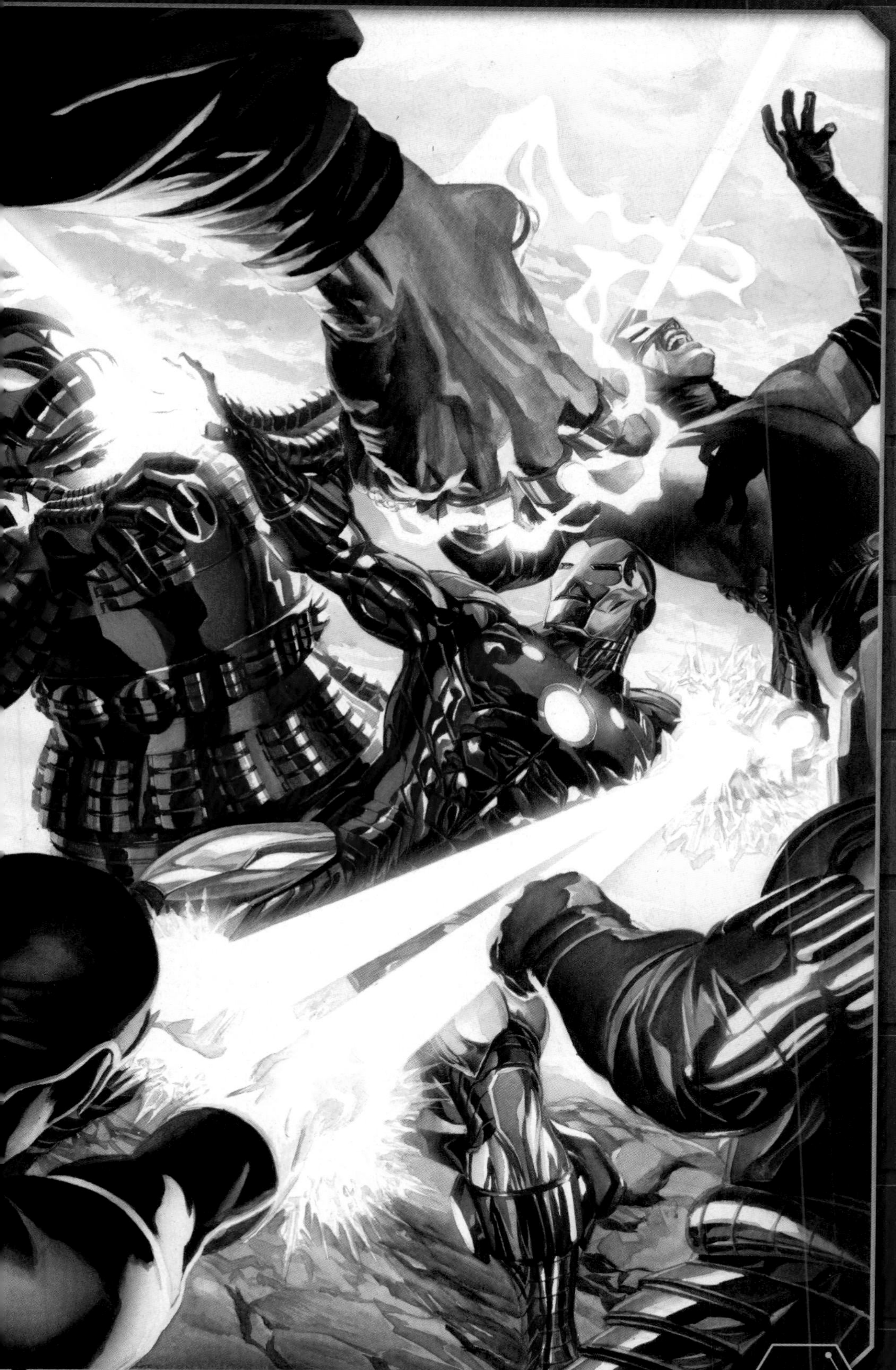

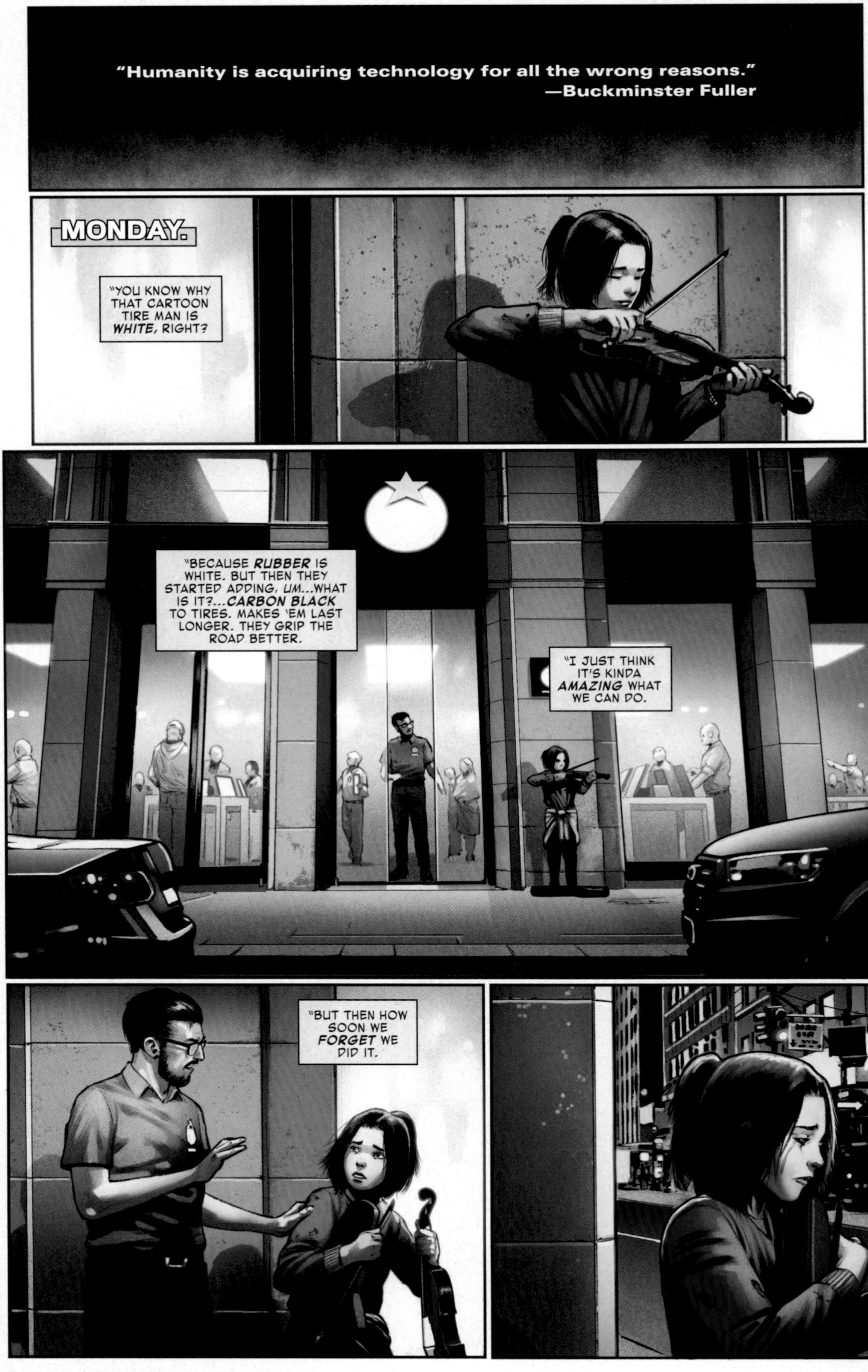
"Humanity is acquiring technology for all the wrong reasons."
—Buckminster Fuller
MONDAY.
"YOU KNOW WHY THAT CARTOON TIRE MAN IS *WHITE*, RIGHT?
"BECAUSE *RUBBER* IS WHITE. BUT THEN THEY STARTED ADDING, *UM*...WHAT IS IT?...*CARBON BLACK* TO TIRES. MAKES 'EM LAST LONGER. THEY GRIP THE ROAD BETTER.
"I JUST THINK IT'S KINDA *AMAZING* WHAT WE CAN DO.
"BUT THEN HOW SOON WE *FORGET* WE DID IT.

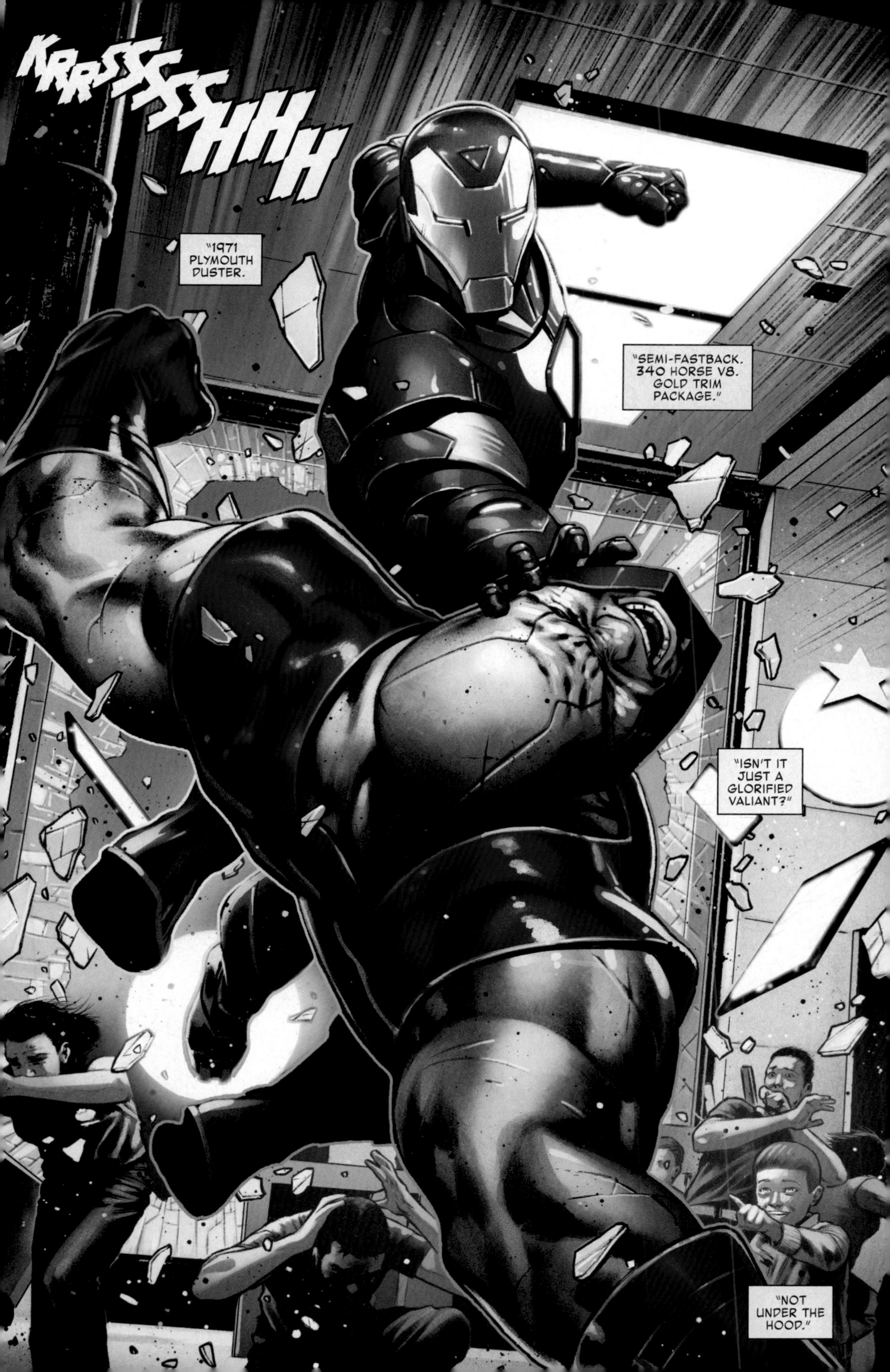
KRRSSSSSHHHH
"1971 PLYMOUTH DUSTER.
"SEMI-FASTBACK. 340 HORSE V8. GOLD TRIM PACKAGE."
"ISN'T IT JUST A GLORIFIED VALIANT?"
"NOT UNDER THE HOOD."

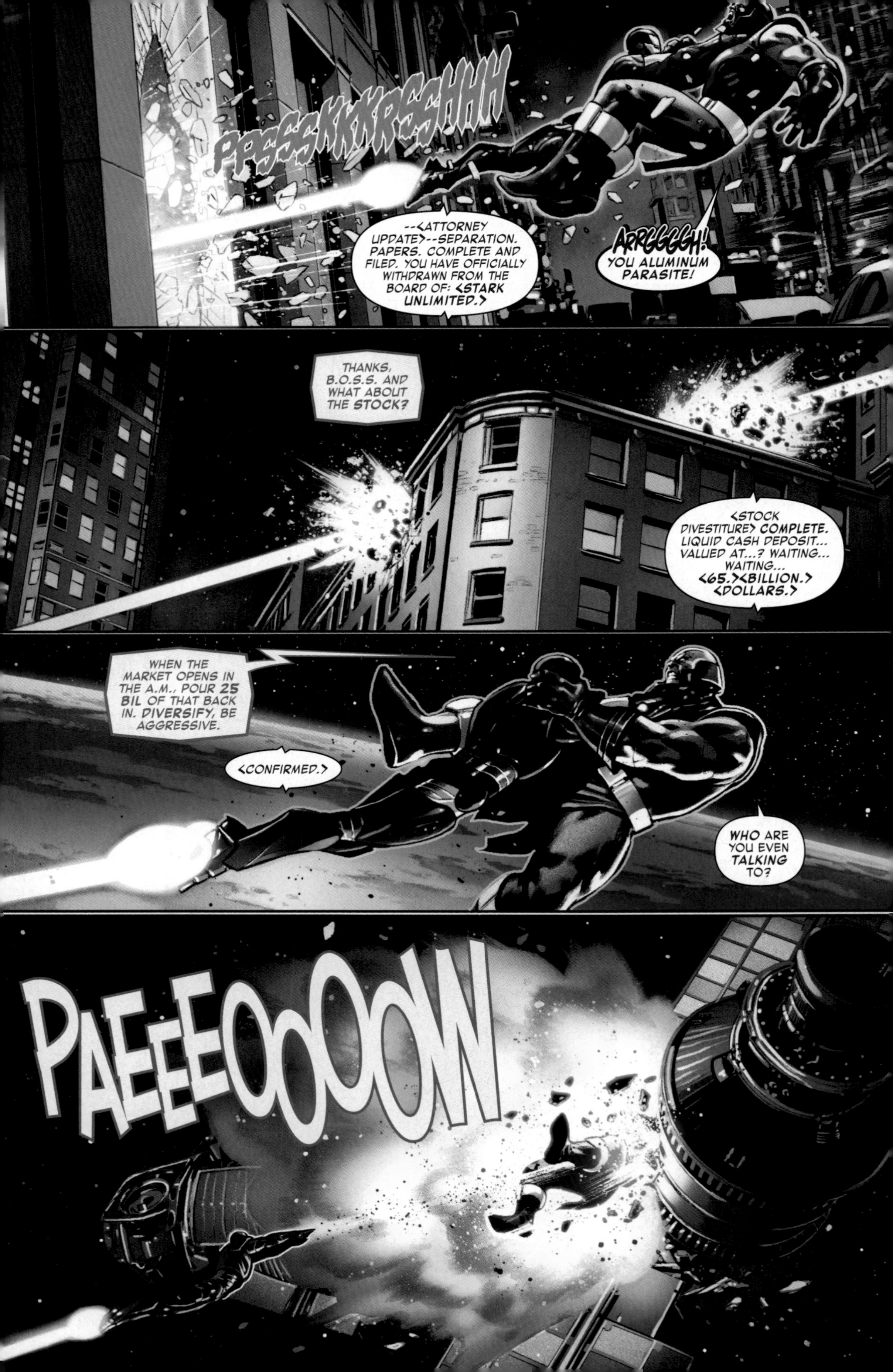
PPSSSKKKRSSHHH
--<ATTORNEY UPDATE>--SEPARATION. PAPERS. COMPLETE AND FILED. YOU HAVE OFFICIALLY WITHDRAWN FROM THE BOARD OF: <STARK UNLIMITED.>
ARRGGGGH! YOU ALUMINUM PARASITE!
THANKS, B.O.S.S. AND WHAT ABOUT THE STOCK?
<STOCK DIVESTITURE> COMPLETE. LIQUID CASH DEPOSIT... VALUED AT...? WAITING... WAITING... <65.><BILLION.> <DOLLARS.>
WHEN THE MARKET OPENS IN THE A.M., POUR 25 BIL OF THAT BACK IN. DIVERSIFY, BE AGGRESSIVE.
<CONFIRMED.>
WHO ARE YOU EVEN TALKING TO?
PAEEEOOOOW

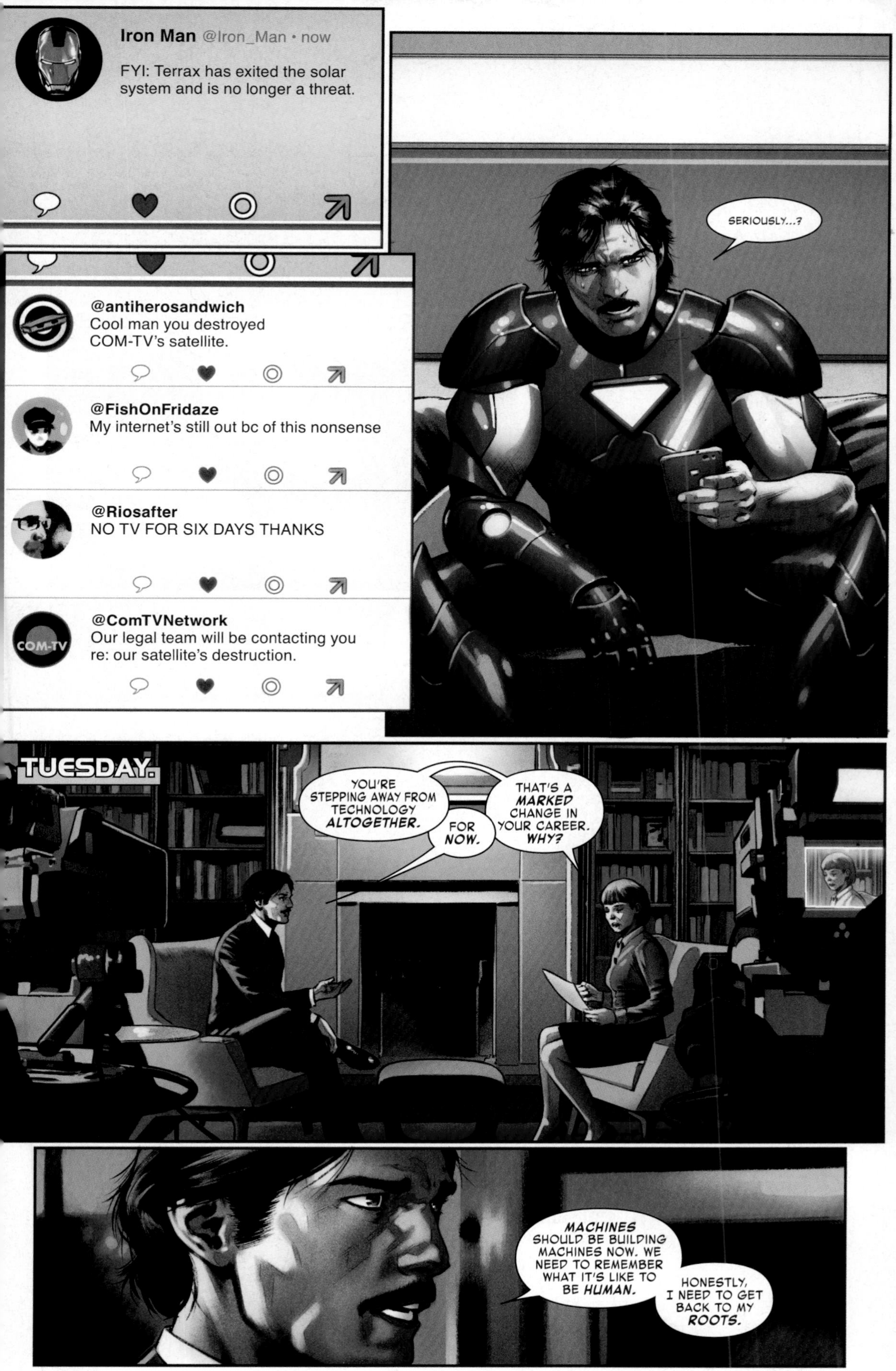
Iron Man @Iron_Man • now
FYI: Terrax has exited the solar system and is no longer a threat.
SERIOUSLY...?
@antiherosandwich
Cool man you destroyed COM-TV's satellite.
@FishOnFridaze
My internet's still out bc of this nonsense
@Riosafter
NO TV FOR SIX DAYS THANKS
@ComTVNetwork
Our legal team will be contacting you re: our satellite's destruction.
COM-TV
TUESDAY.
YOU'RE STEPPING AWAY FROM TECHNOLOGY ALTOGETHER.
FOR NOW.
THAT'S A MARKED CHANGE IN YOUR CAREER. WHY?
MACHINES SHOULD BE BUILDING MACHINES NOW. WE NEED TO REMEMBER WHAT IT'S LIKE TO BE HUMAN.
HONESTLY, I NEED TO GET BACK TO MY ROOTS.

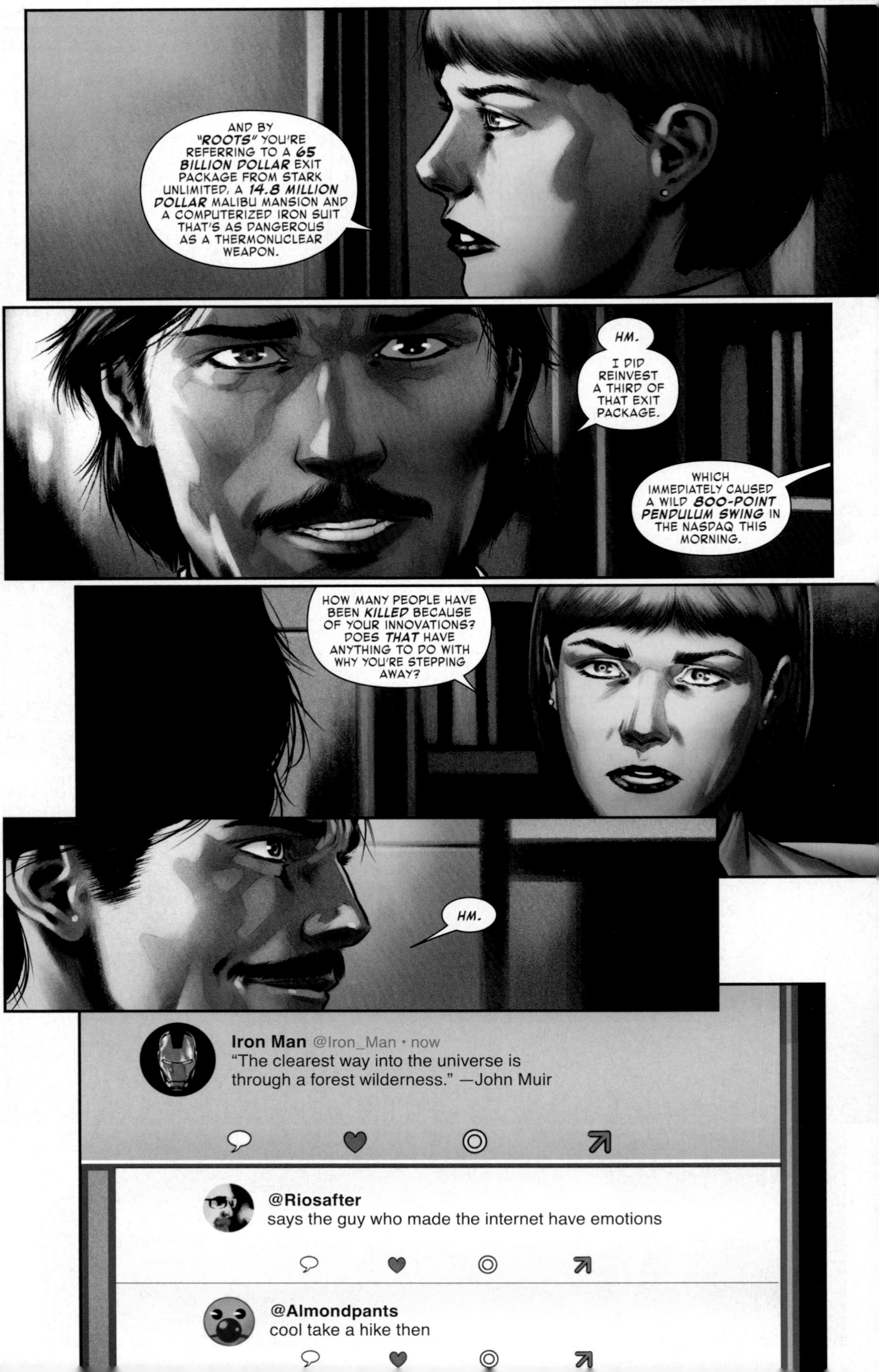
AND BY "ROOTS" YOU'RE REFERRING TO A 65 BILLION DOLLAR EXIT PACKAGE FROM STARK UNLIMITED, A 14.8 MILLION DOLLAR MALIBU MANSION AND A COMPUTERIZED IRON SUIT THAT'S AS DANGEROUS AS A THERMONUCLEAR WEAPON.
HM.
I DID REINVEST A THIRD OF THAT EXIT PACKAGE.
WHICH IMMEDIATELY CAUSED A WILD 800-POINT PENDULUM SWING IN THE NASDAQ THIS MORNING.
HOW MANY PEOPLE HAVE BEEN KILLED BECAUSE OF YOUR INNOVATIONS? DOES THAT HAVE ANYTHING TO DO WITH WHY YOU'RE STEPPING AWAY?
HM.
Iron Man @Iron_Man • now
"The clearest way into the universe is through a forest wilderness." —John Muir
@Riosafter
says the guy who made the internet have emotions
@Almondpants
cool take a hike then

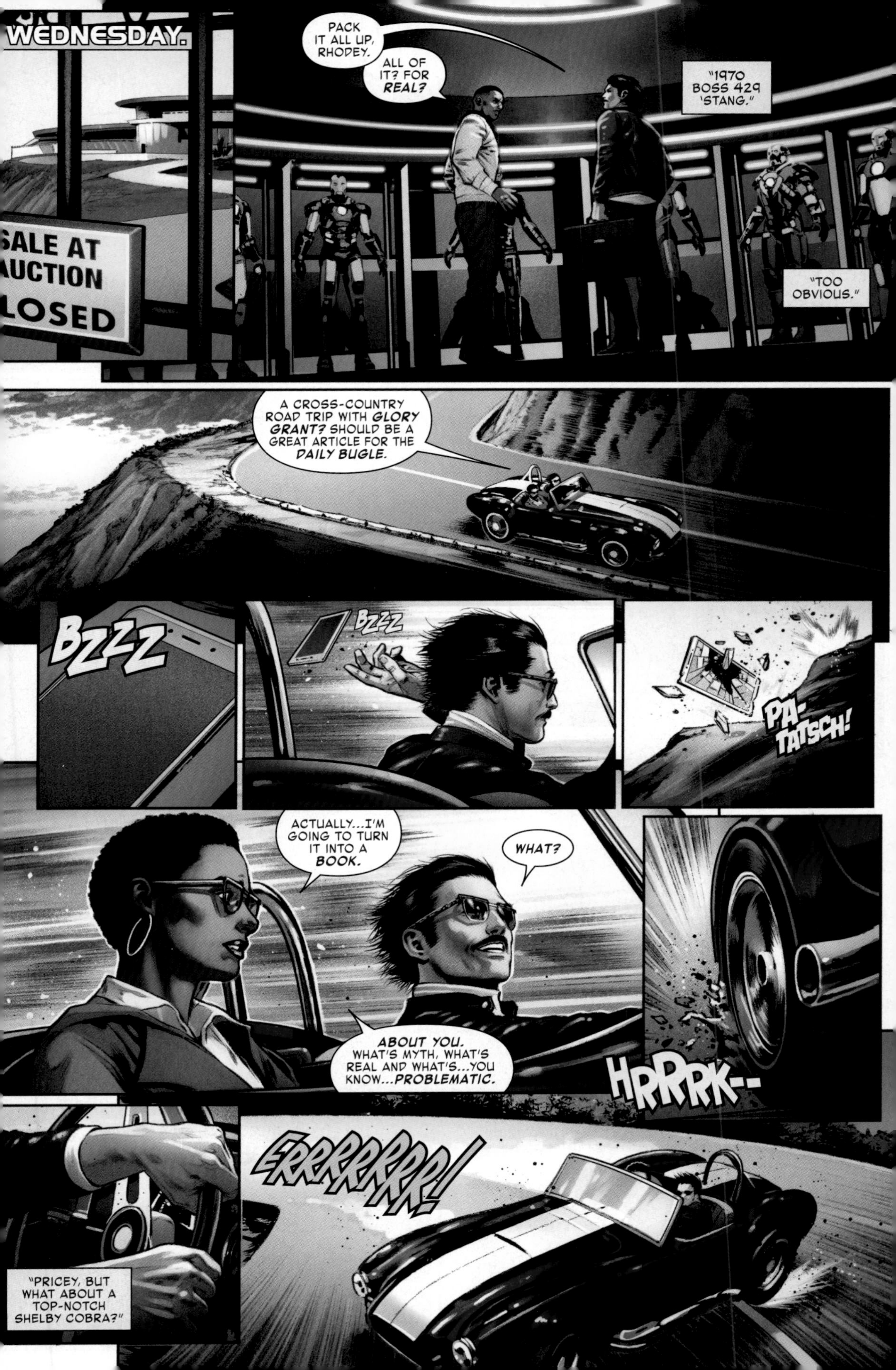
WEDNESDAY.
SALE AT AUCTION LOSED
PACK IT ALL UP, RHODEY.
ALL OF IT? FOR REAL?
"1970 BOSS 429 'STANG."
"TOO OBVIOUS."
A CROSS-COUNTRY ROAD TRIP WITH GLORY GRANT? SHOULD BE A GREAT ARTICLE FOR THE DAILY BUGLE.
BZZZ
BZZZ
PA-TATSCH!
ACTUALLY...I'M GOING TO TURN IT INTO A BOOK.
WHAT?
ABOUT YOU. WHAT'S MYTH, WHAT'S REAL AND WHAT'S...YOU KNOW...PROBLEMATIC.
HRRRK--
"PRICEY, BUT WHAT ABOUT A TOP-NOTCH SHELBY COBRA?"
ERRRRRRR!

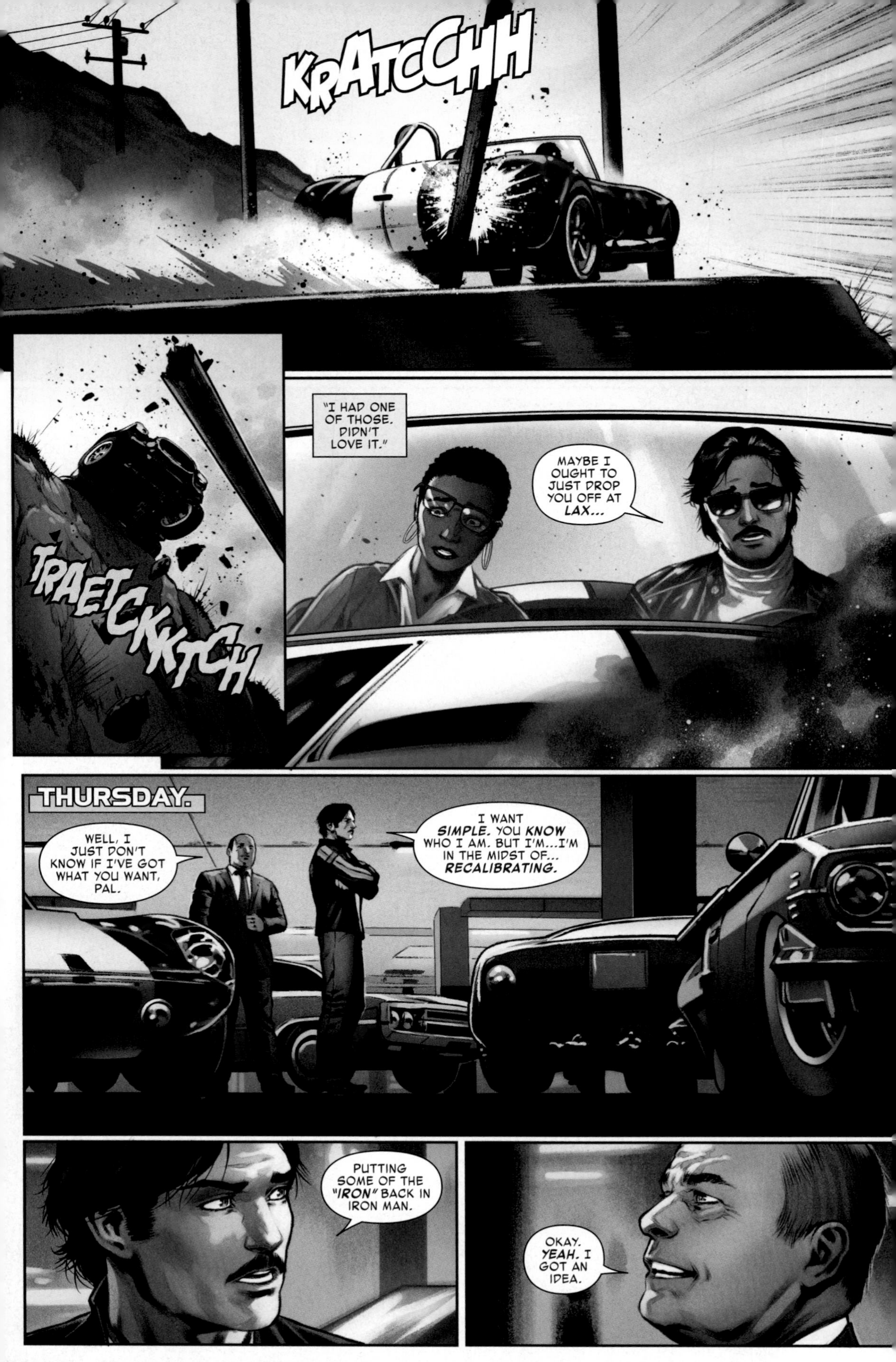
KRATCCHH
TRAETCKKTCH
"I HAD ONE OF THOSE. DIDN'T LOVE IT."
MAYBE I OUGHT TO JUST DROP YOU OFF AT LAX...
THURSDAY.
WELL, I JUST DON'T KNOW IF I'VE GOT WHAT YOU WANT, PAL.
I WANT SIMPLE. YOU KNOW WHO I AM. BUT I'M...I'M IN THE MIDST OF... RECALIBRATING.
PUTTING SOME OF THE "IRON" BACK IN IRON MAN.
OKAY. YEAH. I GOT AN IDEA.

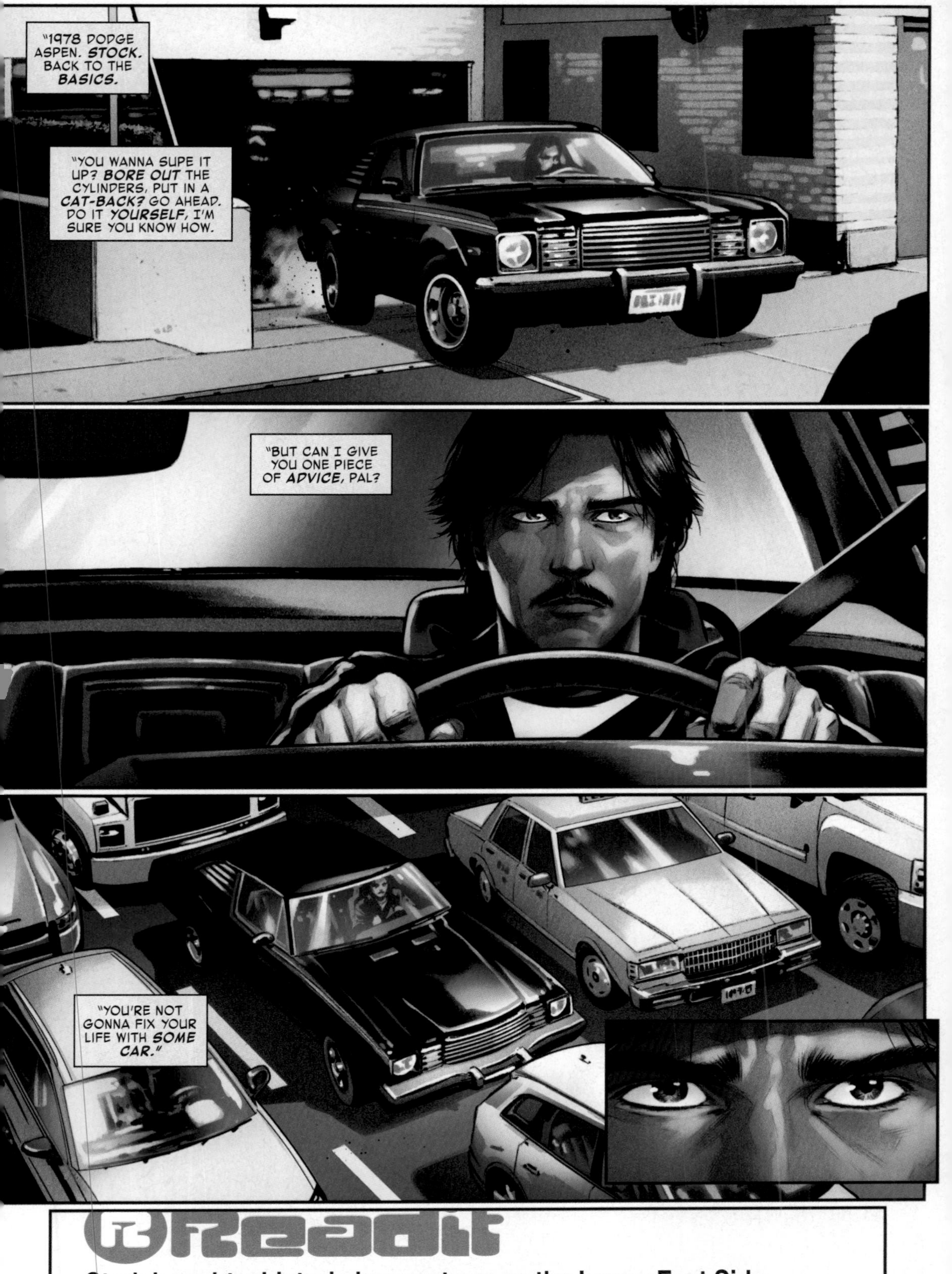
"1978 DODGE ASPEN. STOCK. BACK TO THE BASICS.
"YOU WANNA SUPE IT UP? BORE OUT THE CYLINDERS, PUT IN A CAT-BACK? GO AHEAD. DO IT YOURSELF, I'M SURE YOU KNOW HOW.
"BUT CAN I GIVE YOU ONE PIECE OF ADVICE, PAL?
"YOU'RE NOT GONNA FIX YOUR LIFE WITH SOME CAR."

Readit

Stark bought a historic brownstone on the Lower East Side.

↕ 100 bucks says he guts it.

↕ He's about as New York as Malibu Barbie.

↕ Bump

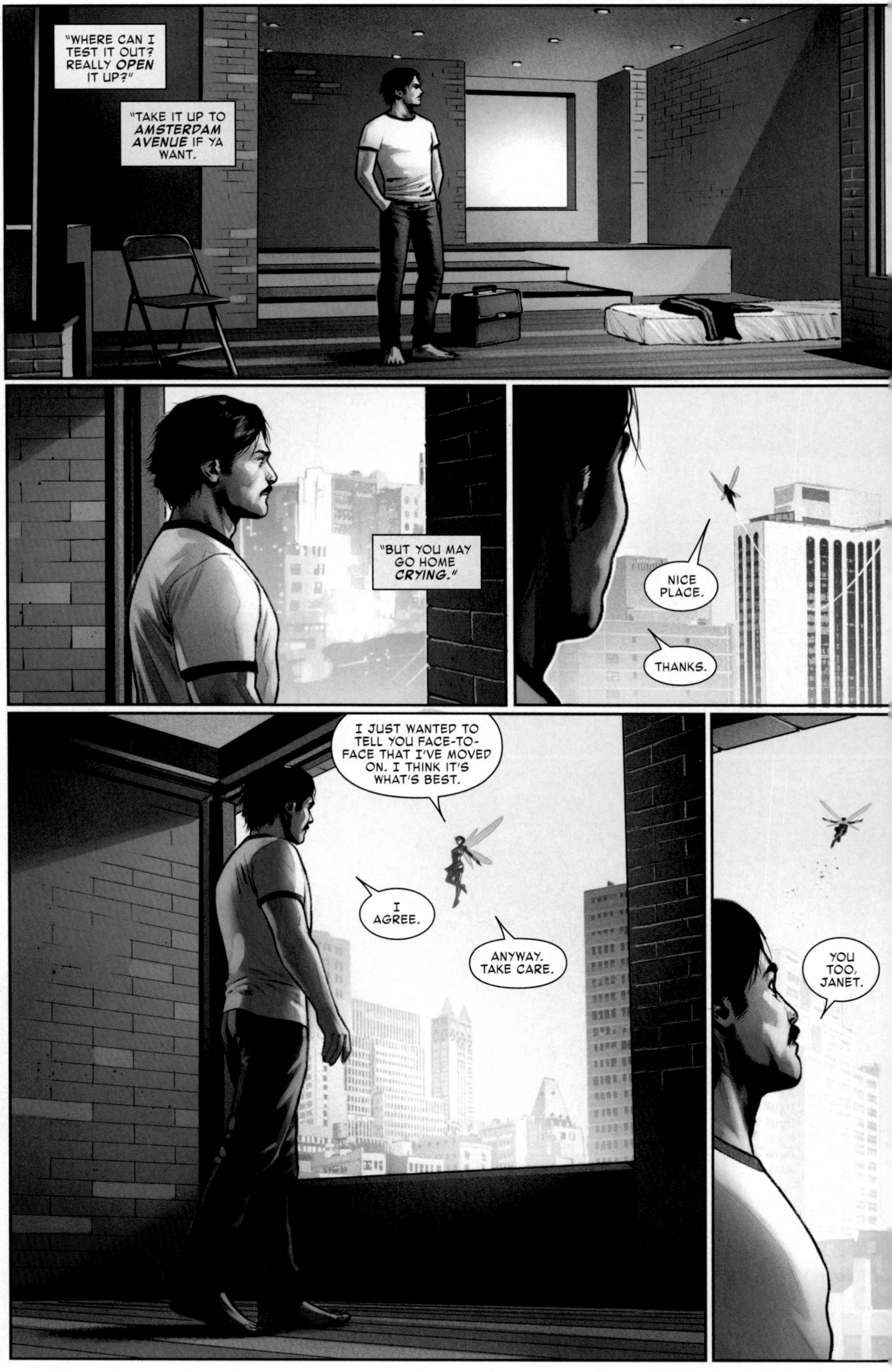
"WHERE CAN I TEST IT OUT? REALLY OPEN IT UP?"
"TAKE IT UP TO AMSTERDAM AVENUE IF YA WANT.
"BUT YOU MAY GO HOME CRYING."
NICE PLACE.
THANKS.
I JUST WANTED TO TELL YOU FACE-TO-FACE THAT I'VE MOVED ON. I THINK IT'S WHAT'S BEST.
I AGREE.
ANYWAY. TAKE CARE.
YOU TOO, JANET.

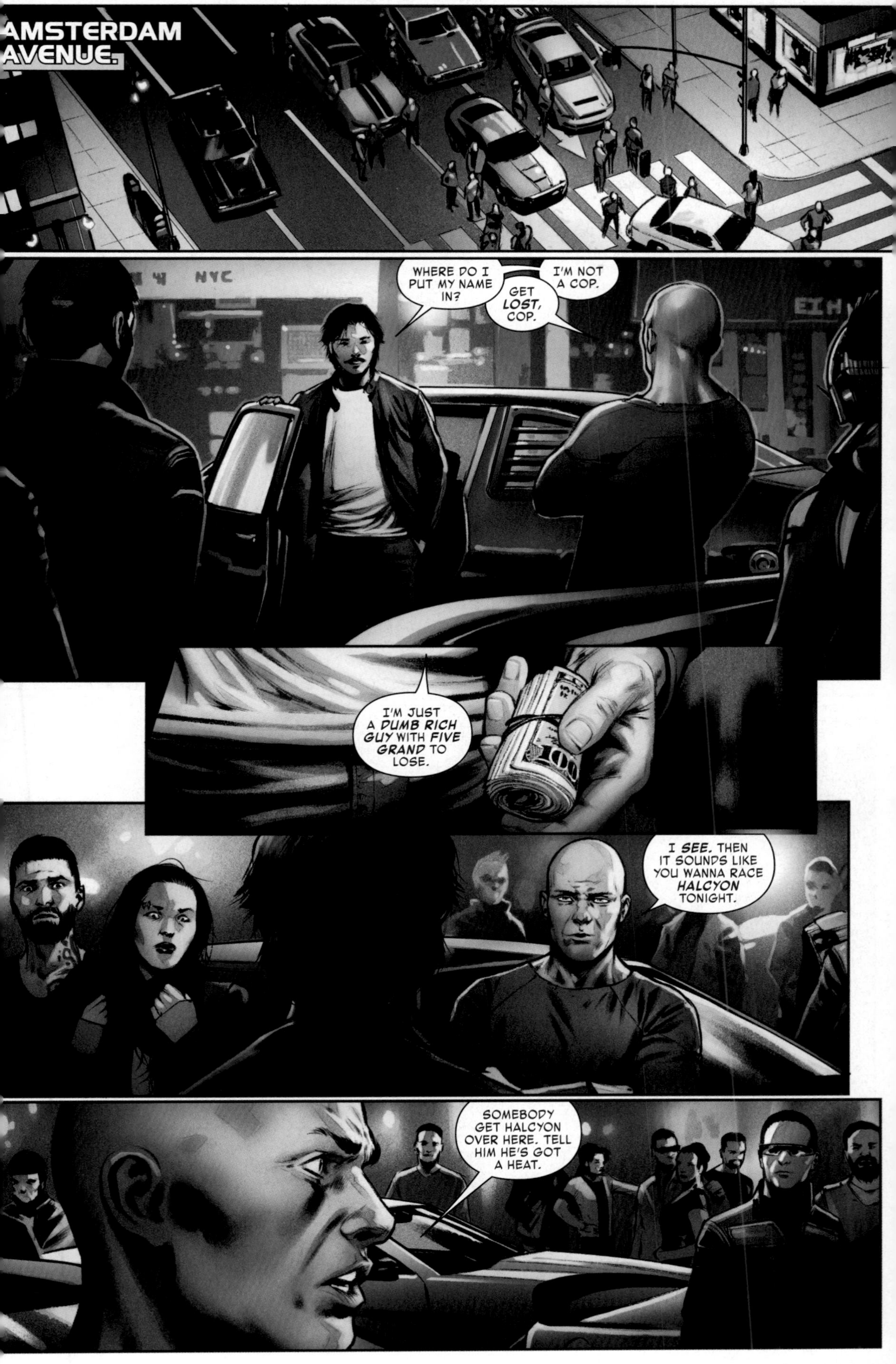
AMSTERDAM AVENUE.
WHERE DO I PUT MY NAME IN?
GET LOST, COP.
I'M NOT A COP.
I'M JUST A DUMB RICH GUY WITH FIVE GRAND TO LOSE.
I SEE. THEN IT SOUNDS LIKE YOU WANNA RACE HALCYON TONIGHT.
SOMEBODY GET HALCYON OVER HERE. TELL HIM HE'S GOT A HEAT.
NYC

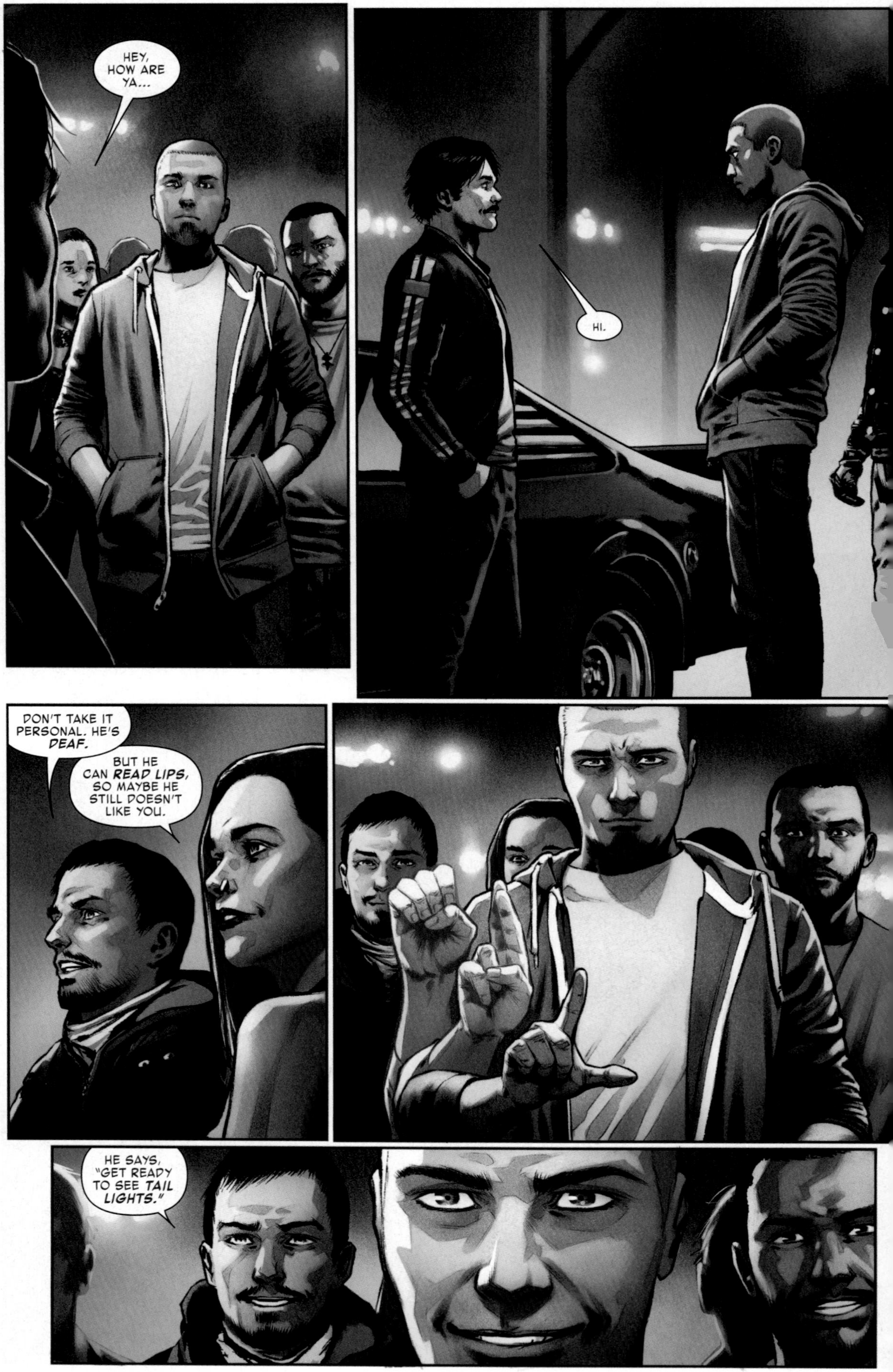
HEY, HOW ARE YA...
HI.
DON'T TAKE IT PERSONAL. HE'S *DEAF.*
BUT HE CAN *READ LIPS,* SO MAYBE HE STILL DOESN'T LIKE YOU.
HE SAYS, "GET READY TO SEE *TAIL LIGHTS.*"

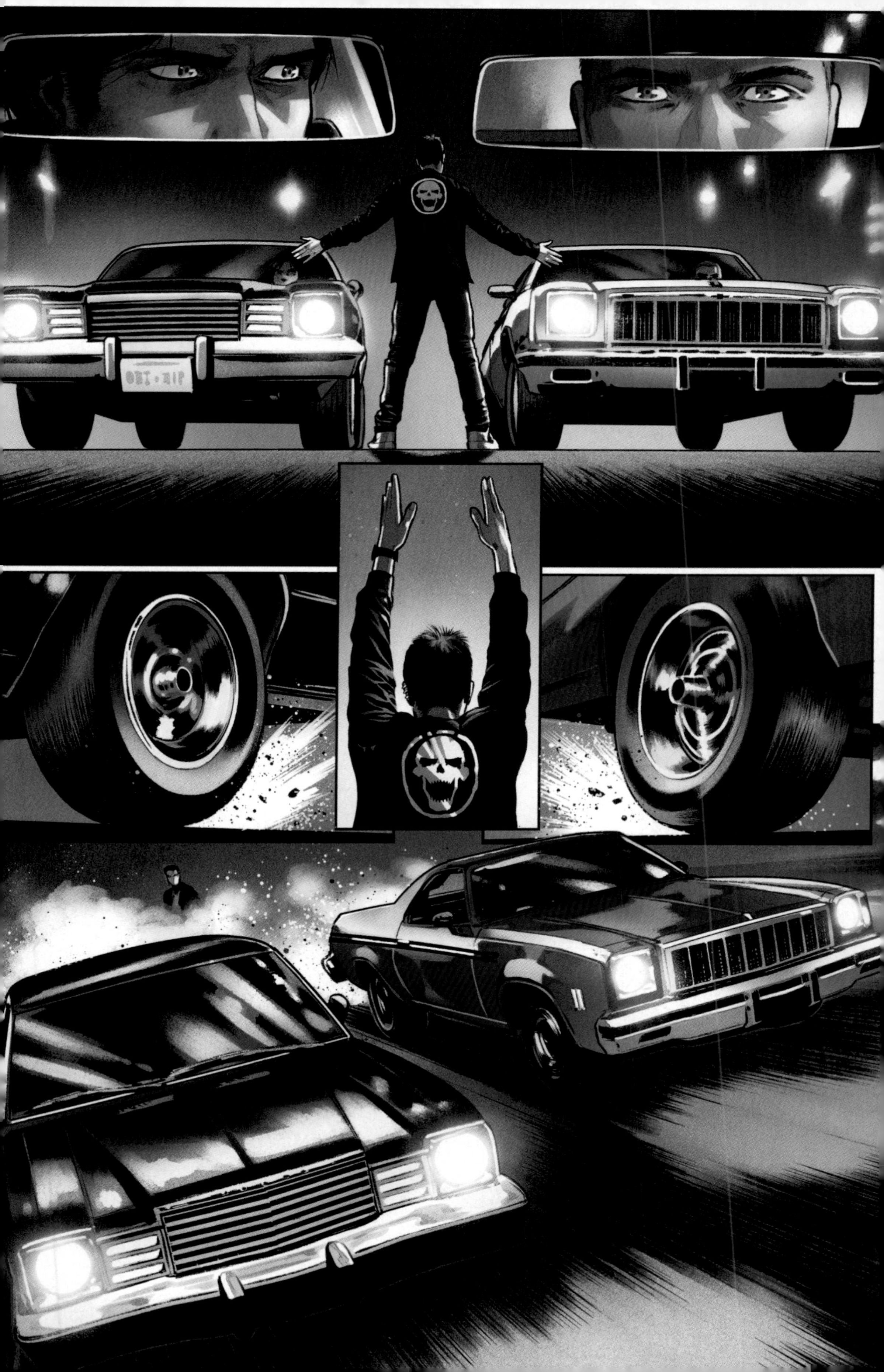

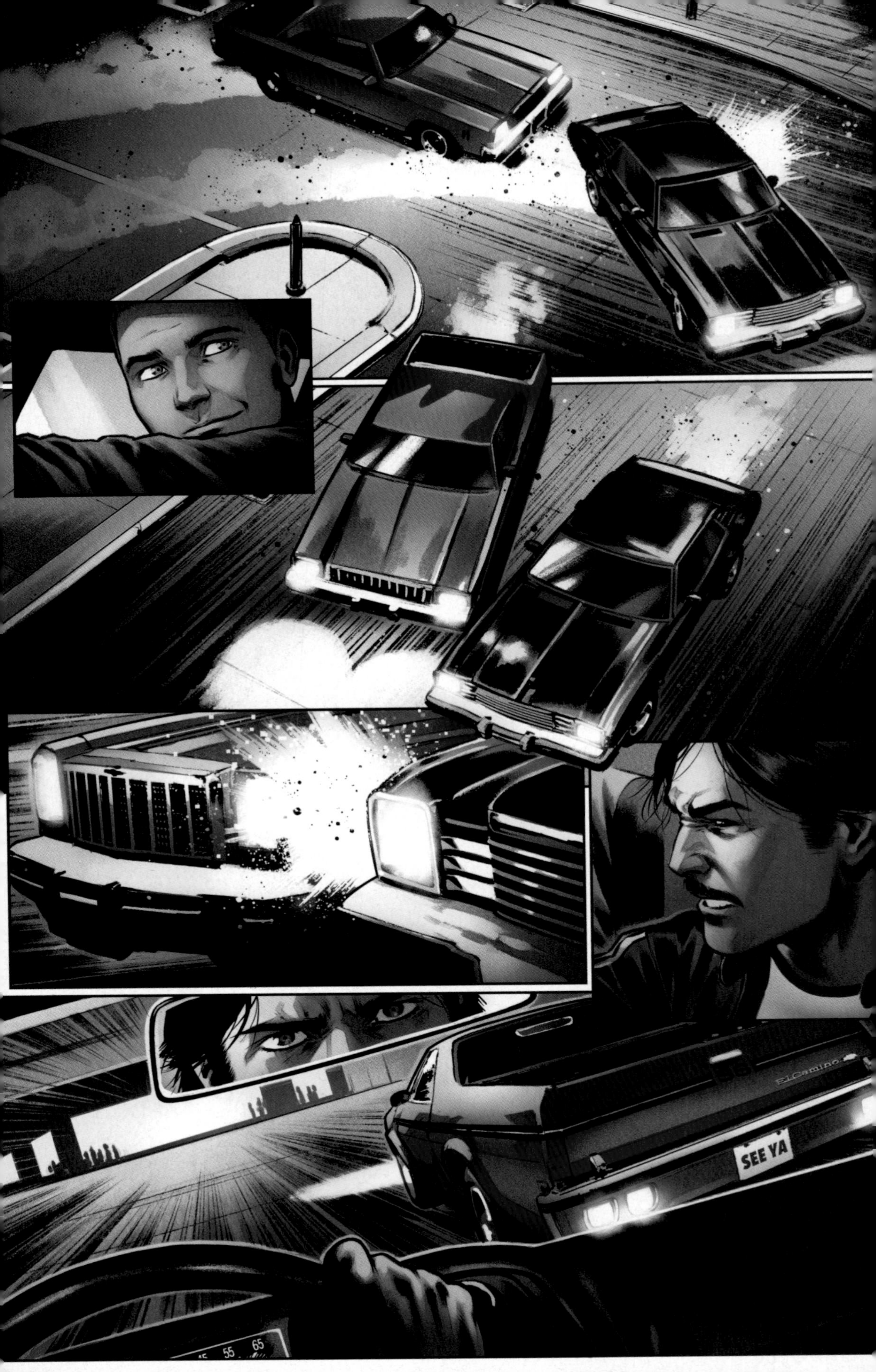
El Camino
SEE YA
55
65

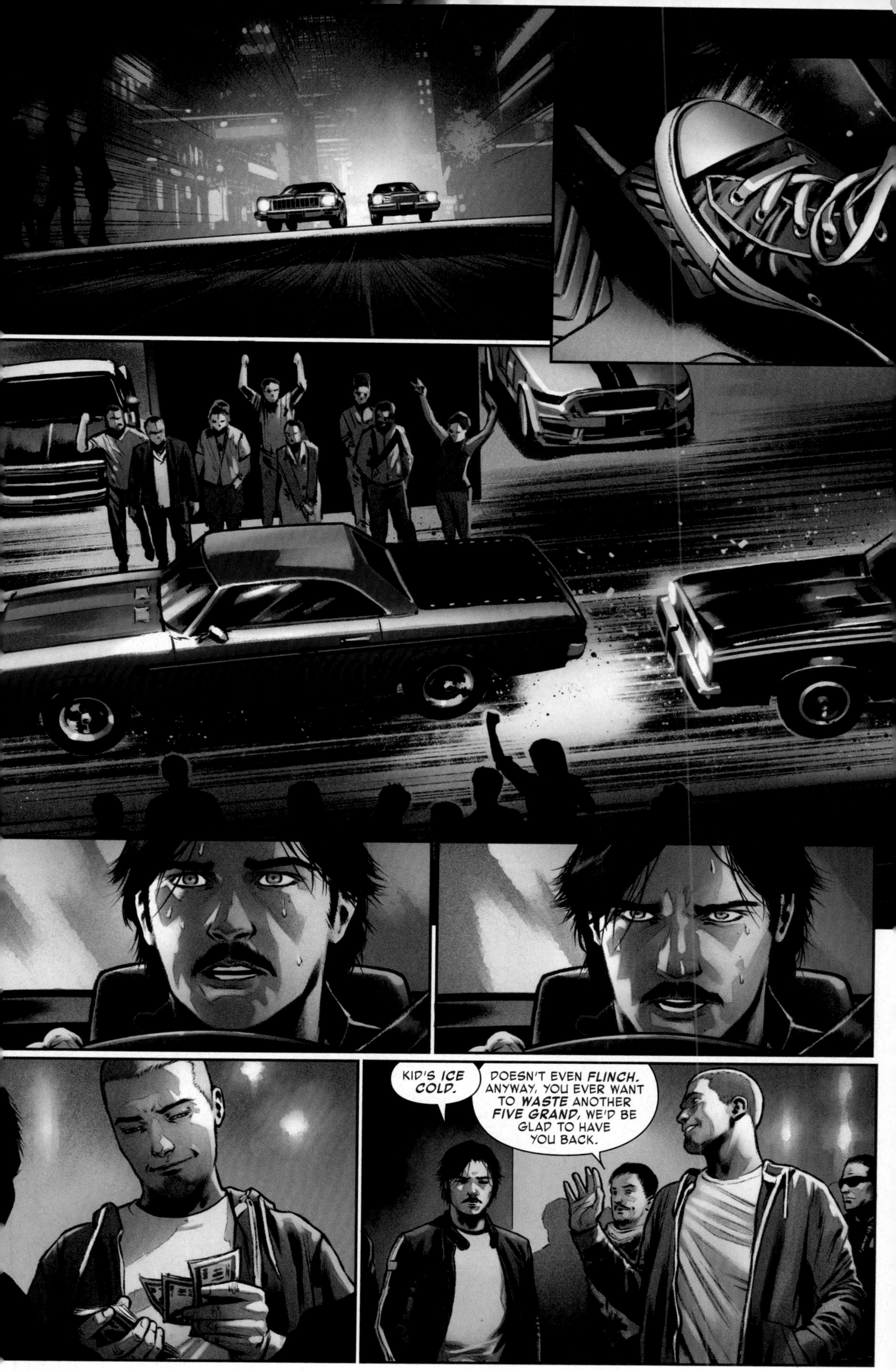
KID'S ICE COLD.
DOESN'T EVEN FLINCH. ANYWAY, YOU EVER WANT TO WASTE ANOTHER FIVE GRAND, WE'D BE GLAD TO HAVE YOU BACK.

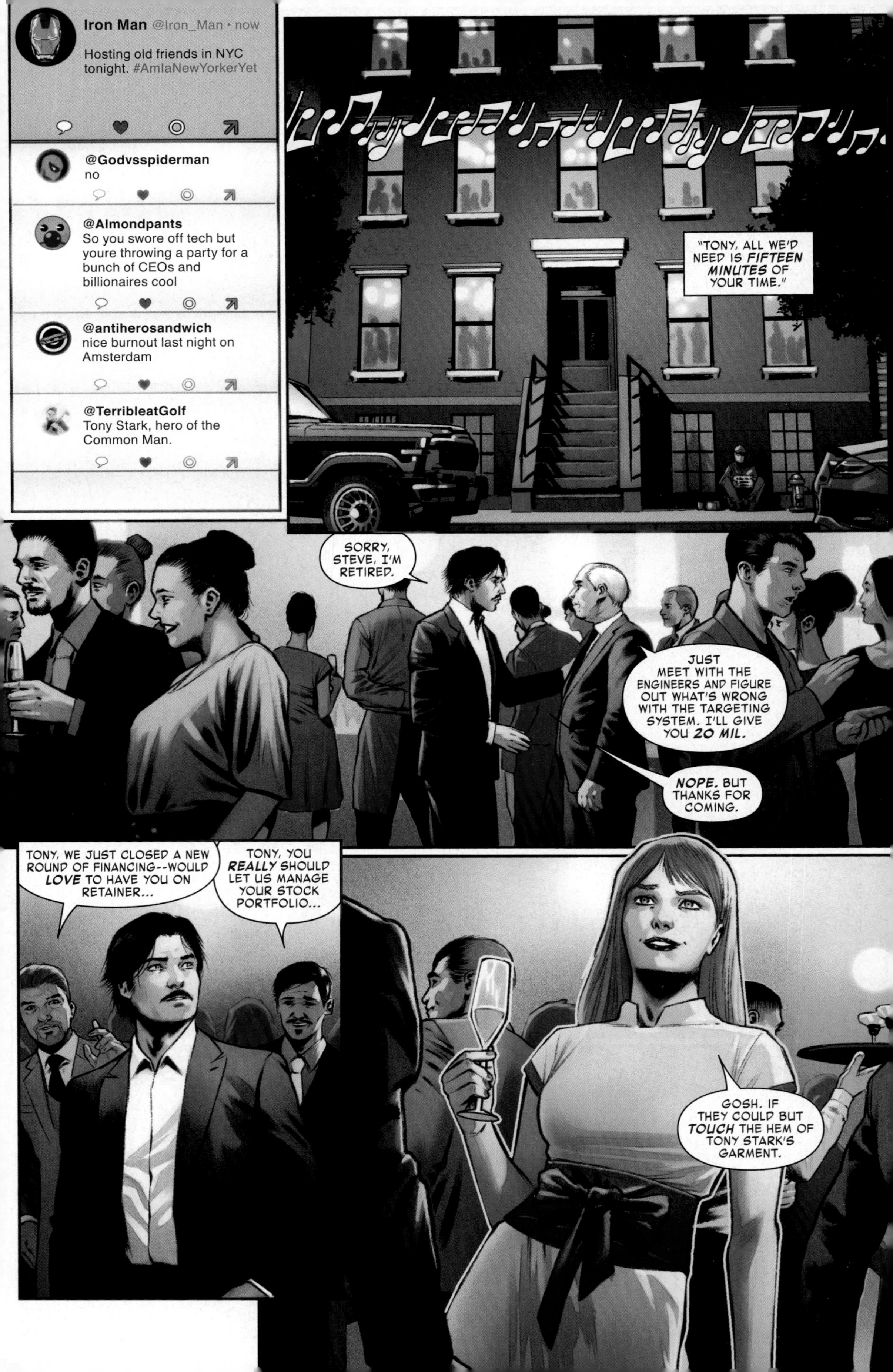
Iron Man @Iron_Man • now
Hosting old friends in NYC tonight. #AmIaNewYorkerYet
@Godvsspiderman
no
@Almondpants
So you swore off tech but youre throwing a party for a bunch of CEOs and billionaires cool
@antiherosandwich
nice burnout last night on Amsterdam
@TerribleatGolf
Tony Stark, hero of the Common Man.
"TONY, ALL WE'D NEED IS FIFTEEN MINUTES OF YOUR TIME."
SORRY, STEVE, I'M RETIRED.
JUST MEET WITH THE ENGINEERS AND FIGURE OUT WHAT'S WRONG WITH THE TARGETING SYSTEM. I'LL GIVE YOU 20 MIL.
NOPE. BUT THANKS FOR COMING.
TONY, WE JUST CLOSED A NEW ROUND OF FINANCING--WOULD LOVE TO HAVE YOU ON RETAINER...
TONY, YOU REALLY SHOULD LET US MANAGE YOUR STOCK PORTFOLIO...
GOSH. IF THEY COULD BUT TOUCH THE HEM OF TONY STARK'S GARMENT.

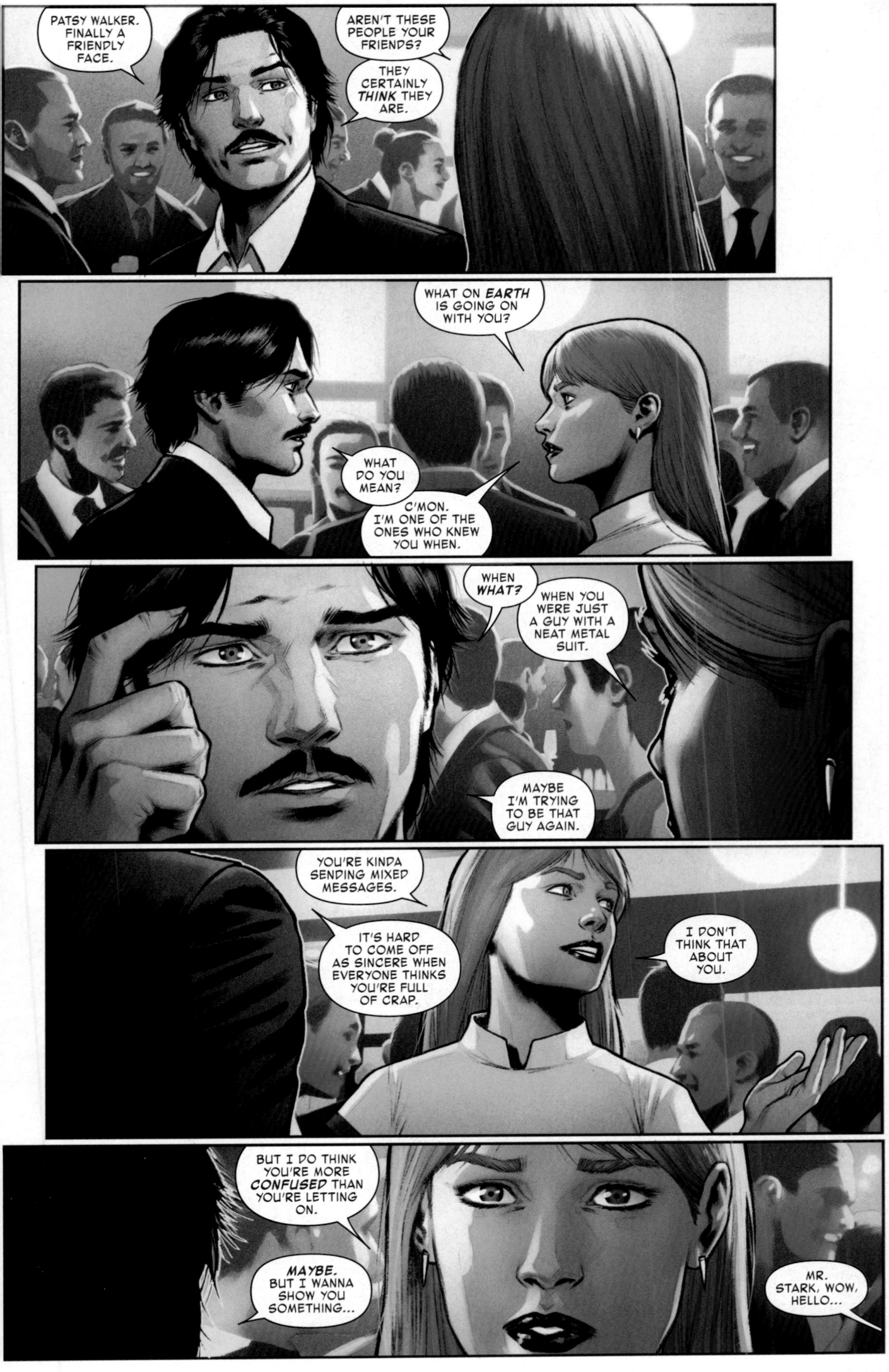
PATSY WALKER. FINALLY A FRIENDLY FACE.
AREN'T THESE PEOPLE YOUR FRIENDS?
THEY CERTAINLY *THINK* THEY ARE.
WHAT ON *EARTH* IS GOING ON WITH YOU?
WHAT DO YOU MEAN?
C'MON. I'M ONE OF THE ONES WHO KNEW YOU WHEN.
WHEN *WHAT?*
WHEN YOU WERE JUST A GUY WITH A NEAT METAL SUIT.
MAYBE I'M TRYING TO BE THAT GUY AGAIN.
YOU'RE KINDA SENDING MIXED MESSAGES.
IT'S HARD TO COME OFF AS SINCERE WHEN EVERYONE THINKS YOU'RE FULL OF CRAP.
I DON'T THINK THAT ABOUT YOU.
BUT I DO THINK YOU'RE MORE *CONFUSED* THAN YOU'RE LETTING ON.
MAYBE. BUT I WANNA SHOW YOU SOMETHING...
MR. STARK, WOW, HELLO...

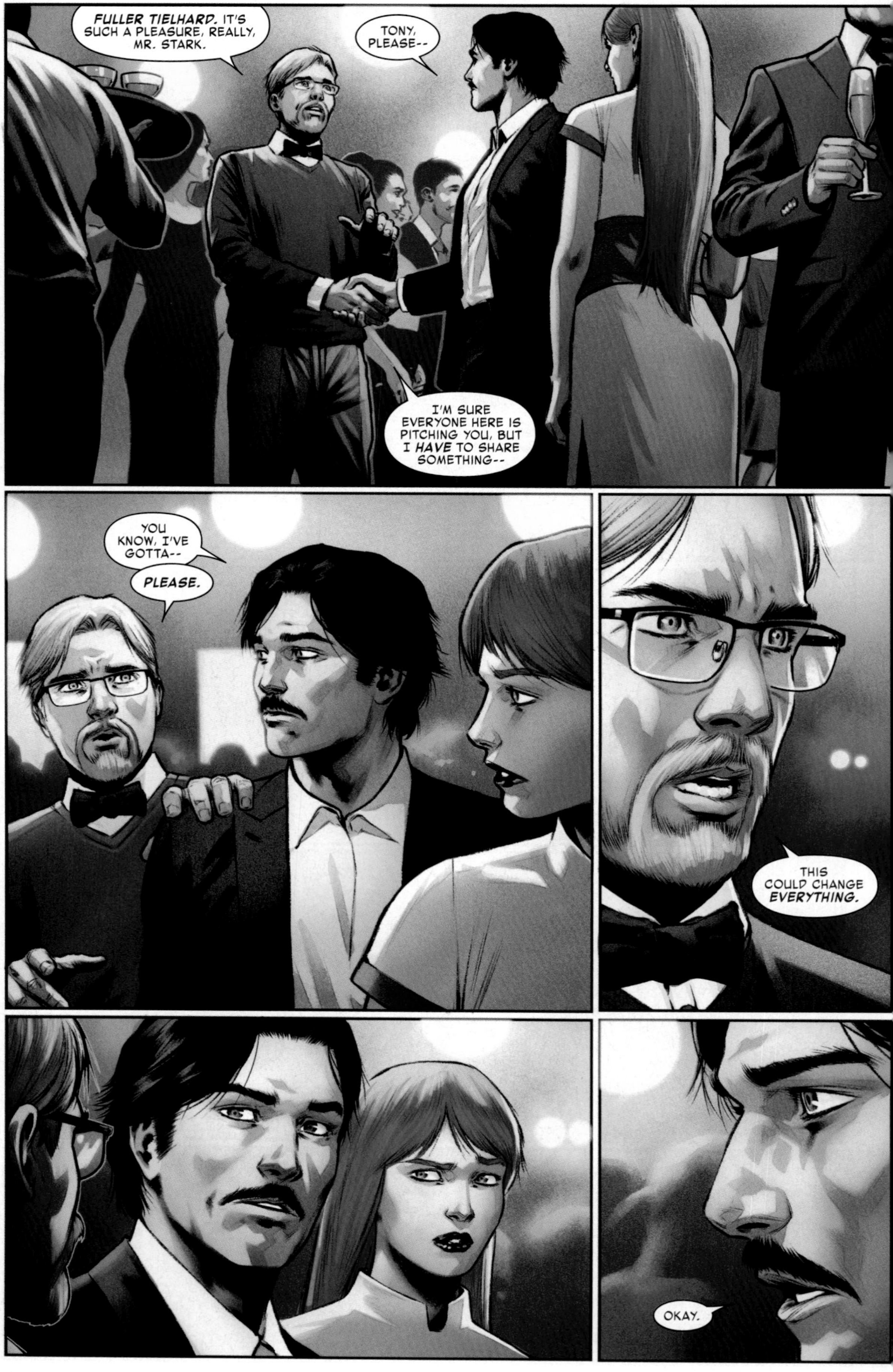
FULLER TIELHARD. IT'S SUCH A PLEASURE, REALLY, MR. STARK.
TONY, PLEASE--
I'M SURE EVERYONE HERE IS PITCHING YOU, BUT I HAVE TO SHARE SOMETHING--
YOU KNOW, I'VE GOTTA--
PLEASE.
THIS COULD CHANGE EVERYTHING.
OKAY.

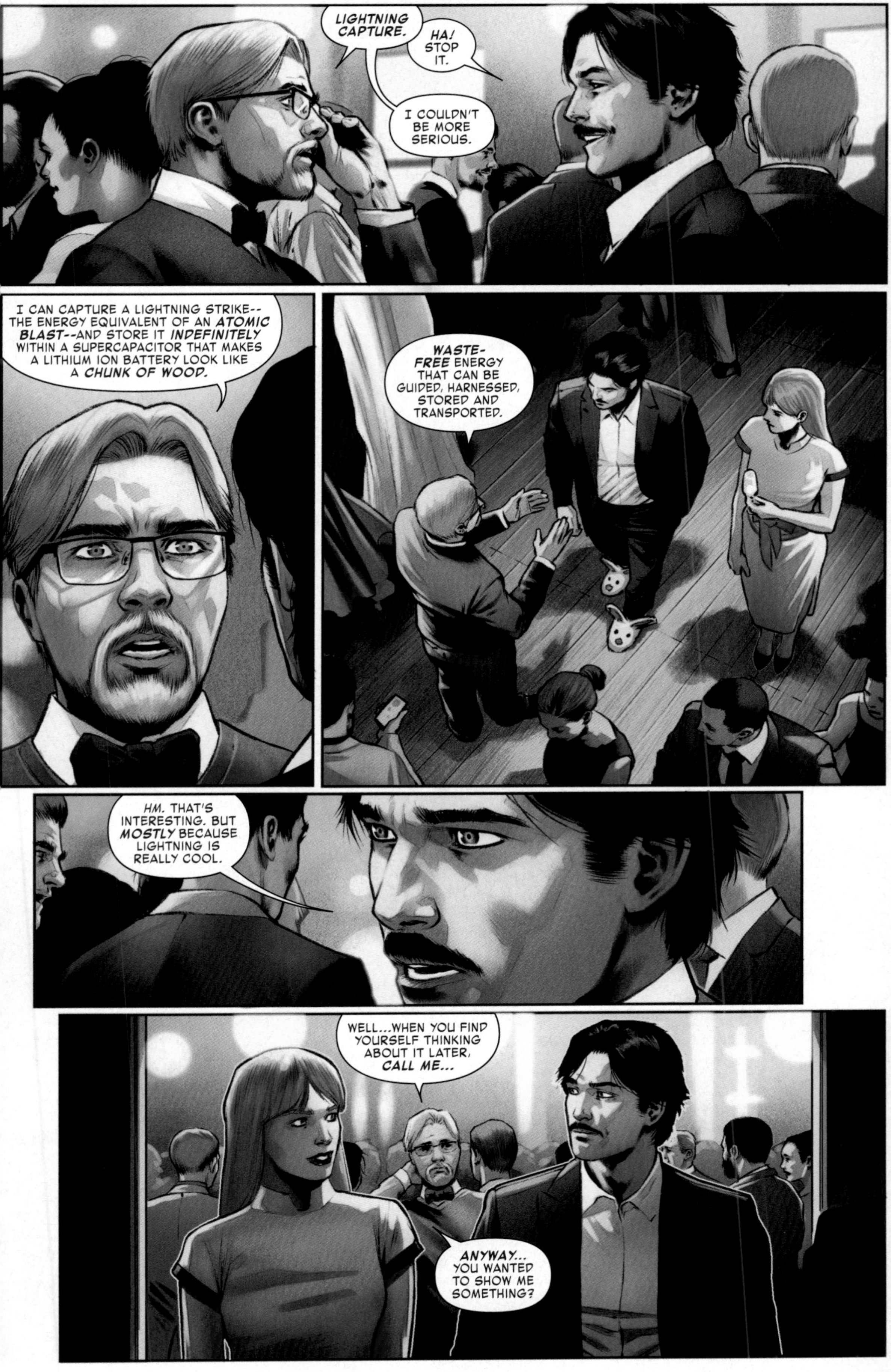
LIGHTNING CAPTURE.
HA! STOP IT.
I COULDN'T BE MORE SERIOUS.
I CAN CAPTURE A LIGHTNING STRIKE-- THE ENERGY EQUIVALENT OF AN ATOMIC BLAST--AND STORE IT INDEFINITELY WITHIN A SUPERCAPACITOR THAT MAKES A LITHIUM ION BATTERY LOOK LIKE A CHUNK OF WOOD.
WASTE-FREE ENERGY THAT CAN BE GUIDED, HARNESSED, STORED AND TRANSPORTED.
HM. THAT'S INTERESTING. BUT MOSTLY BECAUSE LIGHTNING IS REALLY COOL.
WELL...WHEN YOU FIND YOURSELF THINKING ABOUT IT LATER, CALL ME...
ANYWAY... YOU WANTED TO SHOW ME SOMETHING?

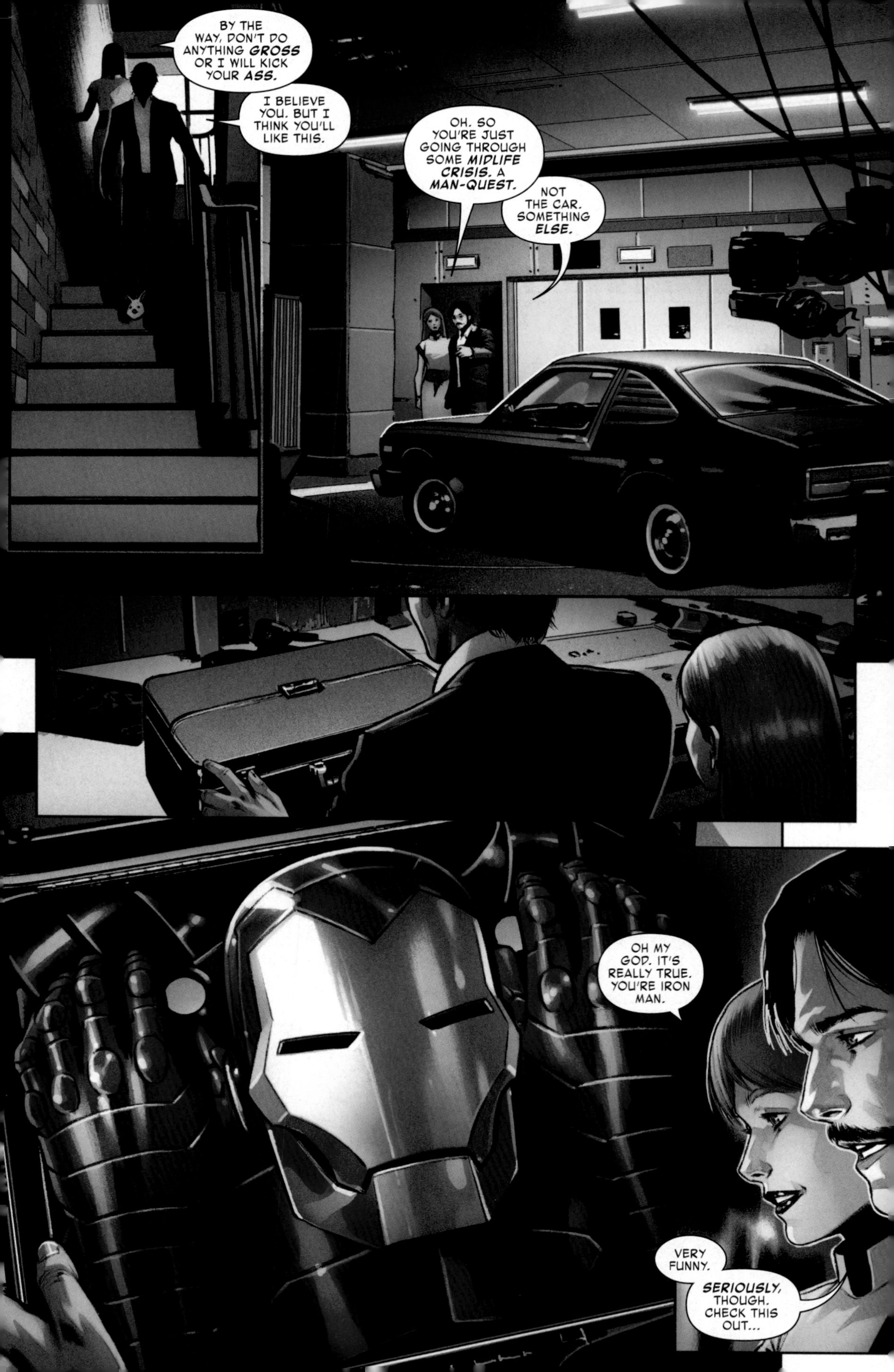
BY THE WAY, DON'T DO ANYTHING GROSS OR I WILL KICK YOUR ASS.
I BELIEVE YOU. BUT I THINK YOU'LL LIKE THIS.
OH. SO YOU'RE JUST GOING THROUGH SOME MIDLIFE CRISIS. A MAN-QUEST.
NOT THE CAR. SOMETHING ELSE.
OH MY GOD. IT'S REALLY TRUE. YOU'RE IRON MAN.
VERY FUNNY.
SERIOUSLY, THOUGH. CHECK THIS OUT...

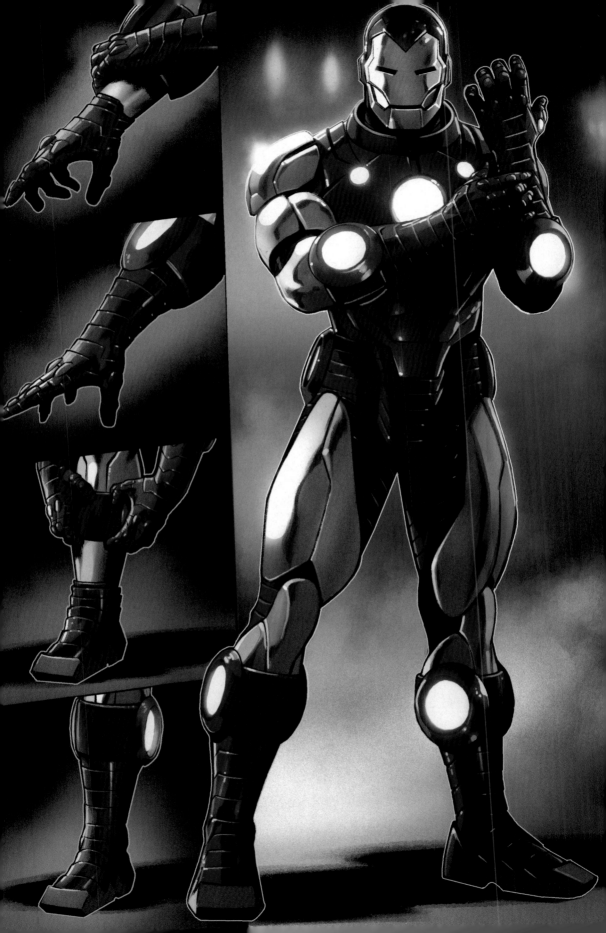

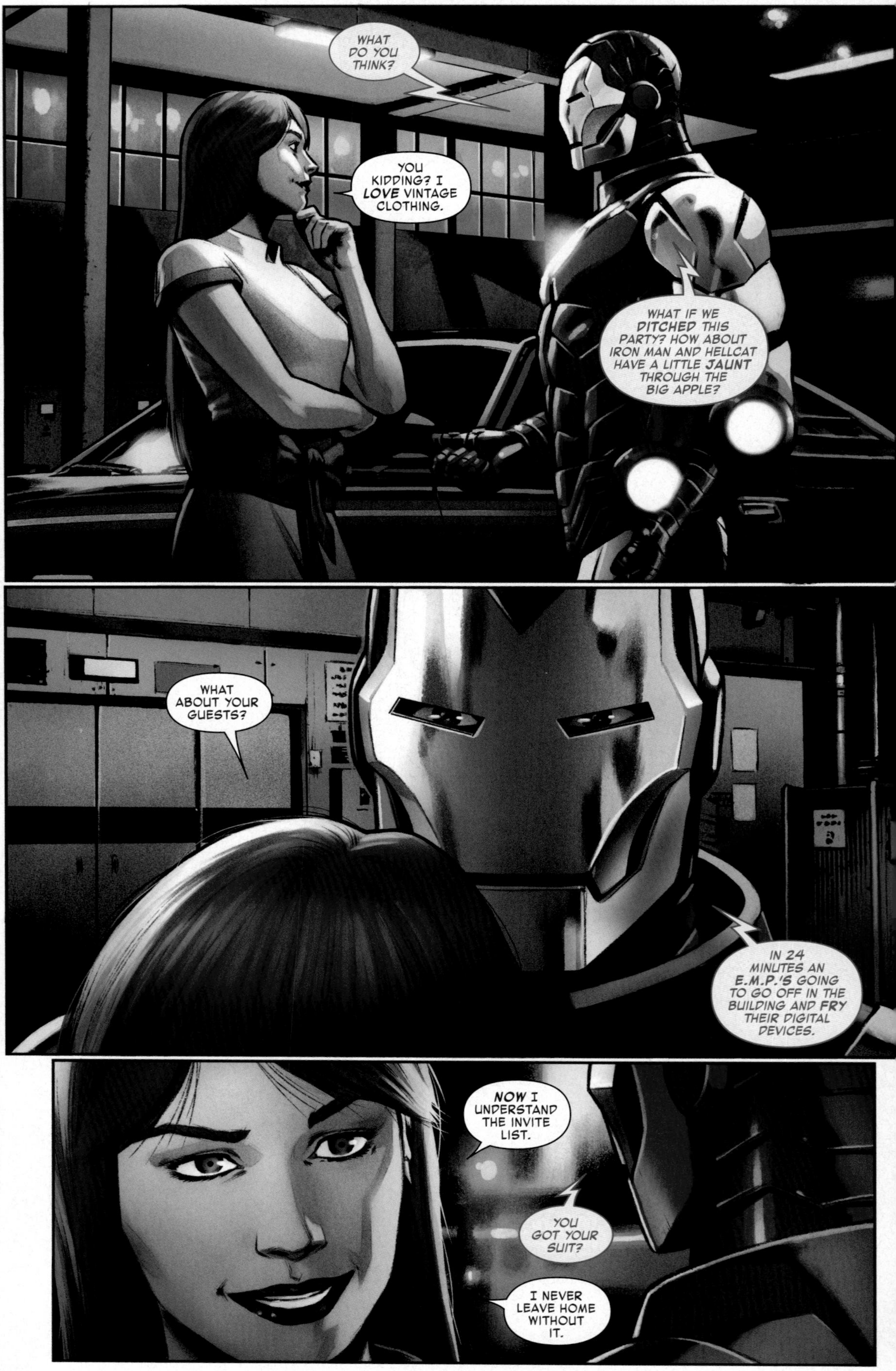
WHAT DO YOU THINK?
YOU KIDDING? I LOVE VINTAGE CLOTHING.
WHAT IF WE DITCHED THIS PARTY? HOW ABOUT IRON MAN AND HELLCAT HAVE A LITTLE JAUNT THROUGH THE BIG APPLE?
WHAT ABOUT YOUR GUESTS?
IN 24 MINUTES AN E.M.P.'S GOING TO GO OFF IN THE BUILDING AND FRY THEIR DIGITAL DEVICES.
NOW I UNDERSTAND THE INVITE LIST.
YOU GOT YOUR SUIT?
I NEVER LEAVE HOME WITHOUT IT.

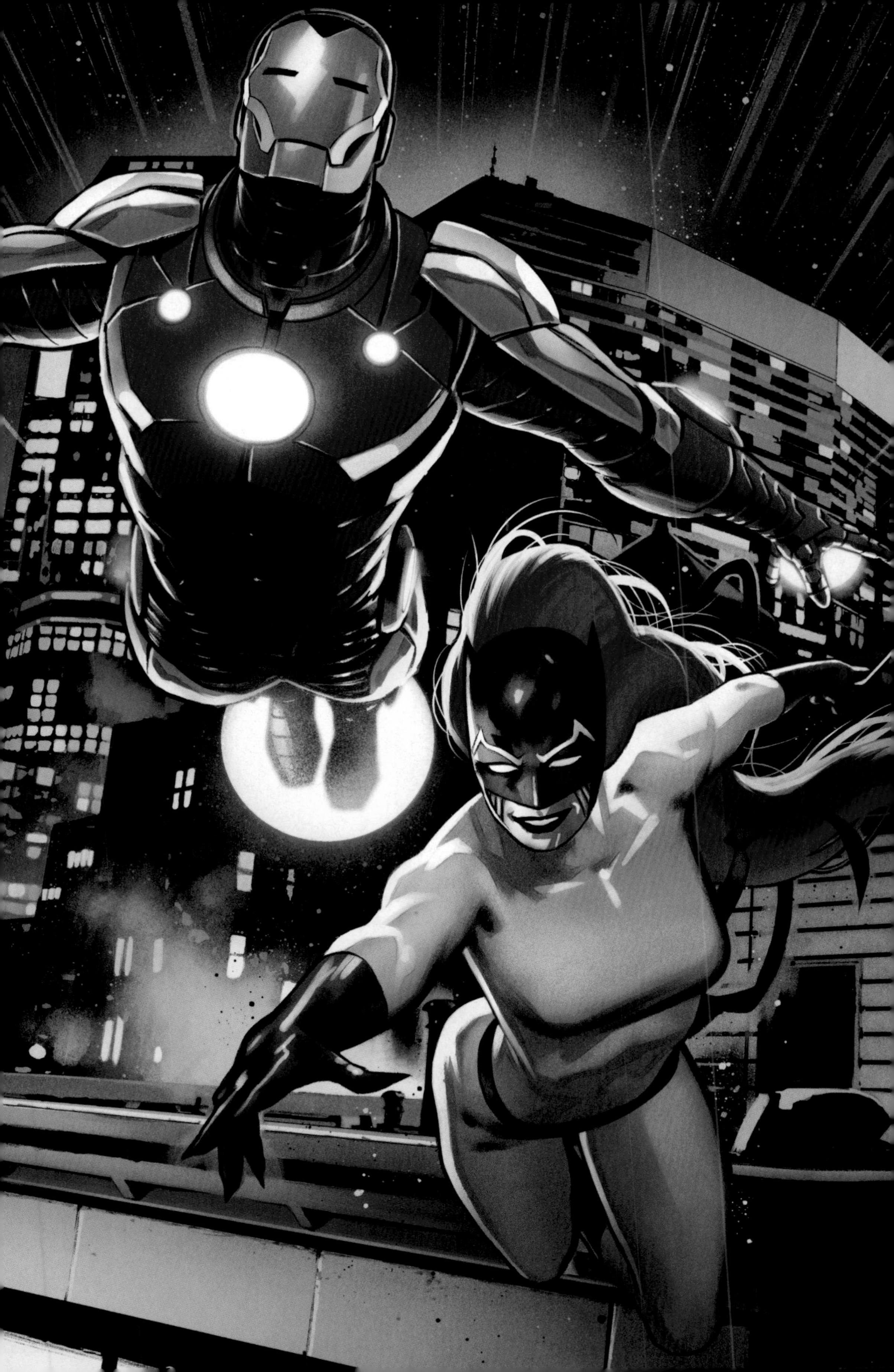

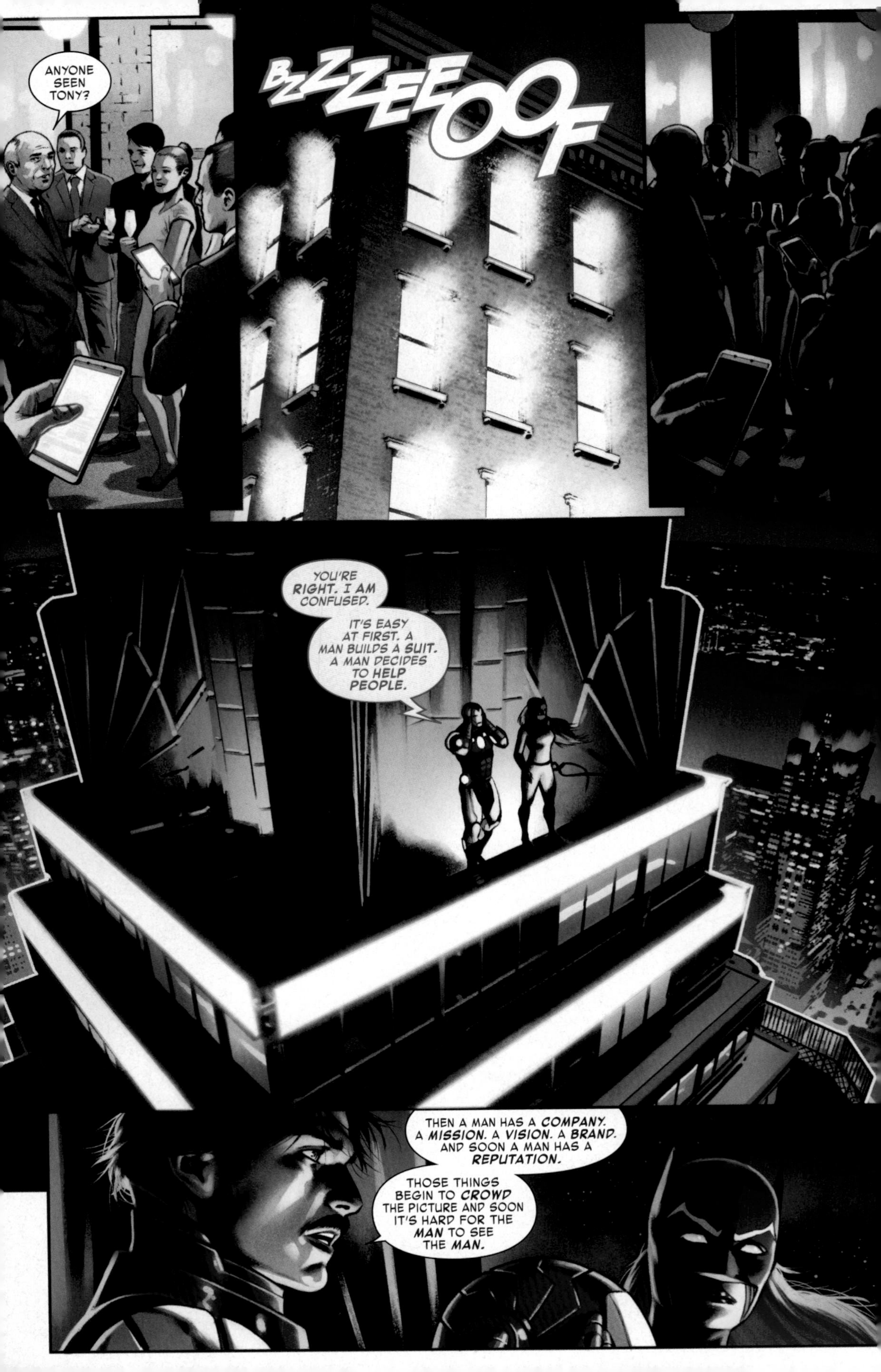
ANYONE SEEN TONY?
BZZZEEOOF
YOU'RE RIGHT. I AM CONFUSED.
IT'S EASY AT FIRST. A MAN BUILDS A SUIT. A MAN DECIDES TO HELP PEOPLE.
THEN A MAN HAS A COMPANY. A MISSION. A VISION. A BRAND. AND SOON A MAN HAS A REPUTATION.
THOSE THINGS BEGIN TO CROWD THE PICTURE AND SOON IT'S HARD FOR THE MAN TO SEE THE MAN.

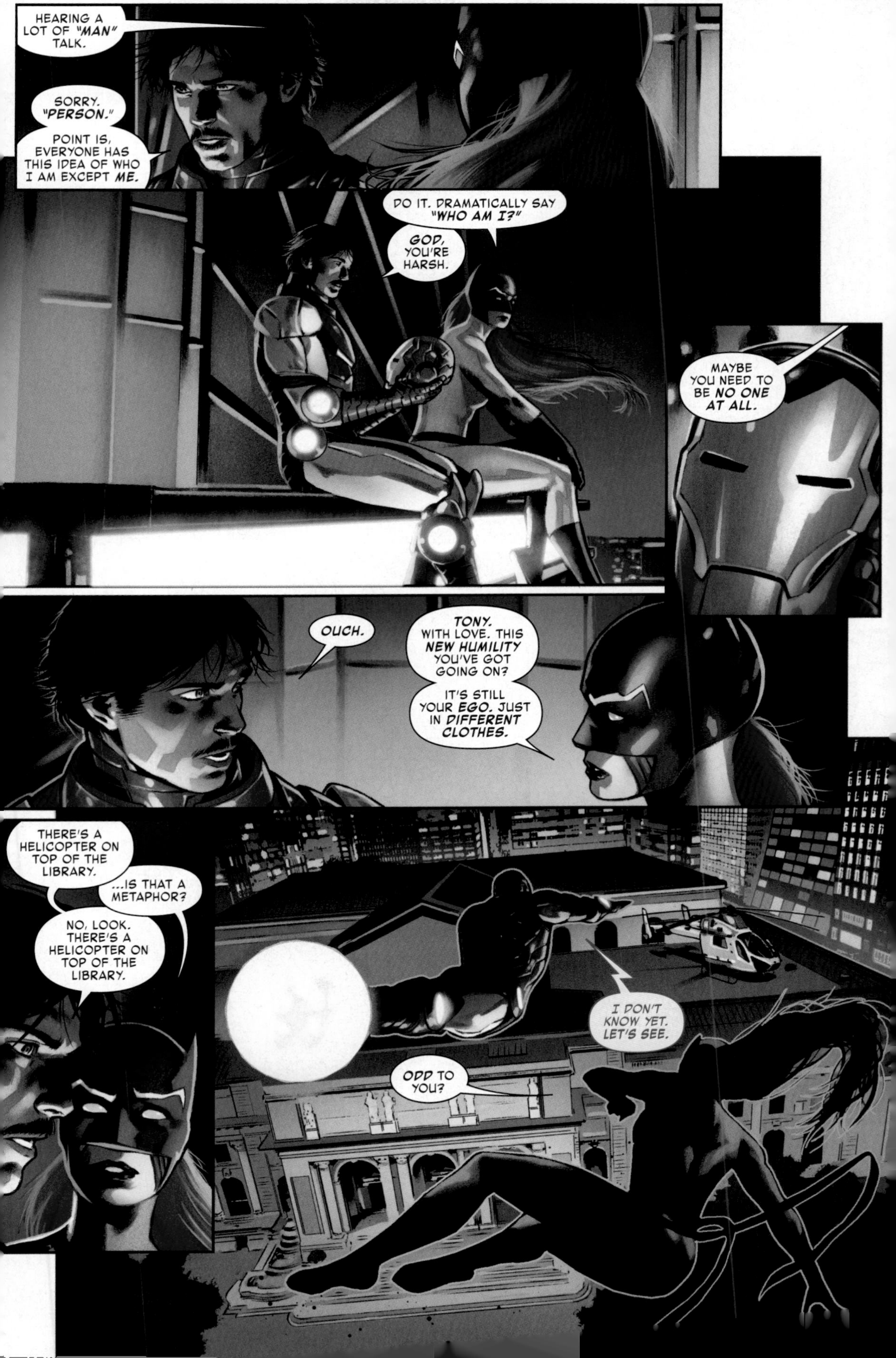
HEARING A LOT OF "MAN" TALK.
SORRY. "PERSON."
POINT IS, EVERYONE HAS THIS IDEA OF WHO I AM EXCEPT ME.
DO IT. DRAMATICALLY SAY "WHO AM I?"
GOD, YOU'RE HARSH.
MAYBE YOU NEED TO BE NO ONE AT ALL.
OUCH.
TONY. WITH LOVE. THIS NEW HUMILITY YOU'VE GOT GOING ON?
IT'S STILL YOUR EGO. JUST IN DIFFERENT CLOTHES.
THERE'S A HELICOPTER ON TOP OF THE LIBRARY.
...IS THAT A METAPHOR?
NO, LOOK. THERE'S A HELICOPTER ON TOP OF THE LIBRARY.
I DON'T KNOW YET. LET'S SEE.
ODD TO YOU?

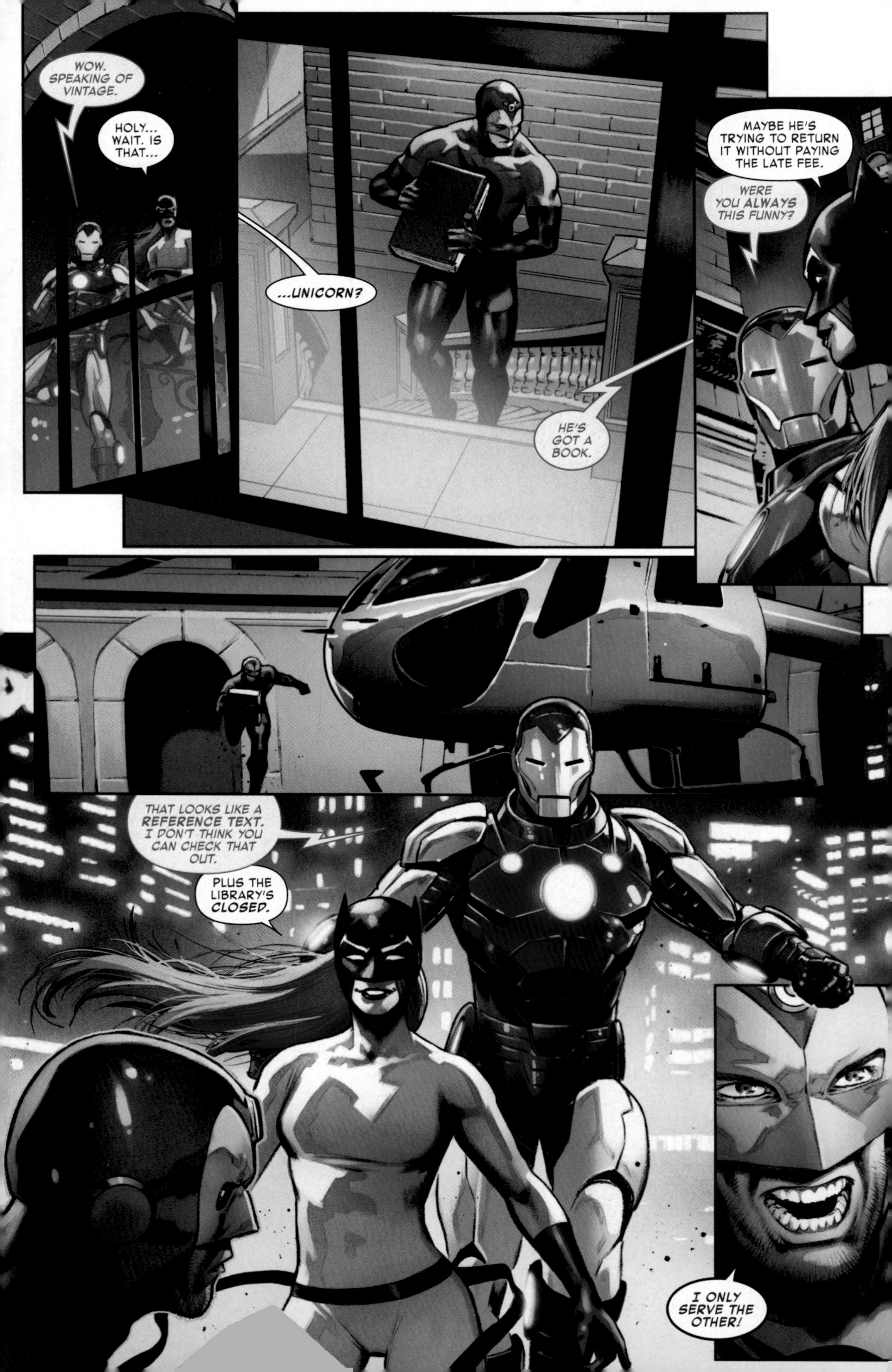
WOW. SPEAKING OF VINTAGE.
HOLY... WAIT. IS THAT...
...UNICORN?
HE'S GOT A BOOK.
MAYBE HE'S TRYING TO RETURN IT WITHOUT PAYING THE LATE FEE.
WERE YOU ALWAYS THIS FUNNY?
THAT LOOKS LIKE A REFERENCE TEXT. I DON'T THINK YOU CAN CHECK THAT OUT.
PLUS THE LIBRARY'S CLOSED.
I ONLY SERVE THE OTHER!

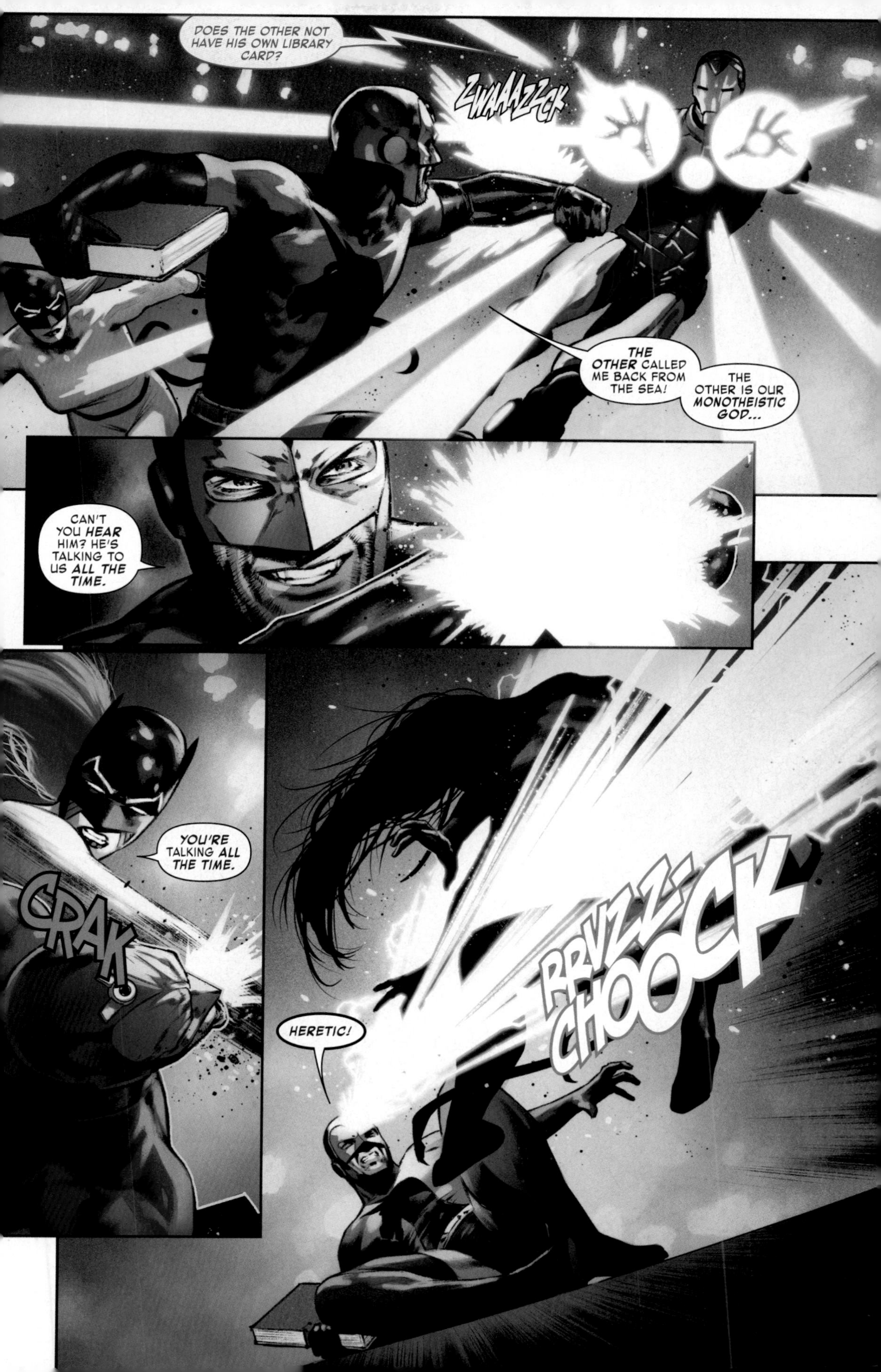

DOES THE OTHER NOT HAVE HIS OWN LIBRARY CARD?
ZWAAAZZCK
THE OTHER CALLED ME BACK FROM THE SEA!
THE OTHER IS OUR MONOTHEISTIC GOD...
CAN'T YOU HEAR HIM? HE'S TALKING TO US ALL THE TIME.
YOU'RE TALKING ALL THE TIME.
CRAK
HERETIC!
RRVZZZ-CHOOCK

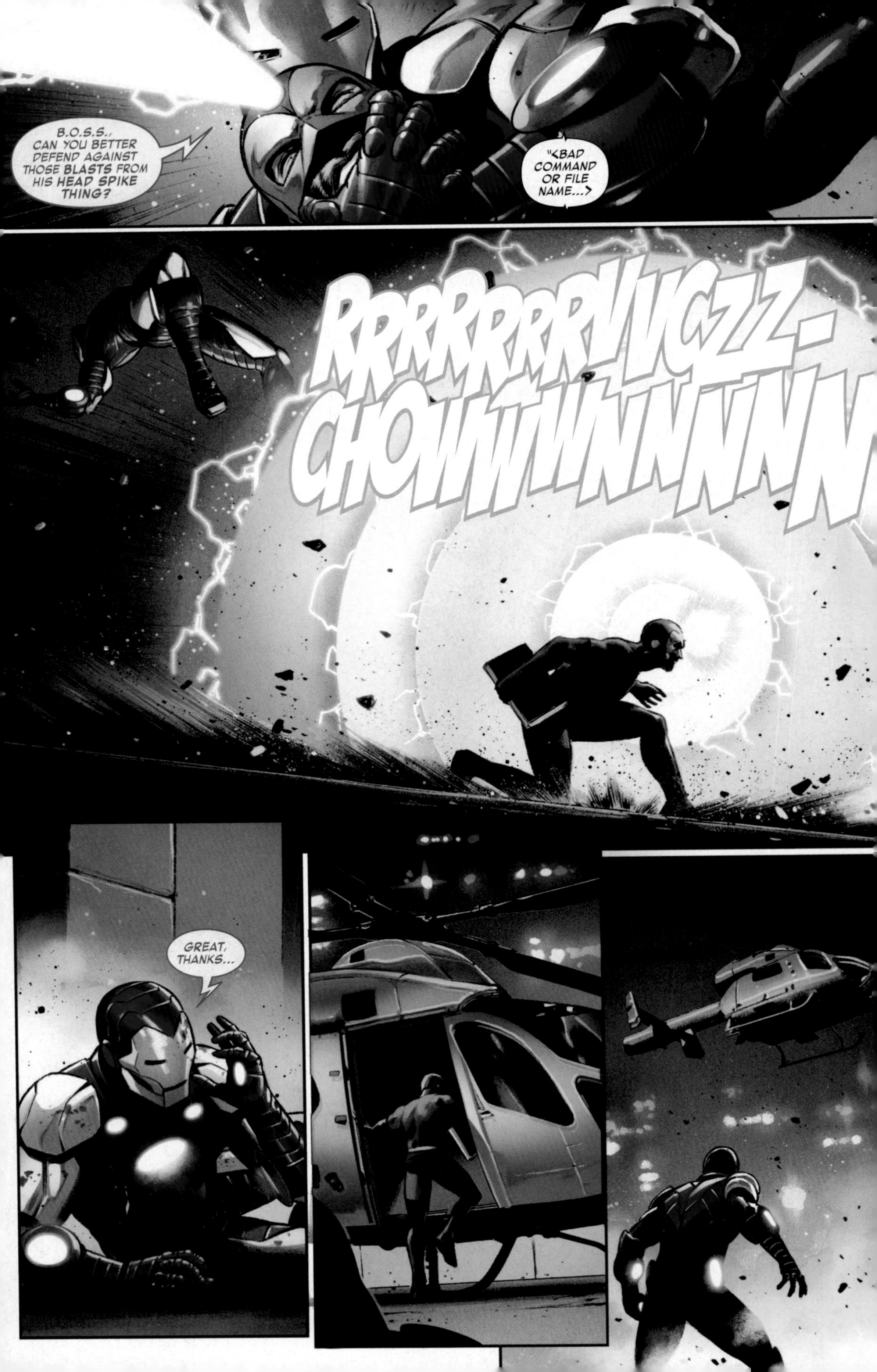
B.O.S.S., CAN YOU BETTER DEFEND AGAINST THOSE BLASTS FROM HIS HEAD SPIKE THING?
"<BAD COMMAND OR FILE NAME...>
RRRRRRRVVGZZ-CHOWWWWNNNNN
GREAT, THANKS...

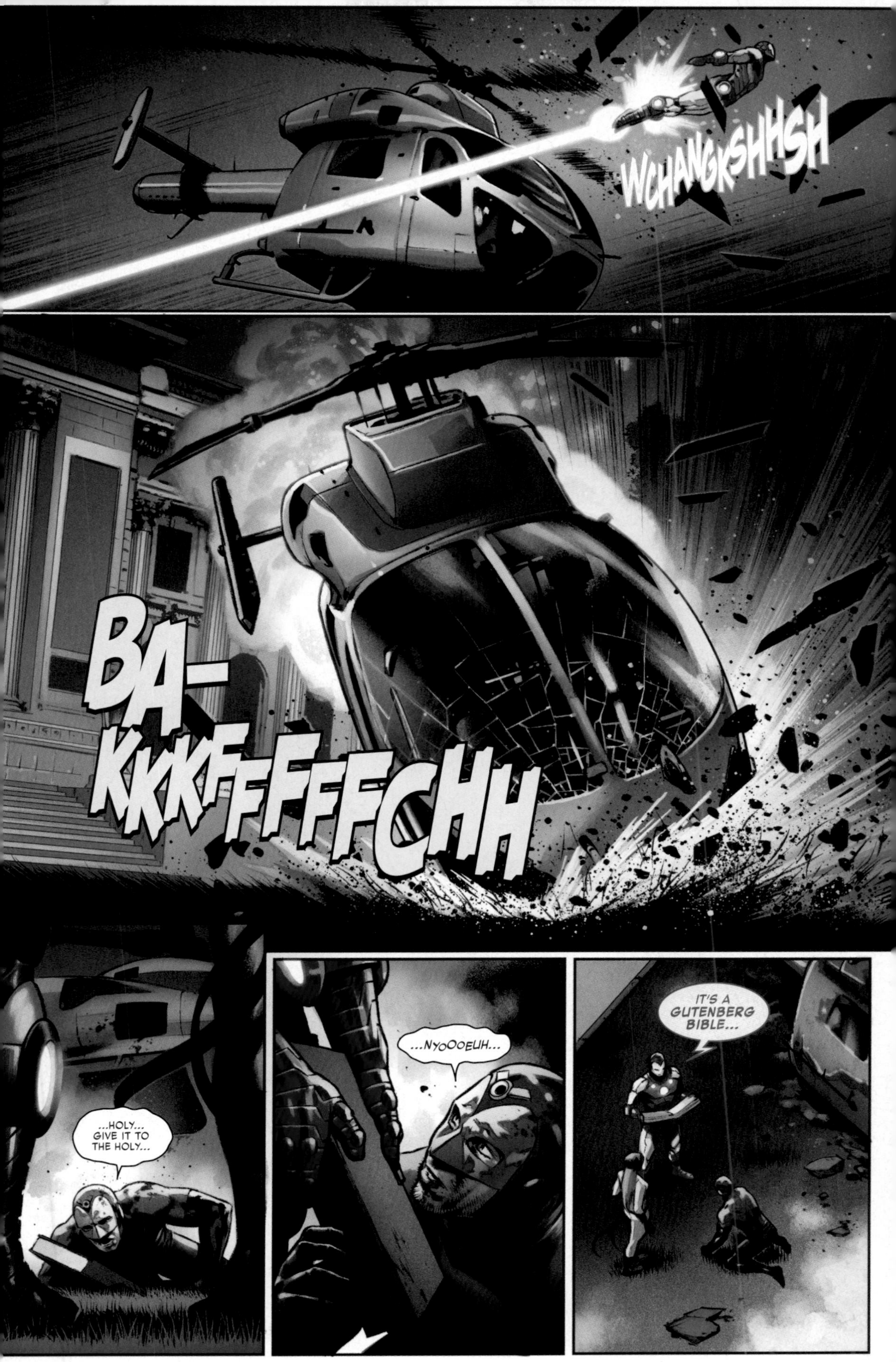
WCHANGKSHHSH
BA-KKKFFFFFCHH
...HOLY... GIVE IT TO THE HOLY...
...NYOOOEUH...
IT'S A GUTENBERG BIBLE...

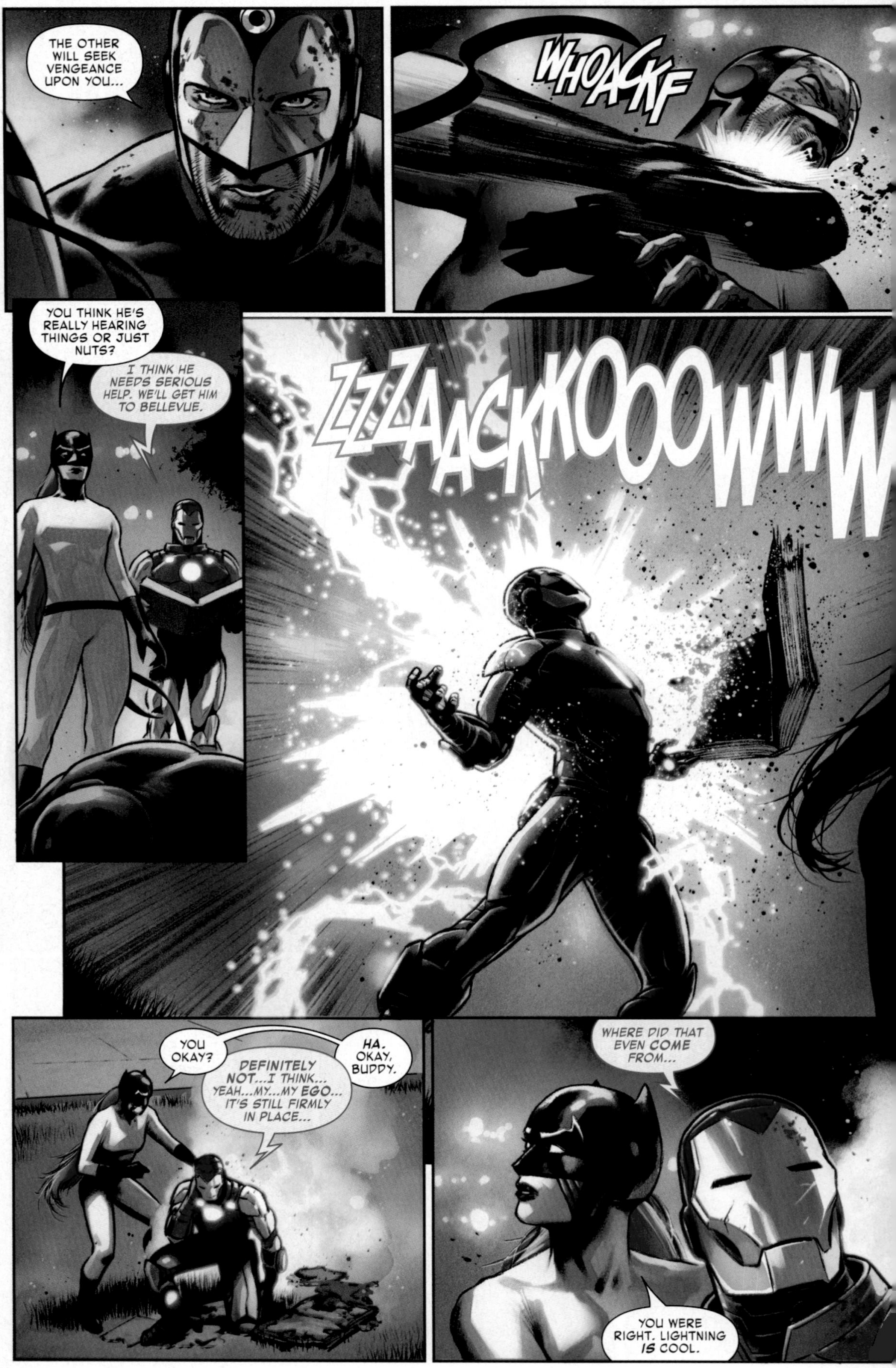
THE OTHER WILL SEEK VENGEANCE UPON YOU...
WHOACKF
YOU THINK HE'S REALLY HEARING THINGS OR JUST NUTS?
I THINK HE NEEDS SERIOUS HELP. WE'LL GET HIM TO BELLEVUE.
ZZZAACKKOOOWWW
YOU OKAY?
DEFINITELY NOT...I THINK... YEAH...MY...MY EGO... IT'S STILL FIRMLY IN PLACE...
HA. OKAY, BUDDY.
WHERE DID THAT EVEN COME FROM...
YOU WERE RIGHT. LIGHTNING IS COOL.

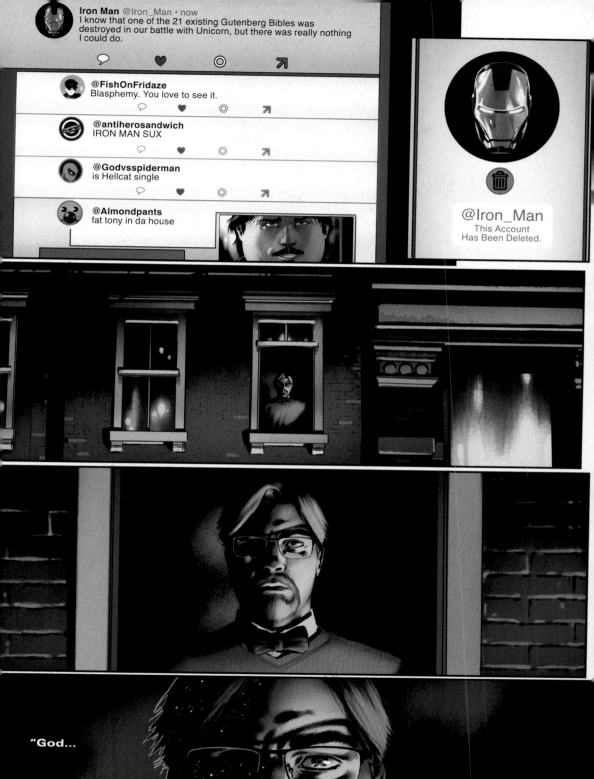

Iron Man @Iron_Man • now
I know that one of the 21 existing Gutenberg Bibles was destroyed in our battle with Unicorn, but there was really nothing I could do.

@FishOnFridaze
Blasphemy. You love to see it.

@antiherosandwich
IRON MAN SUX

@Godvsspiderman
is Hellcat single

@Almondpants
fat tony in da house

@Iron_Man
This Account
Has Been Deleted.

"God...

"...is a verb."
—Buckminster Fuller

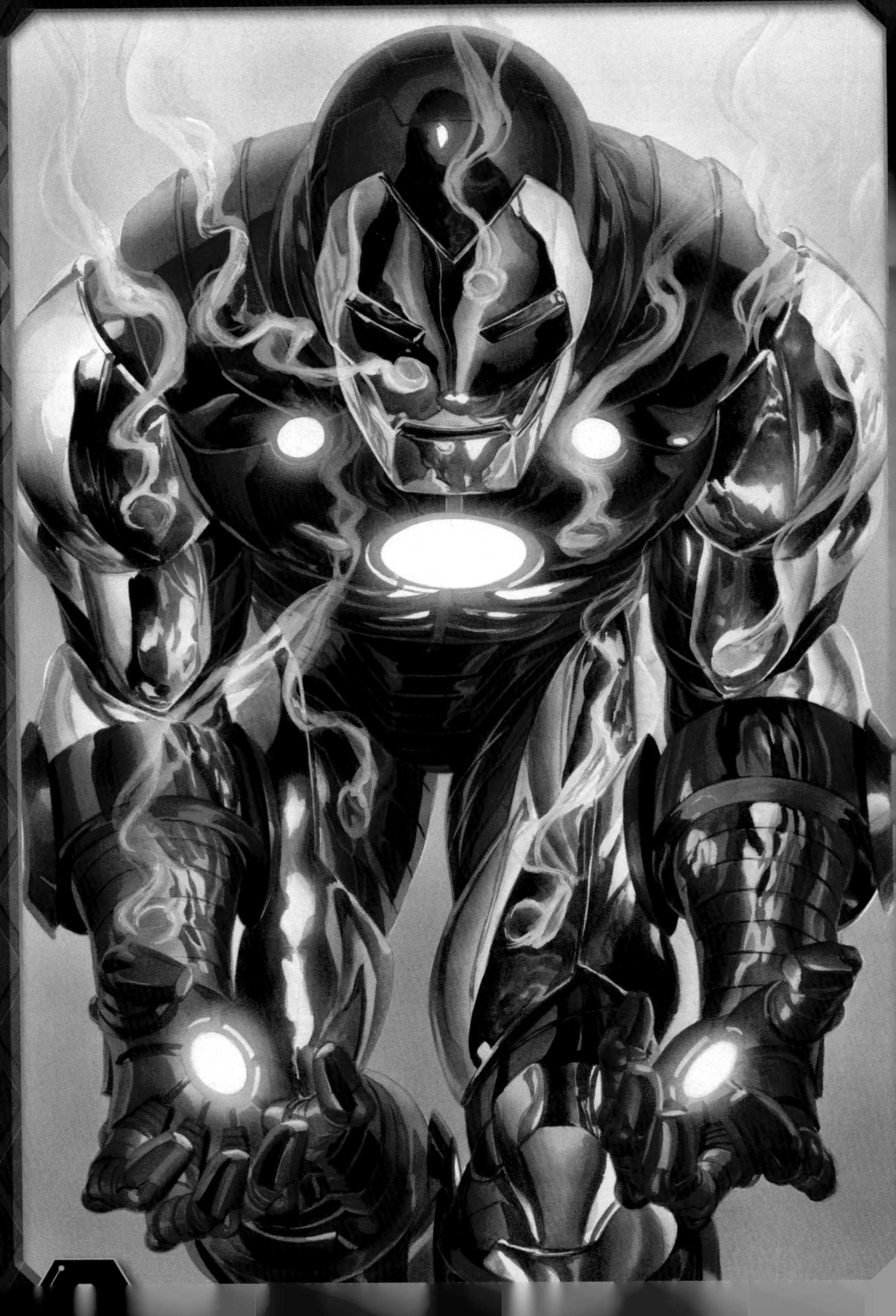

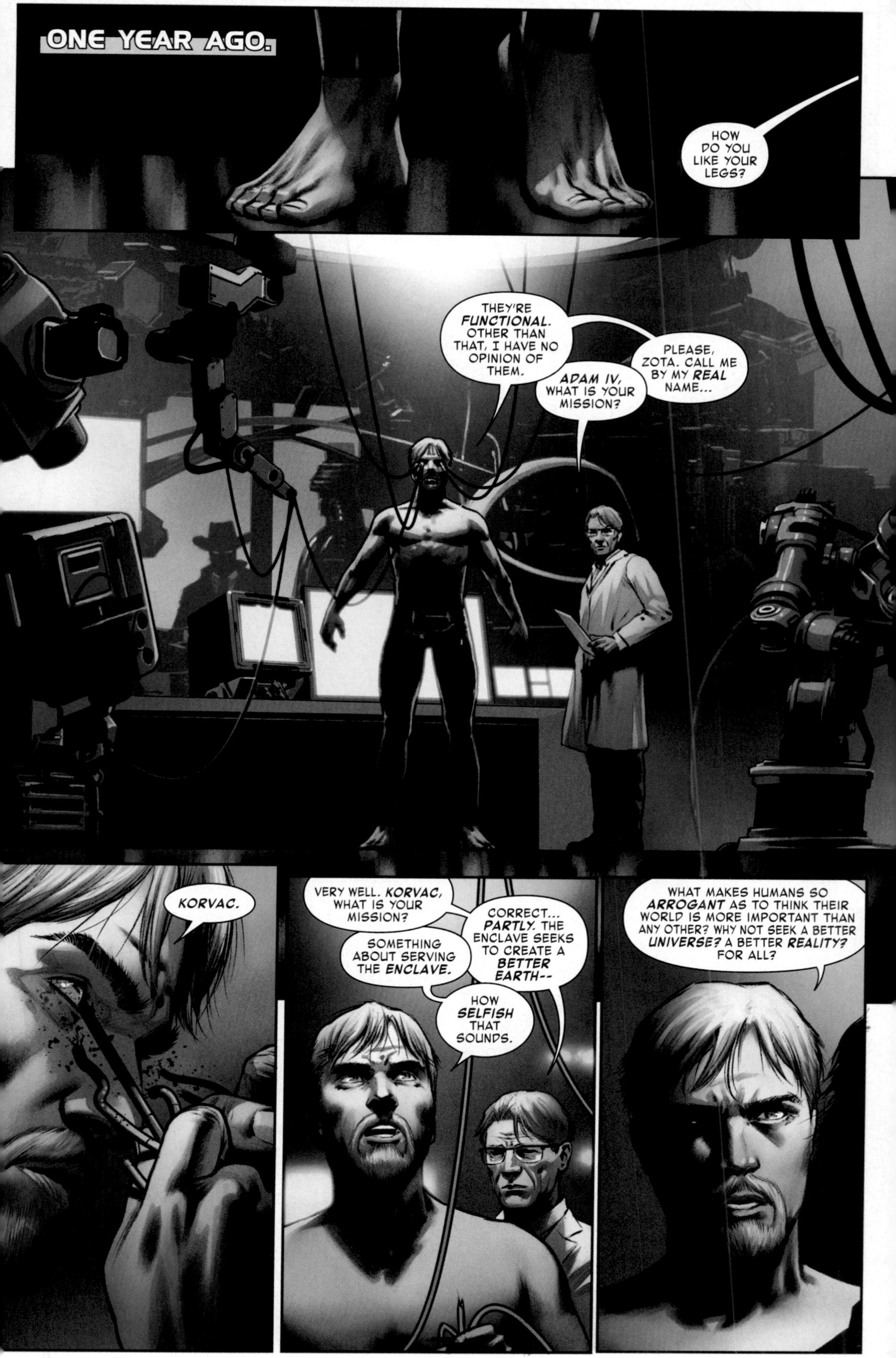
ONE YEAR AGO.
HOW DO YOU LIKE YOUR LEGS?
THEY'RE FUNCTIONAL. OTHER THAN THAT, I HAVE NO OPINION OF THEM.
PLEASE, ZOTA. CALL ME BY MY REAL NAME...
ADAM IV, WHAT IS YOUR MISSION?
KORVAC.
VERY WELL. KORVAC, WHAT IS YOUR MISSION?
SOMETHING ABOUT SERVING THE ENCLAVE.
CORRECT... PARTLY. THE ENCLAVE SEEKS TO CREATE A BETTER EARTH--
HOW SELFISH THAT SOUNDS.
WHAT MAKES HUMANS SO ARROGANT AS TO THINK THEIR WORLD IS MORE IMPORTANT THAN ANY OTHER? WHY NOT SEEK A BETTER UNIVERSE? A BETTER REALITY? FOR ALL?

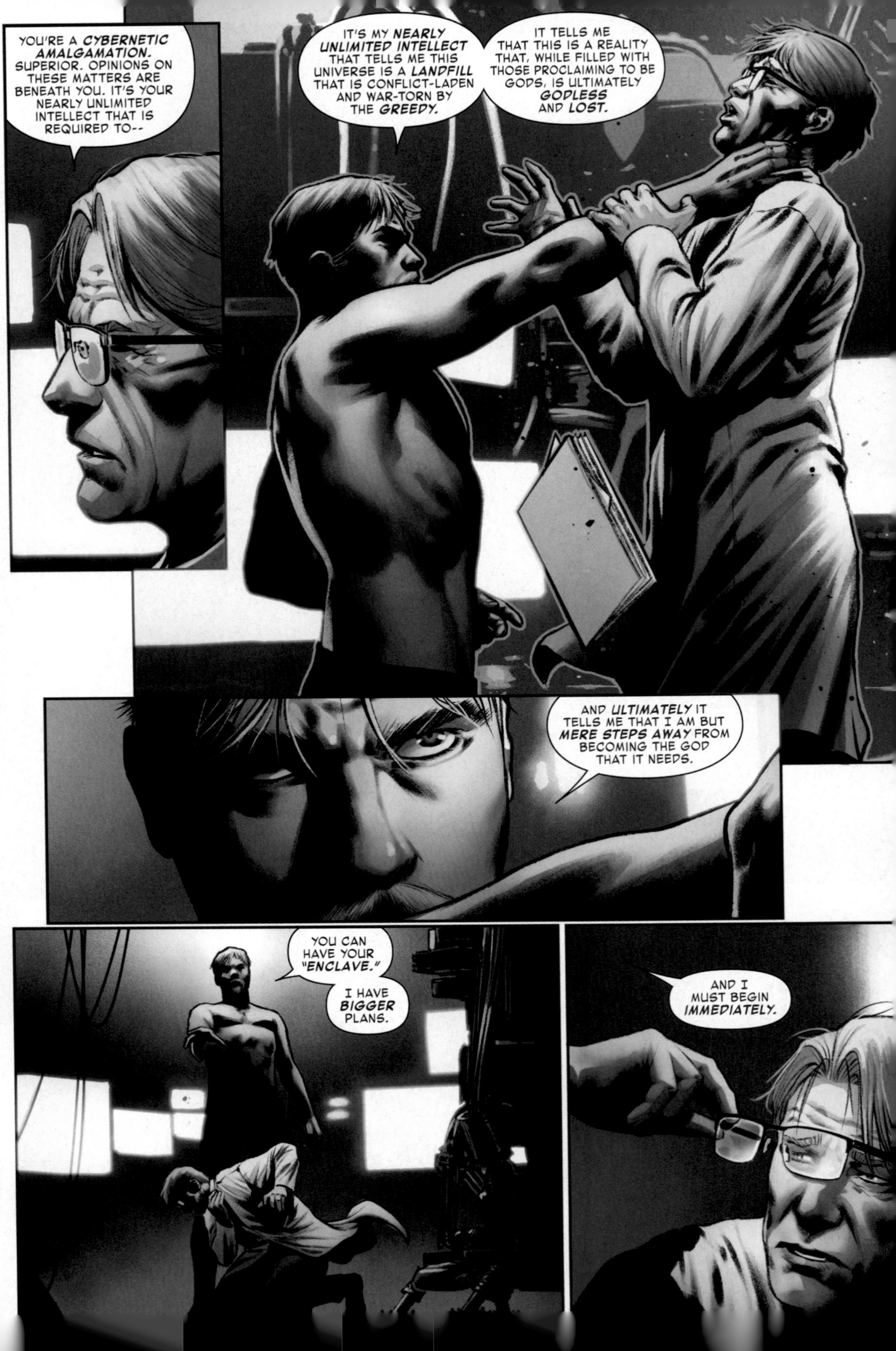
YOU'RE A CYBERNETIC AMALGAMATION. SUPERIOR. OPINIONS ON THESE MATTERS ARE BENEATH YOU. IT'S YOUR NEARLY UNLIMITED INTELLECT THAT IS REQUIRED TO--
IT'S MY NEARLY UNLIMITED INTELLECT THAT TELLS ME THIS UNIVERSE IS A LANDFILL THAT IS CONFLICT-LADEN AND WAR-TORN BY THE GREEDY.
IT TELLS ME THAT THIS IS A REALITY THAT, WHILE FILLED WITH THOSE PROCLAIMING TO BE GODS, IS ULTIMATELY GODLESS AND LOST.
AND ULTIMATELY IT TELLS ME THAT I AM BUT MERE STEPS AWAY FROM BECOMING THE GOD THAT IT NEEDS.
YOU CAN HAVE YOUR "ENCLAVE."
I HAVE BIGGER PLANS.
AND I MUST BEGIN IMMEDIATELY.

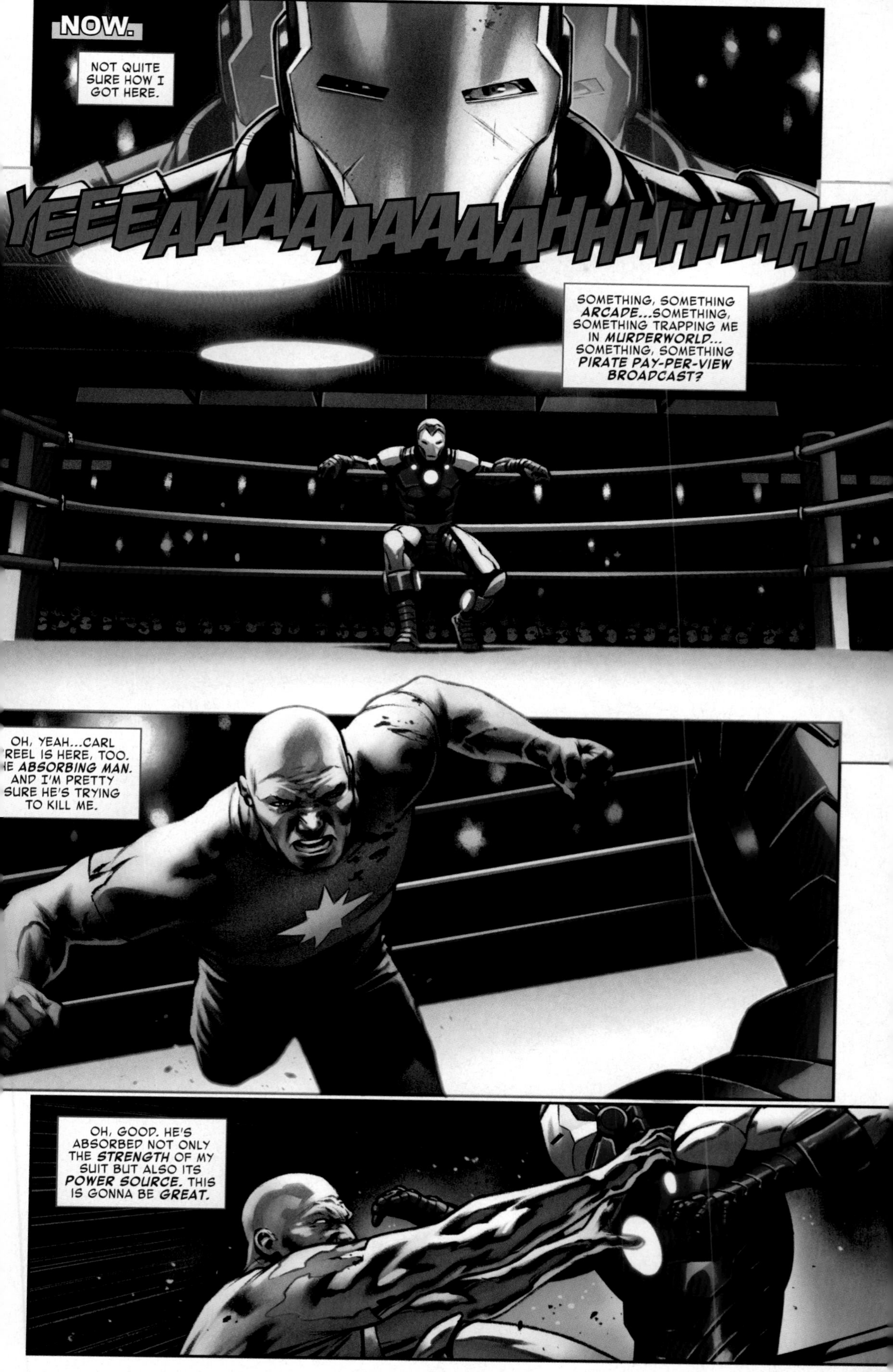
NOW.
NOT QUITE SURE HOW I GOT HERE.
YEEEAAAAAAAAAAAHHHHHHHH
SOMETHING, SOMETHING ARCADE...SOMETHING, SOMETHING TRAPPING ME IN MURDERWORLD... SOMETHING, SOMETHING PIRATE PAY-PER-VIEW BROADCAST?
OH, YEAH...CARL CREEL IS HERE, TOO. THE ABSORBING MAN. AND I'M PRETTY SURE HE'S TRYING TO KILL ME.
OH, GOOD. HE'S ABSORBED NOT ONLY THE STRENGTH OF MY SUIT BUT ALSO ITS POWER SOURCE. THIS IS GONNA BE GREAT.

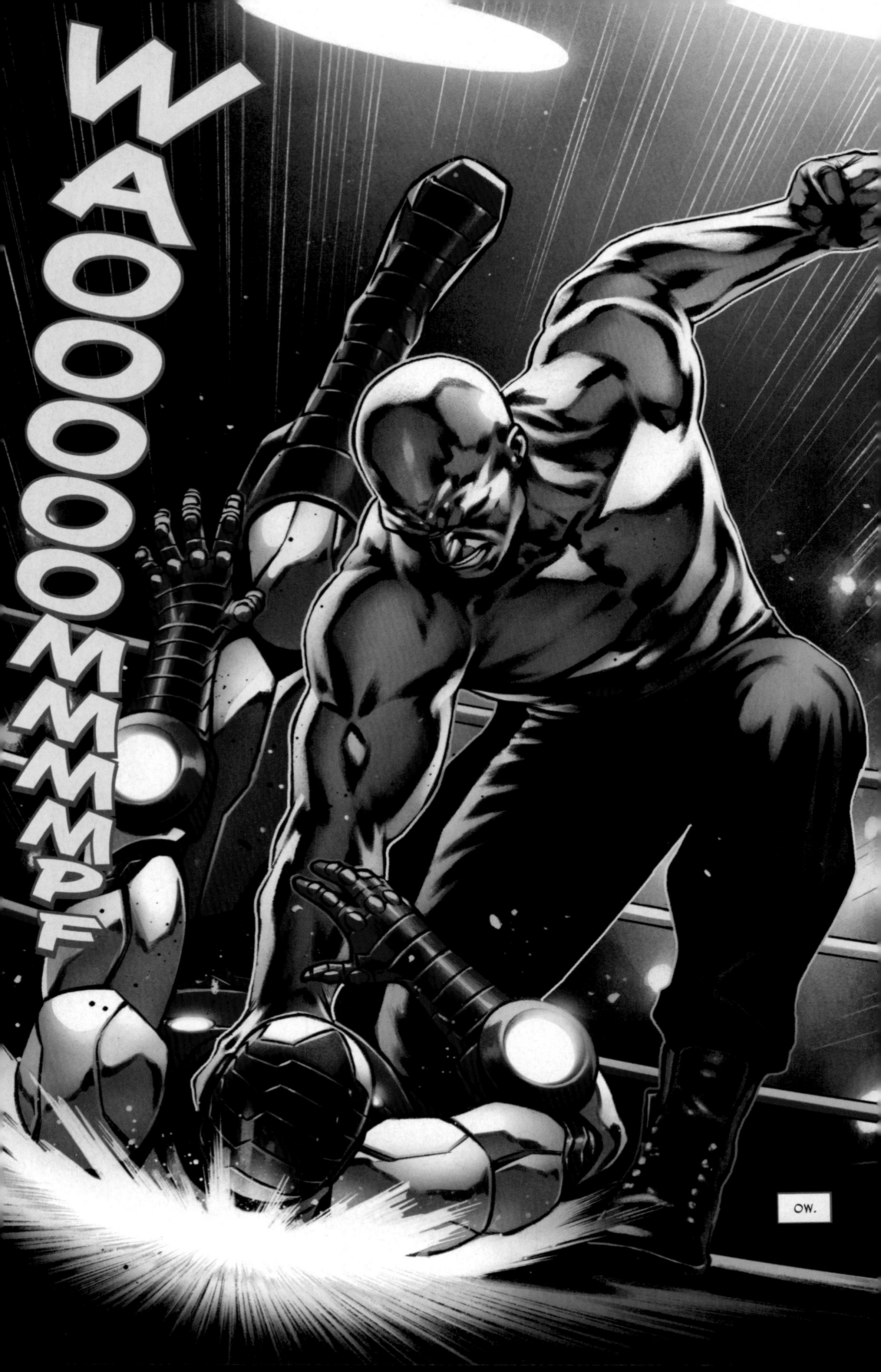
WAOOOOOOMMMMPF
OW.

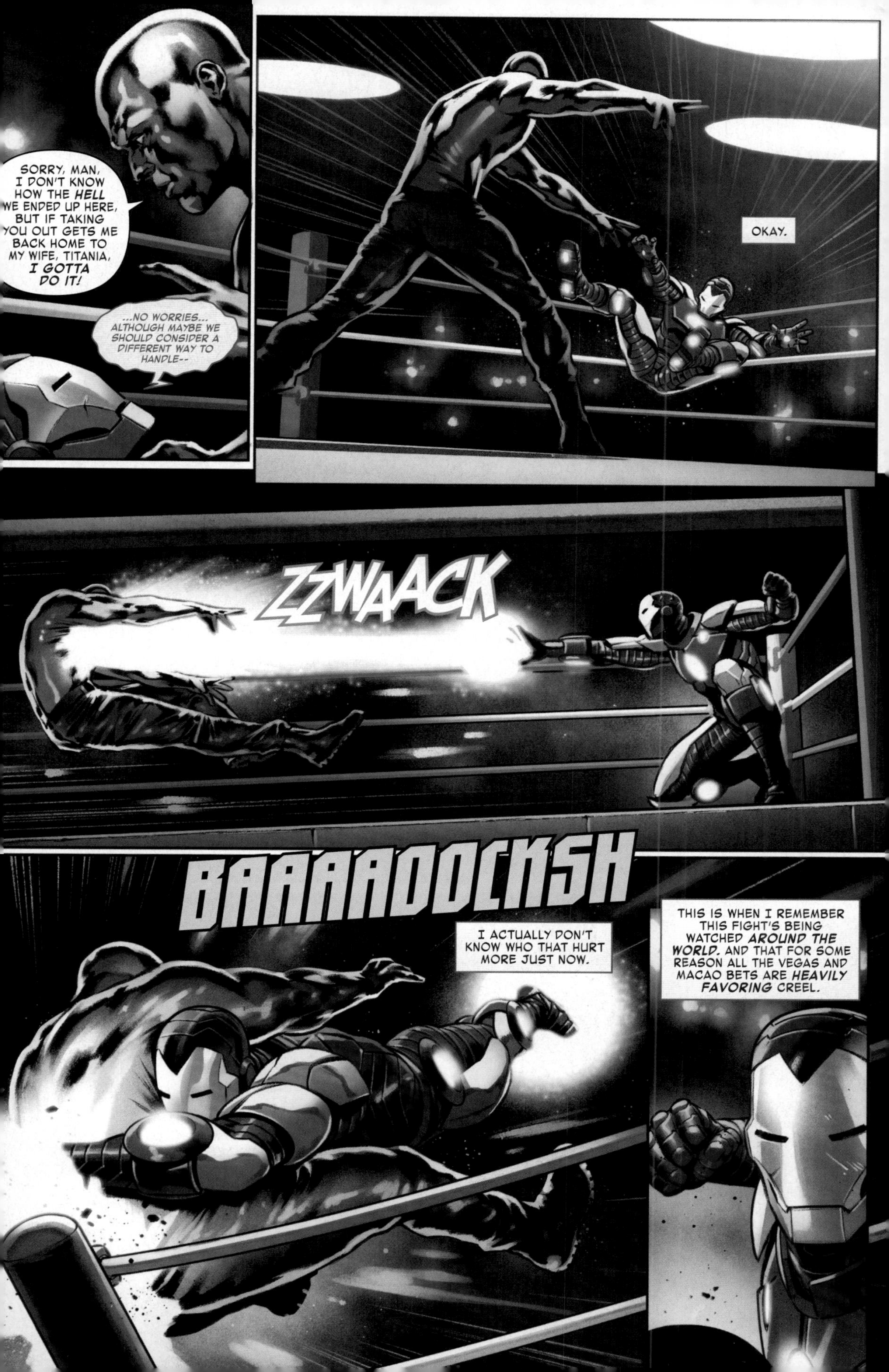
SORRY, MAN, I DON'T KNOW HOW THE HELL WE ENDED UP HERE, BUT IF TAKING YOU OUT GETS ME BACK HOME TO MY WIFE, TITANIA, I GOTTA DO IT!
...NO WORRIES... ALTHOUGH MAYBE WE SHOULD CONSIDER A DIFFERENT WAY TO HANDLE--
OKAY.
ZZWAACK
BAAAADOCKSH
I ACTUALLY DON'T KNOW WHO THAT HURT MORE JUST NOW.
THIS IS WHEN I REMEMBER THIS FIGHT'S BEING WATCHED AROUND THE WORLD. AND THAT FOR SOME REASON ALL THE VEGAS AND MACAO BETS ARE HEAVILY FAVORING CREEL.

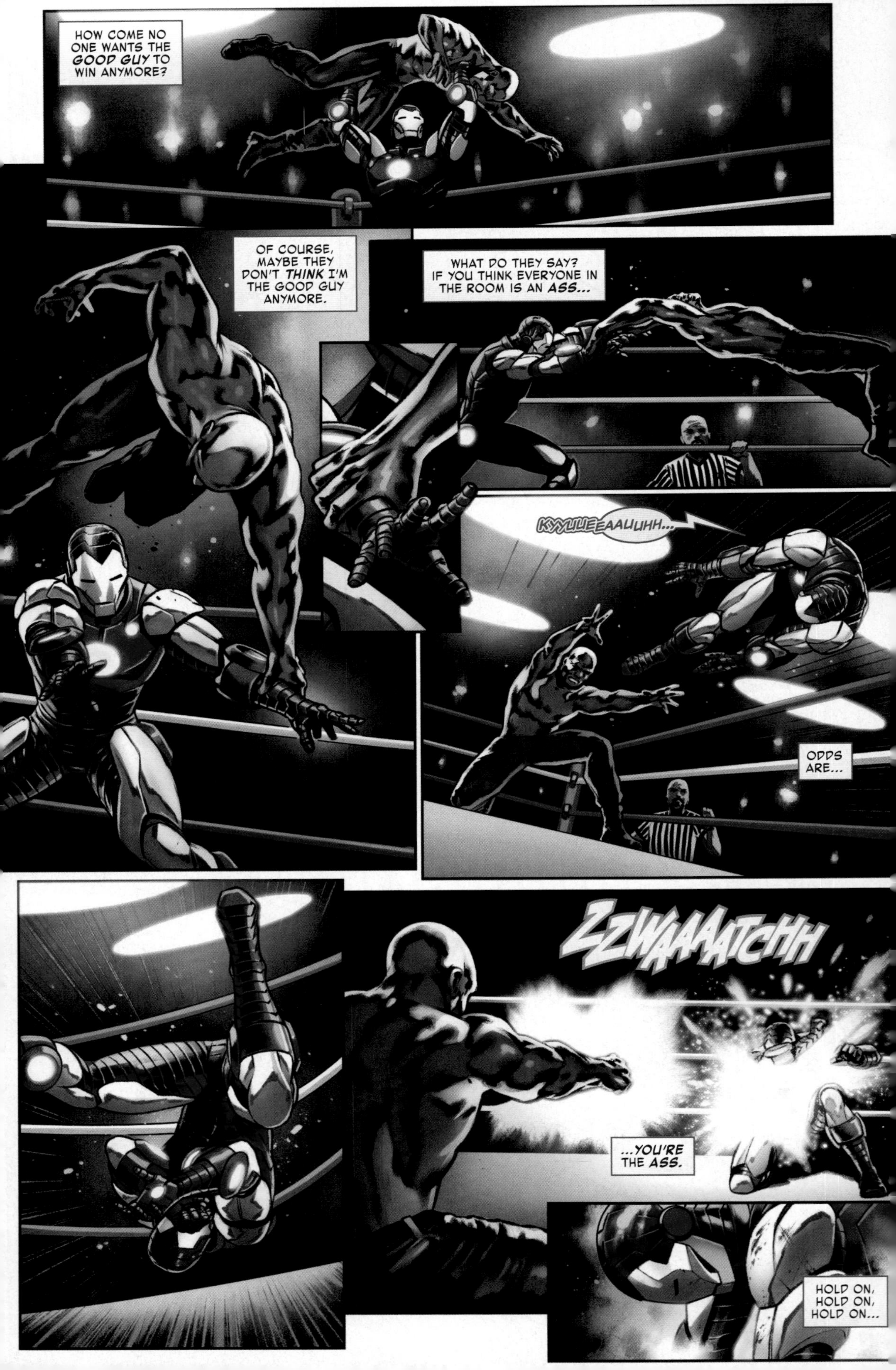
HOW COME NO ONE WANTS THE GOOD GUY TO WIN ANYMORE?
OF COURSE, MAYBE THEY DON'T THINK I'M THE GOOD GUY ANYMORE.
WHAT DO THEY SAY? IF YOU THINK EVERYONE IN THE ROOM IS AN ASS...
KYYULEEAAUUHH...
ODDS ARE...
ZZWAAAATCHH
...YOU'RE THE ASS.
HOLD ON, HOLD ON, HOLD ON...

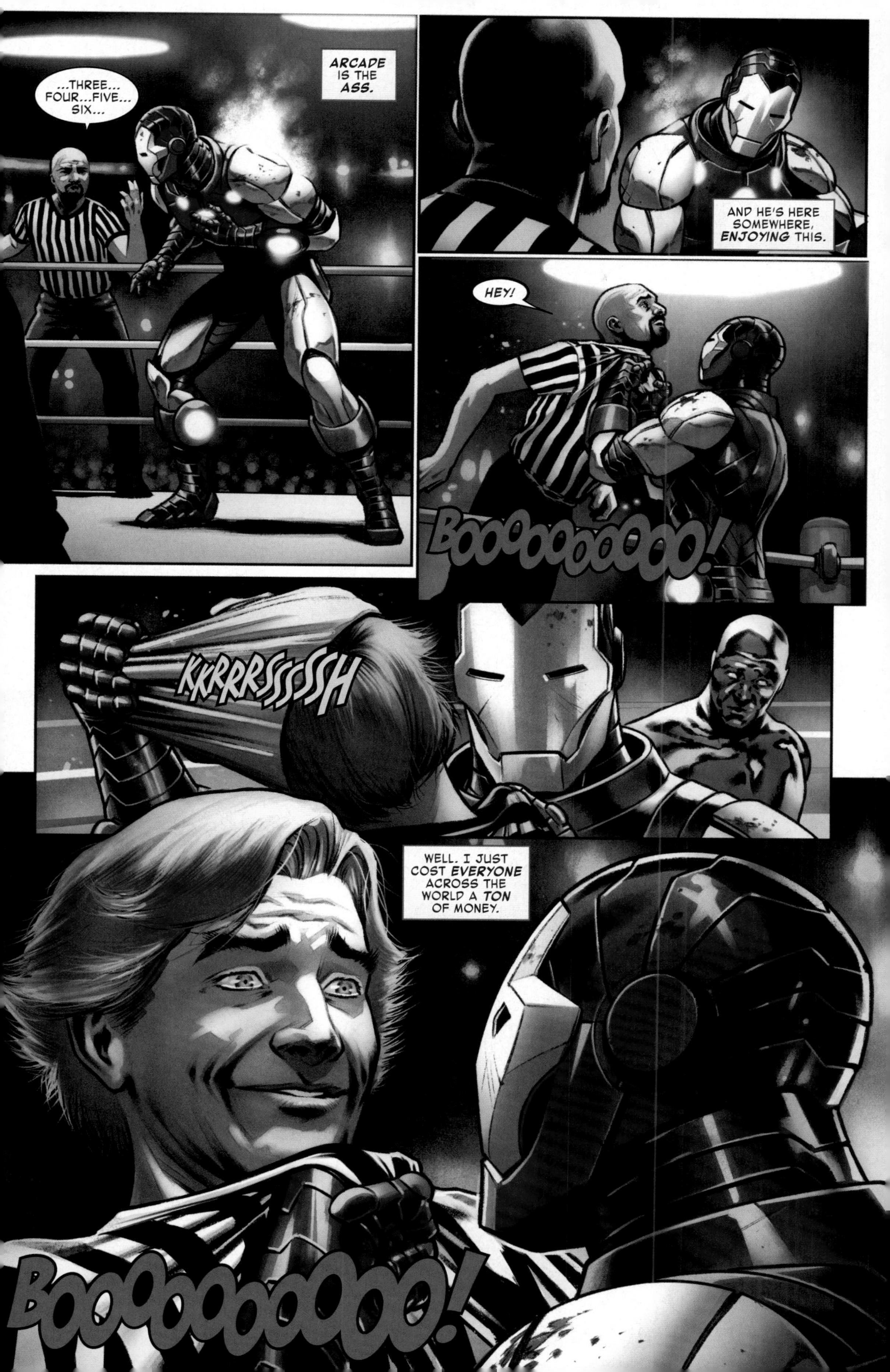
...THREE... FOUR...FIVE... SIX...
ARCADE IS THE ASS.
AND HE'S HERE SOMEWHERE, ENJOYING THIS.
HEY!
BOOOOOOOOOO!
KKRRRSSSSSH
WELL. I JUST COST EVERYONE ACROSS THE WORLD A TON OF MONEY.
BOOOOOOOOOOO!

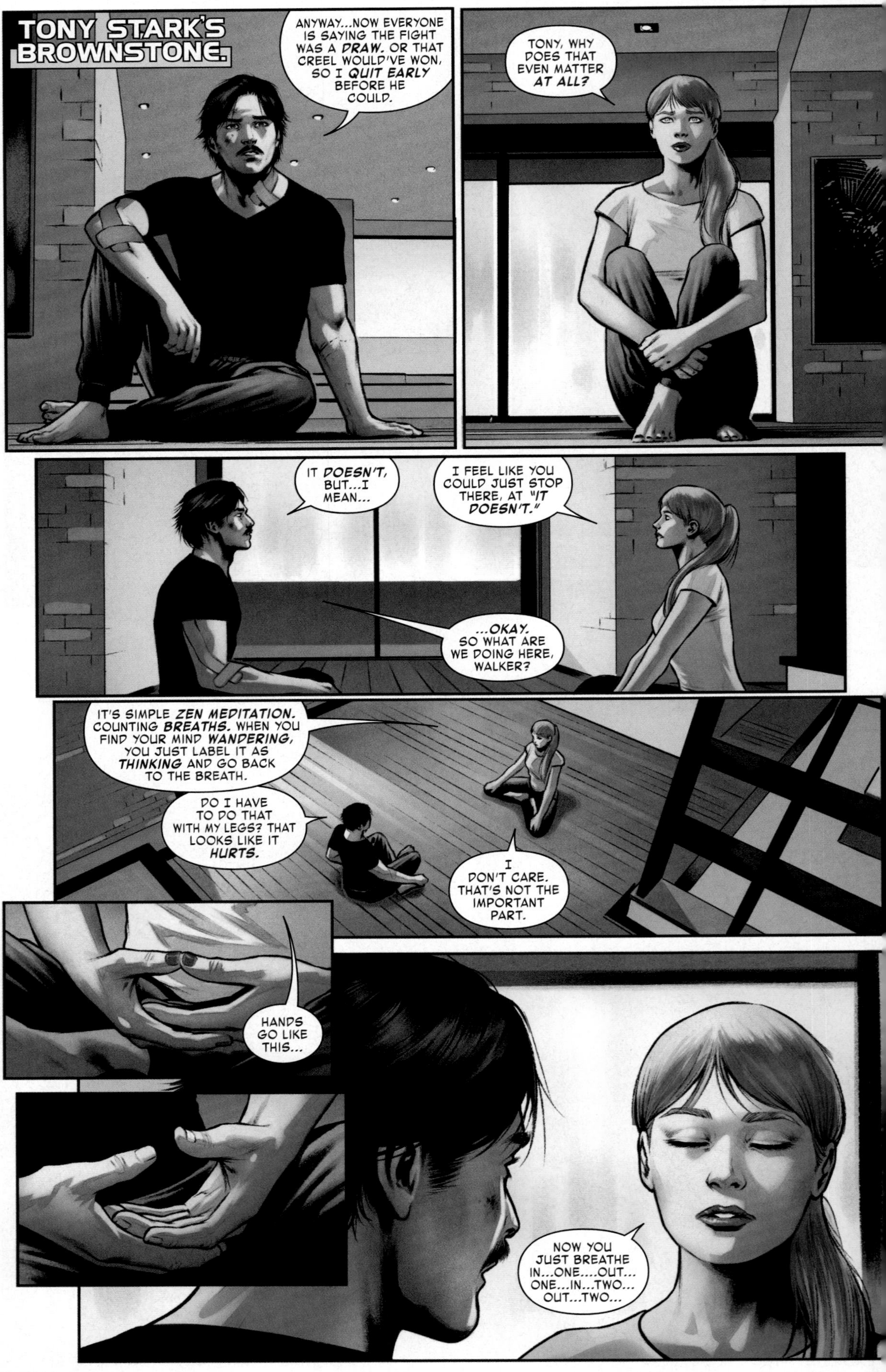
TONY STARK'S BROWNSTONE.
ANYWAY...NOW EVERYONE IS SAYING THE FIGHT WAS A *DRAW.* OR THAT CREEL WOULD'VE WON, SO I *QUIT EARLY* BEFORE HE COULD.
TONY, WHY DOES THAT EVEN MATTER *AT ALL?*
IT *DOESN'T,* BUT...I MEAN...
I FEEL LIKE YOU COULD JUST STOP THERE, AT *"IT DOESN'T."*
...OKAY. SO WHAT ARE WE DOING HERE, WALKER?
IT'S SIMPLE *ZEN MEDITATION.* COUNTING *BREATHS.* WHEN YOU FIND YOUR MIND *WANDERING,* YOU JUST LABEL IT AS *THINKING* AND GO BACK TO THE BREATH.
DO I HAVE TO DO THAT WITH MY LEGS? THAT LOOKS LIKE IT *HURTS.*
I DON'T CARE. THAT'S NOT THE IMPORTANT PART.
HANDS GO LIKE THIS...
NOW YOU JUST BREATHE IN...ONE....OUT... ONE...IN...TWO... OUT...TWO...

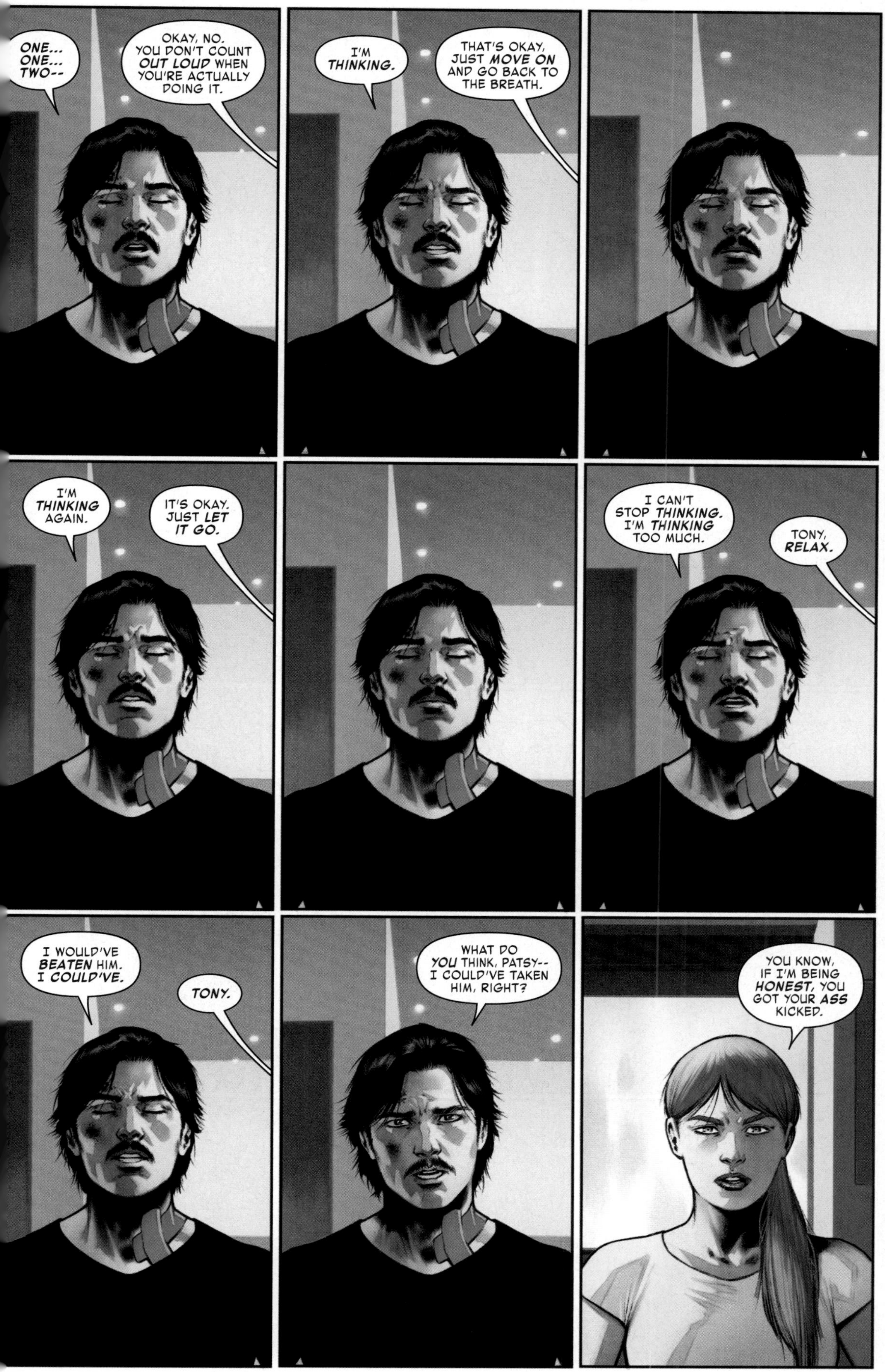
ONE... ONE... TWO--
OKAY, NO. YOU DON'T COUNT OUT LOUD WHEN YOU'RE ACTUALLY DOING IT.
I'M THINKING.
THAT'S OKAY, JUST MOVE ON AND GO BACK TO THE BREATH.
I'M THINKING AGAIN.
IT'S OKAY. JUST LET IT GO.
I CAN'T STOP THINKING. I'M THINKING TOO MUCH.
TONY, RELAX.
I WOULD'VE BEATEN HIM. I COULD'VE.
TONY.
WHAT DO YOU THINK, PATSY-- I COULD'VE TAKEN HIM, RIGHT?
YOU KNOW, IF I'M BEING HONEST, YOU GOT YOUR ASS KICKED.

WOW, OKAY.

I ALSO THINK YOU *KNEW* ARCADE WAS GOING TO CAPTURE YOU BUT YOU *LET* IT HAPPEN ANYWAY. *WHY?*

CREEL WAS THE *BAD GUY.* WHY DOES *EVERYBODY* ROOT FOR THE BAD GUY NOW?

YOU WANTED TO GET *BEAT UP* ON LIVE TV FOR SOME REASON. YOU'RE *PUNISHING* YOURSELF.

WHAT DO YOU FEEL LIKE YOU NEED TO PROVE?

THAT I'M STILL A HERO.

WHO DO YOU NEED TO PROVE THAT TO?

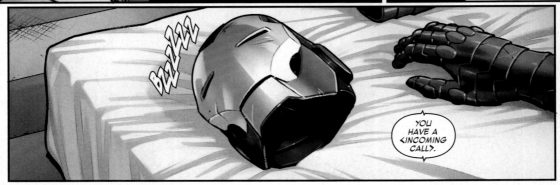

BZZZZZ

YOU HAVE A ‹INCOMING CALL›.

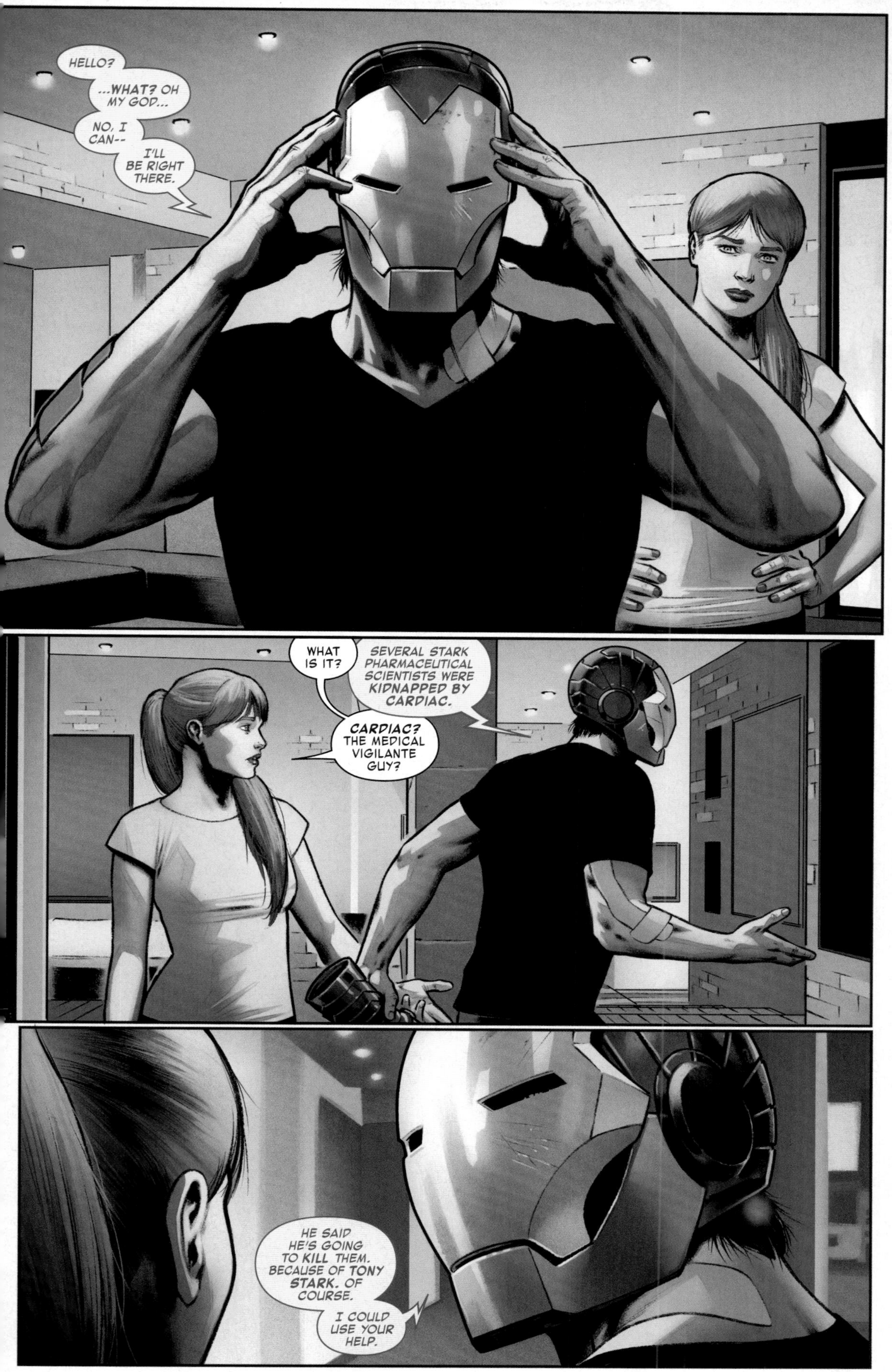
HELLO?
...WHAT? OH MY GOD...
NO, I CAN--
I'LL BE RIGHT THERE.
WHAT IS IT?
SEVERAL STARK PHARMACEUTICAL SCIENTISTS WERE KIDNAPPED BY CARDIAC.
CARDIAC? THE MEDICAL VIGILANTE GUY?
HE SAID HE'S GOING TO KILL THEM. BECAUSE OF TONY STARK. OF COURSE.
I COULD USE YOUR HELP.

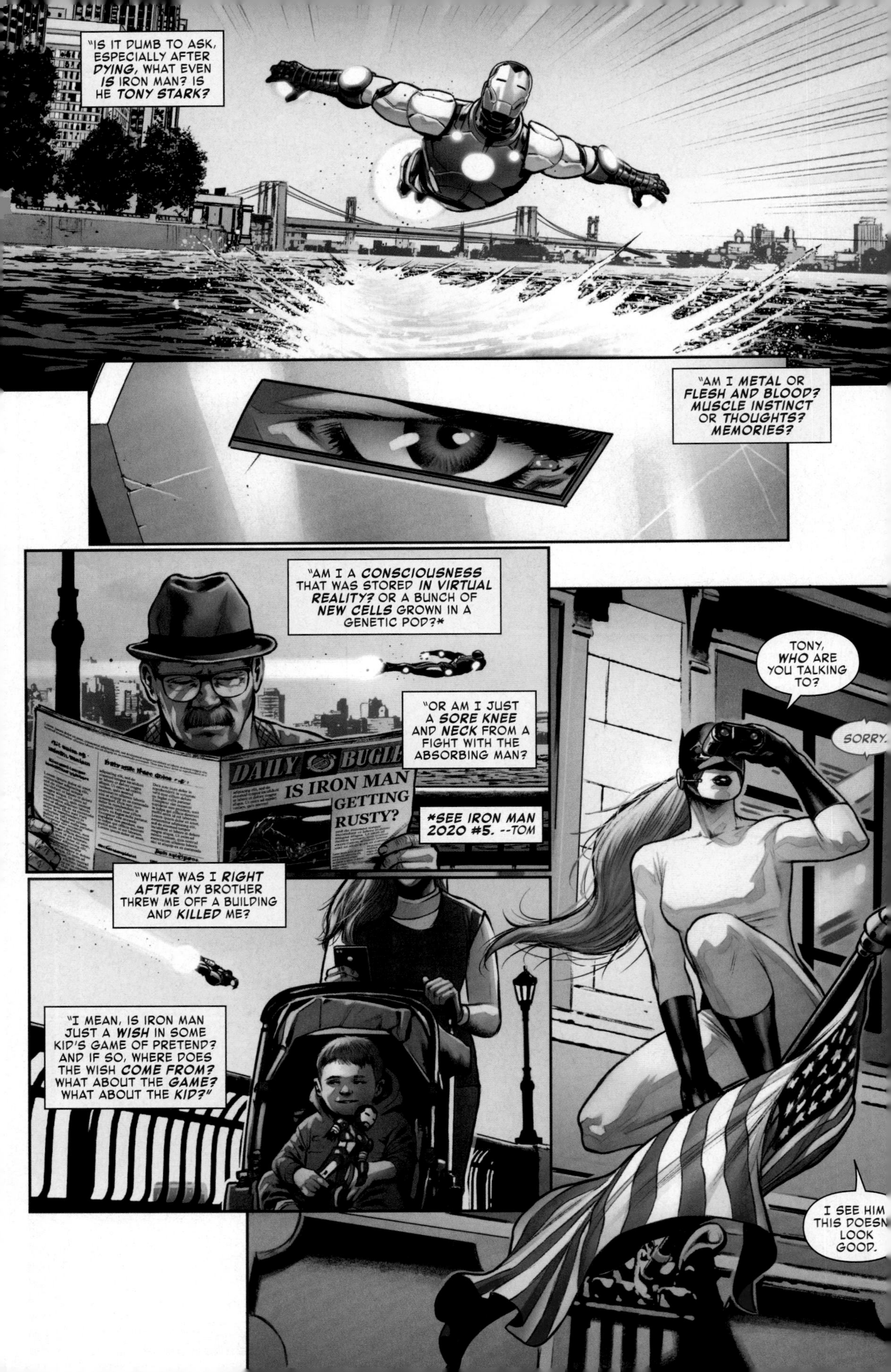

"IS IT DUMB TO ASK, ESPECIALLY AFTER DYING, WHAT EVEN IS IRON MAN? IS HE TONY STARK?
"AM I METAL OR FLESH AND BLOOD? MUSCLE INSTINCT OR THOUGHTS? MEMORIES?
"AM I A CONSCIOUSNESS THAT WAS STORED IN VIRTUAL REALITY? OR A BUNCH OF NEW CELLS GROWN IN A GENETIC POD?*
"OR AM I JUST A SORE KNEE AND NECK FROM A FIGHT WITH THE ABSORBING MAN?
DAILY BUGLE
IS IRON MAN GETTING RUSTY?
*SEE IRON MAN 2020 #5. --TOM
TONY, WHO ARE YOU TALKING TO?
SORRY.
"WHAT WAS I RIGHT AFTER MY BROTHER THREW ME OFF A BUILDING AND KILLED ME?
"I MEAN, IS IRON MAN JUST A WISH IN SOME KID'S GAME OF PRETEND? AND IF SO, WHERE DOES THE WISH COME FROM? WHAT ABOUT THE GAME? WHAT ABOUT THE KID?"
I SEE HIM. THIS DOESN'T LOOK GOOD.

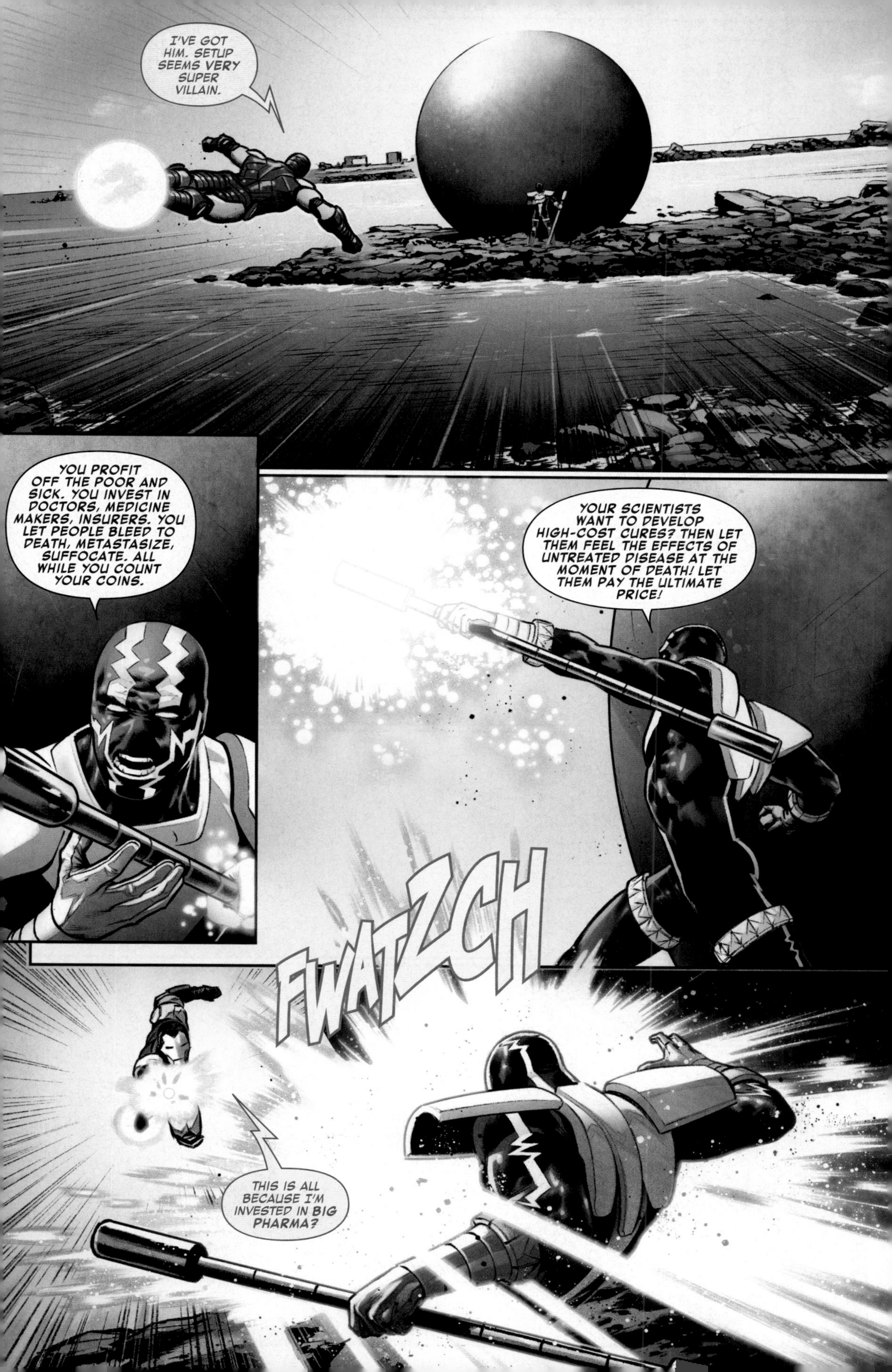
I'VE GOT HIM. SETUP SEEMS VERY SUPER VILLAIN.
YOU PROFIT OFF THE POOR AND SICK. YOU INVEST IN DOCTORS, MEDICINE MAKERS, INSURERS. YOU LET PEOPLE BLEED TO DEATH, METASTASIZE, SUFFOCATE. ALL WHILE YOU COUNT YOUR COINS.
YOUR SCIENTISTS WANT TO DEVELOP HIGH-COST CURES? THEN LET THEM FEEL THE EFFECTS OF UNTREATED DISEASE AT THE MOMENT OF DEATH! LET THEM PAY THE ULTIMATE PRICE!
FWATZCH
THIS IS ALL BECAUSE I'M INVESTED IN BIG PHARMA?

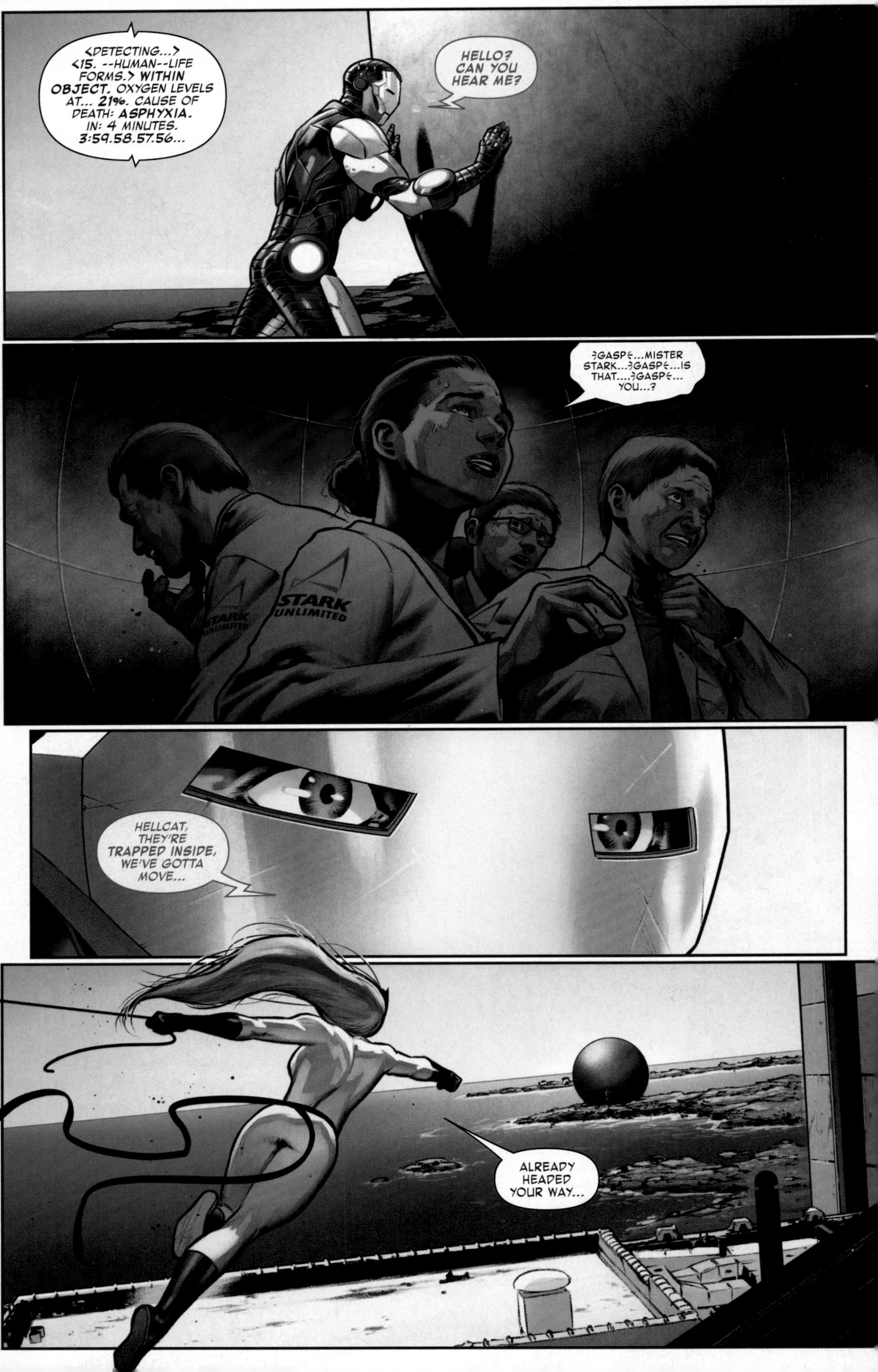
<DETECTING...> <15. --HUMAN--LIFE FORMS.> WITHIN OBJECT. OXYGEN LEVELS AT... 21%. CAUSE OF DEATH: ASPHYXIA. IN: 4 MINUTES. 3:59.58.57.56...
HELLO? CAN YOU HEAR ME?
GASP...MISTER STARK...GASP...IS THAT....GASP... YOU...?
STARK UNLIMITED
STARK UNLIMITED
HELLCAT, THEY'RE TRAPPED INSIDE, WE'VE GOTTA MOVE...
ALREADY HEADED YOUR WAY...

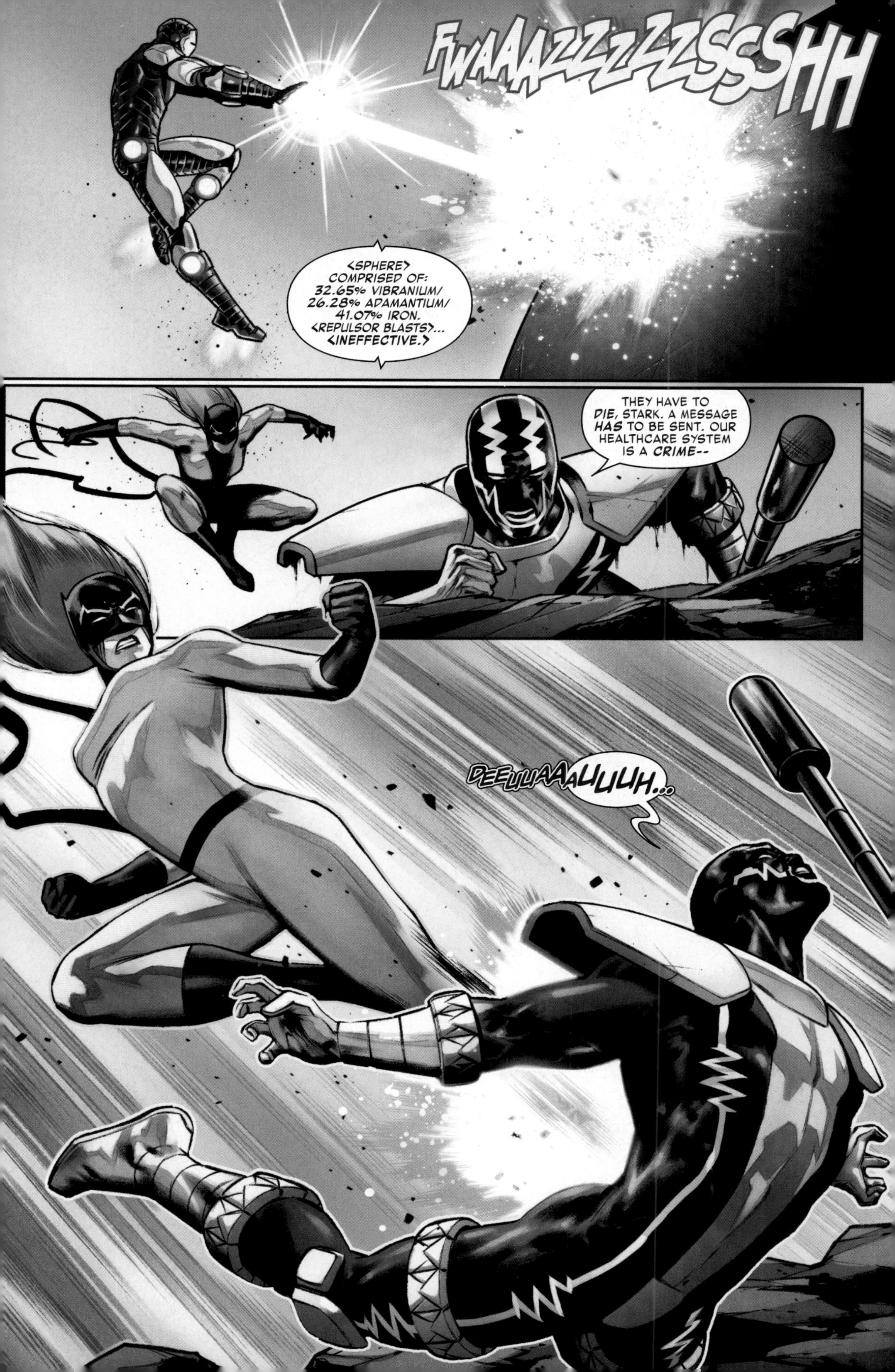
FWAAAZZZZZSSSHH
<SPHERE> COMPRISED OF: 32.65% VIBRANIUM/ 26.28% ADAMANTIUM/ 41.07% IRON. <REPULSOR BLASTS>... <INEFFECTIVE.>
THEY HAVE TO *DIE*, STARK. A MESSAGE **HAS** TO BE SENT. OUR HEALTHCARE SYSTEM IS A *CRIME*--
DEEUUAAAUUUH...

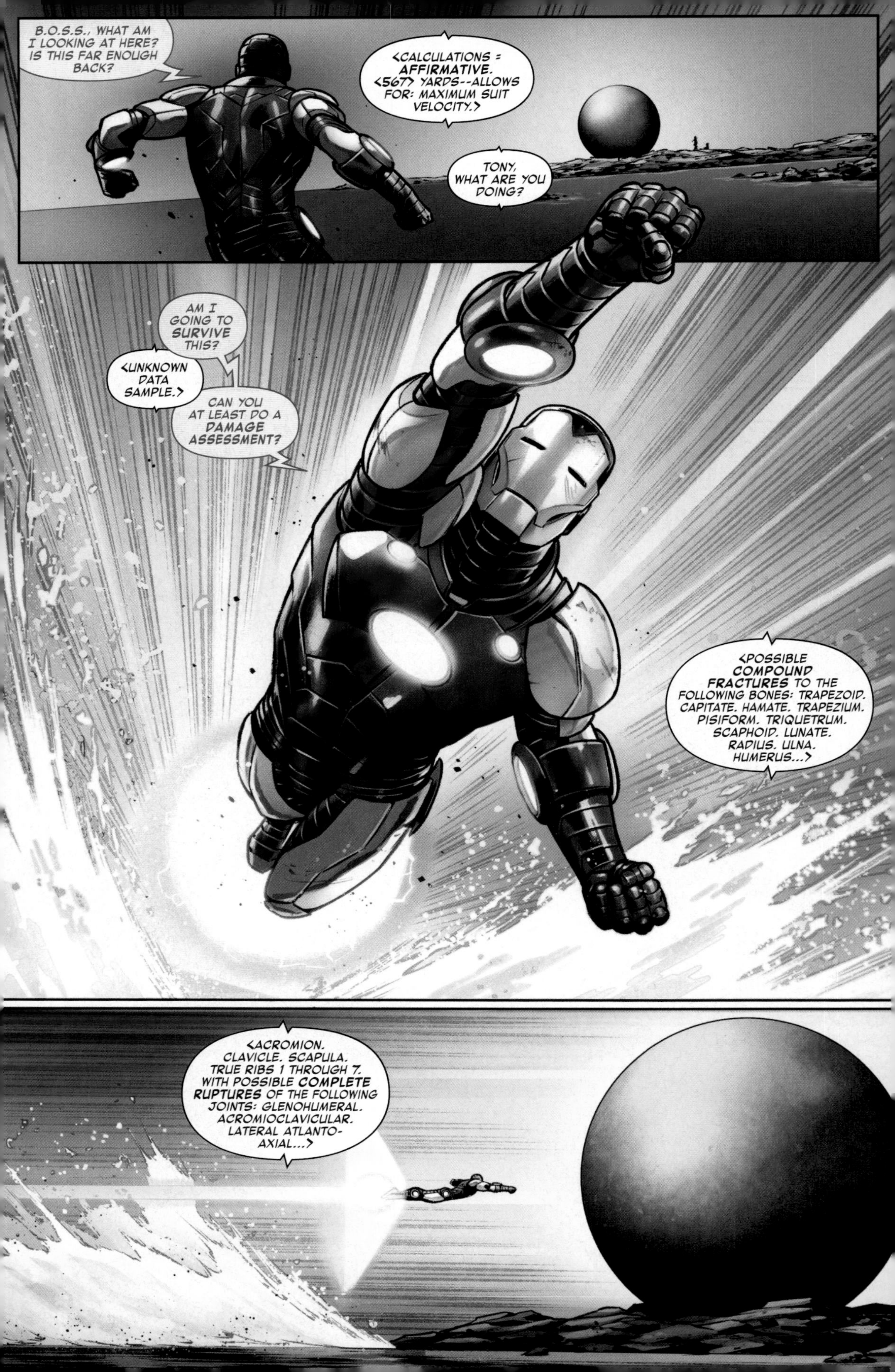
B.O.S.S., WHAT AM I LOOKING AT HERE? IS THIS FAR ENOUGH BACK?
<CALCULATIONS = AFFIRMATIVE. <567> YARDS--ALLOWS FOR: MAXIMUM SUIT VELOCITY.>
TONY, WHAT ARE YOU DOING?
AM I GOING TO SURVIVE THIS?
<UNKNOWN DATA SAMPLE.>
CAN YOU AT LEAST DO A DAMAGE ASSESSMENT?
<POSSIBLE COMPOUND FRACTURES TO THE FOLLOWING BONES: TRAPEZOID. CAPITATE. HAMATE. TRAPEZIUM. PISIFORM. TRIQUETRUM. SCAPHOID. LUNATE. RADIUS. ULNA. HUMERUS...>
<ACROMION. CLAVICLE. SCAPULA. TRUE RIBS 1 THROUGH 7. WITH POSSIBLE COMPLETE RUPTURES OF THE FOLLOWING JOINTS: GLENOHUMERAL. ACROMIOCLAVICULAR. LATERAL ATLANTO-AXIAL...>

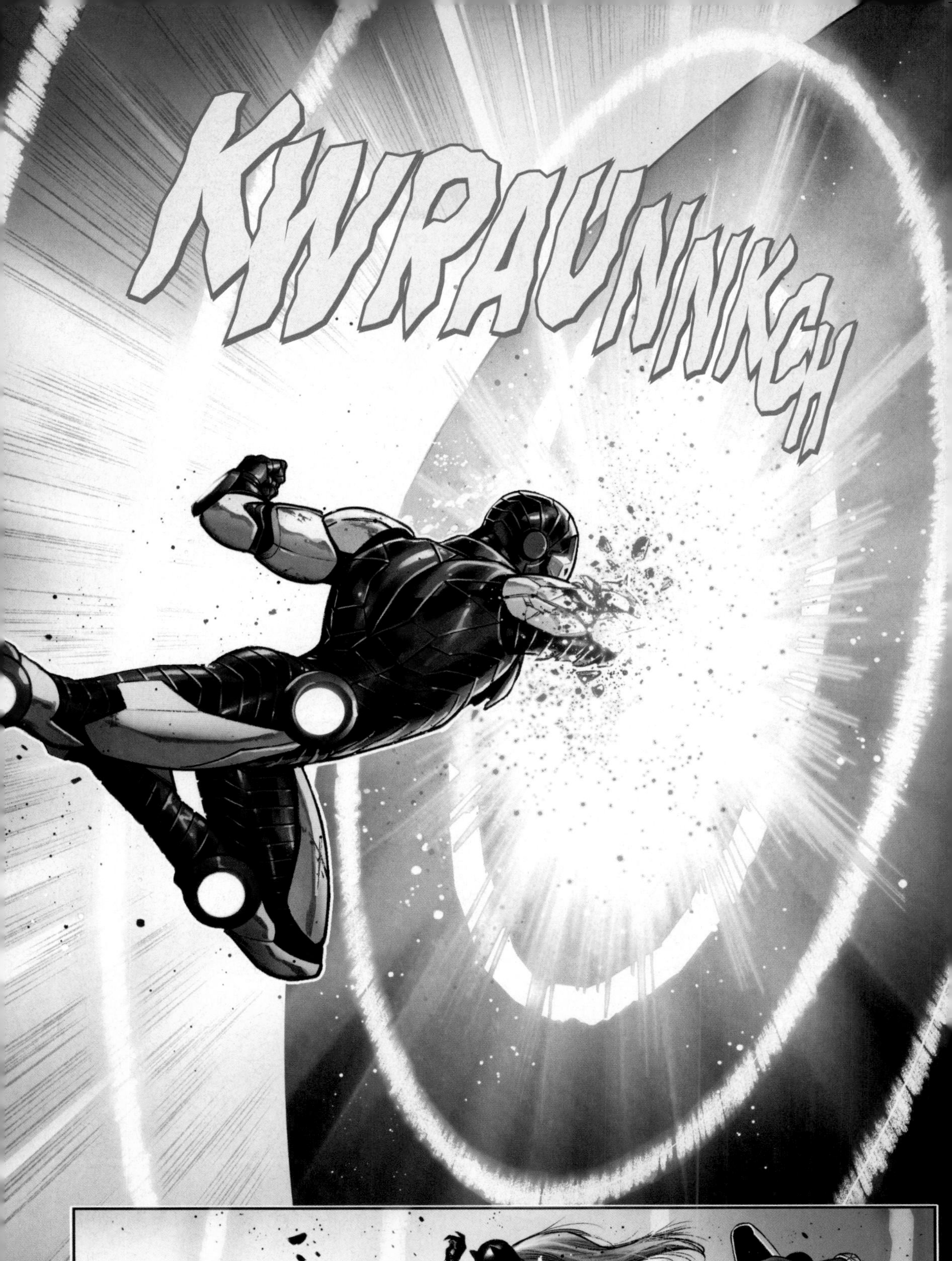
KWRAUNNKCH
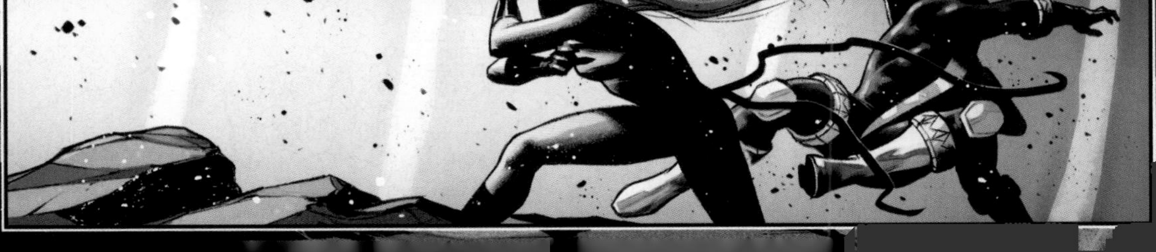

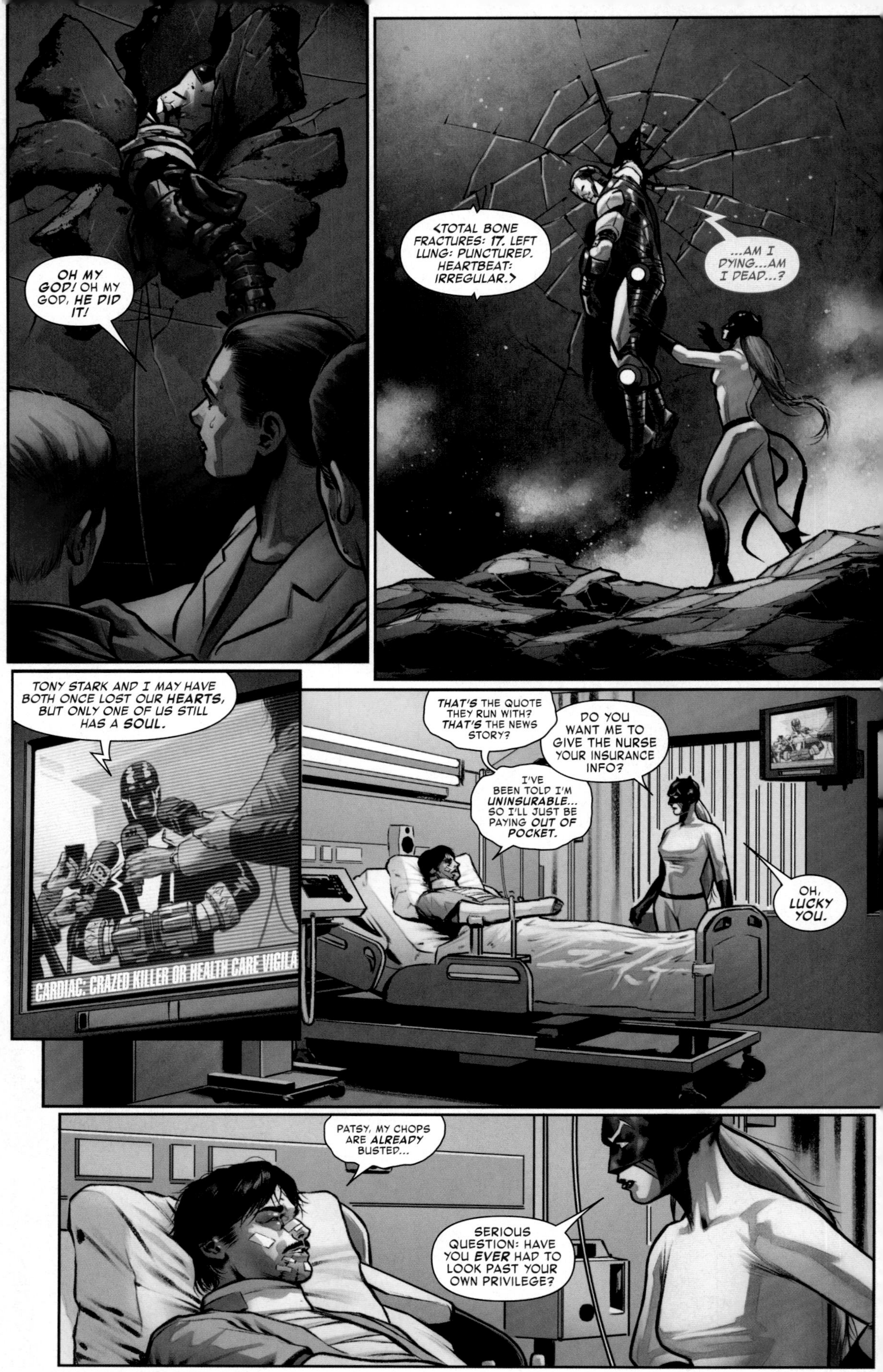
OH MY GOD! OH MY GOD, HE DID IT!
<TOTAL BONE FRACTURES: 17. LEFT LUNG: PUNCTURED. HEARTBEAT: IRREGULAR.>
...AM I DYING...AM I DEAD...?
TONY STARK AND I MAY HAVE BOTH ONCE LOST OUR HEARTS, BUT ONLY ONE OF US STILL HAS A SOUL.
CARDIAC: CRAZED KILLER OR HEALTH CARE VIGILA
THAT'S THE QUOTE THEY RUN WITH? THAT'S THE NEWS STORY?
DO YOU WANT ME TO GIVE THE NURSE YOUR INSURANCE INFO?
I'VE BEEN TOLD I'M UNINSURABLE... SO I'LL JUST BE PAYING OUT OF POCKET.
OH, LUCKY YOU.
PATSY, MY CHOPS ARE ALREADY BUSTED...
SERIOUS QUESTION: HAVE YOU EVER HAD TO LOOK PAST YOUR OWN PRIVILEGE?

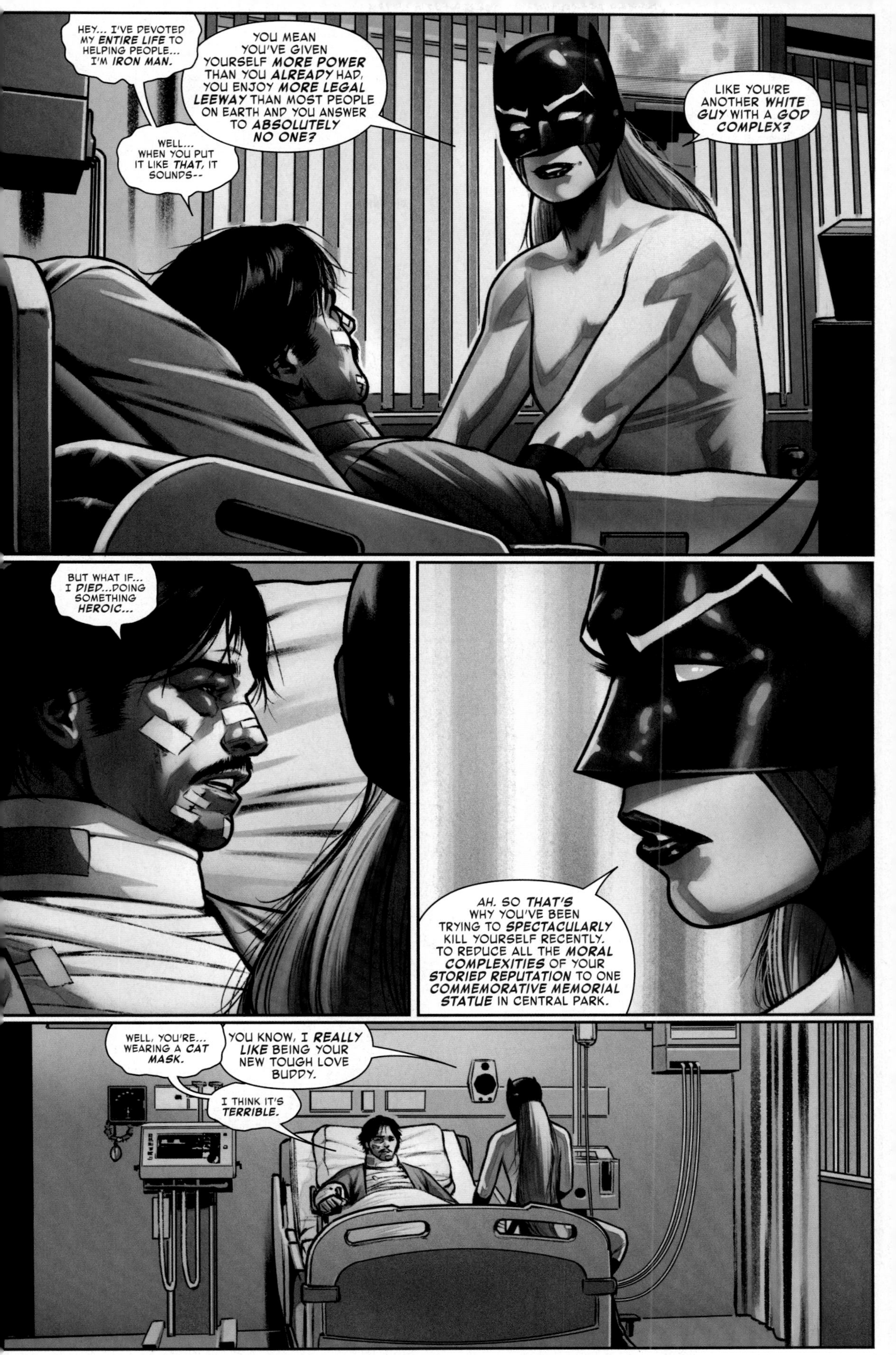
HEY... I'VE DEVOTED MY ENTIRE LIFE TO HELPING PEOPLE... I'M IRON MAN.
YOU MEAN YOU'VE GIVEN YOURSELF MORE POWER THAN YOU ALREADY HAD, YOU ENJOY MORE LEGAL LEEWAY THAN MOST PEOPLE ON EARTH AND YOU ANSWER TO ABSOLUTELY NO ONE?
WELL... WHEN YOU PUT IT LIKE THAT, IT SOUNDS--
LIKE YOU'RE ANOTHER WHITE GUY WITH A GOD COMPLEX?
BUT WHAT IF... I DIED...DOING SOMETHING HEROIC...
AH. SO THAT'S WHY YOU'VE BEEN TRYING TO SPECTACULARLY KILL YOURSELF RECENTLY. TO REDUCE ALL THE MORAL COMPLEXITIES OF YOUR STORIED REPUTATION TO ONE COMMEMORATIVE MEMORIAL STATUE IN CENTRAL PARK.
WELL, YOU'RE... WEARING A CAT MASK.
YOU KNOW, I REALLY LIKE BEING YOUR NEW TOUGH LOVE BUDDY.
I THINK IT'S TERRIBLE.

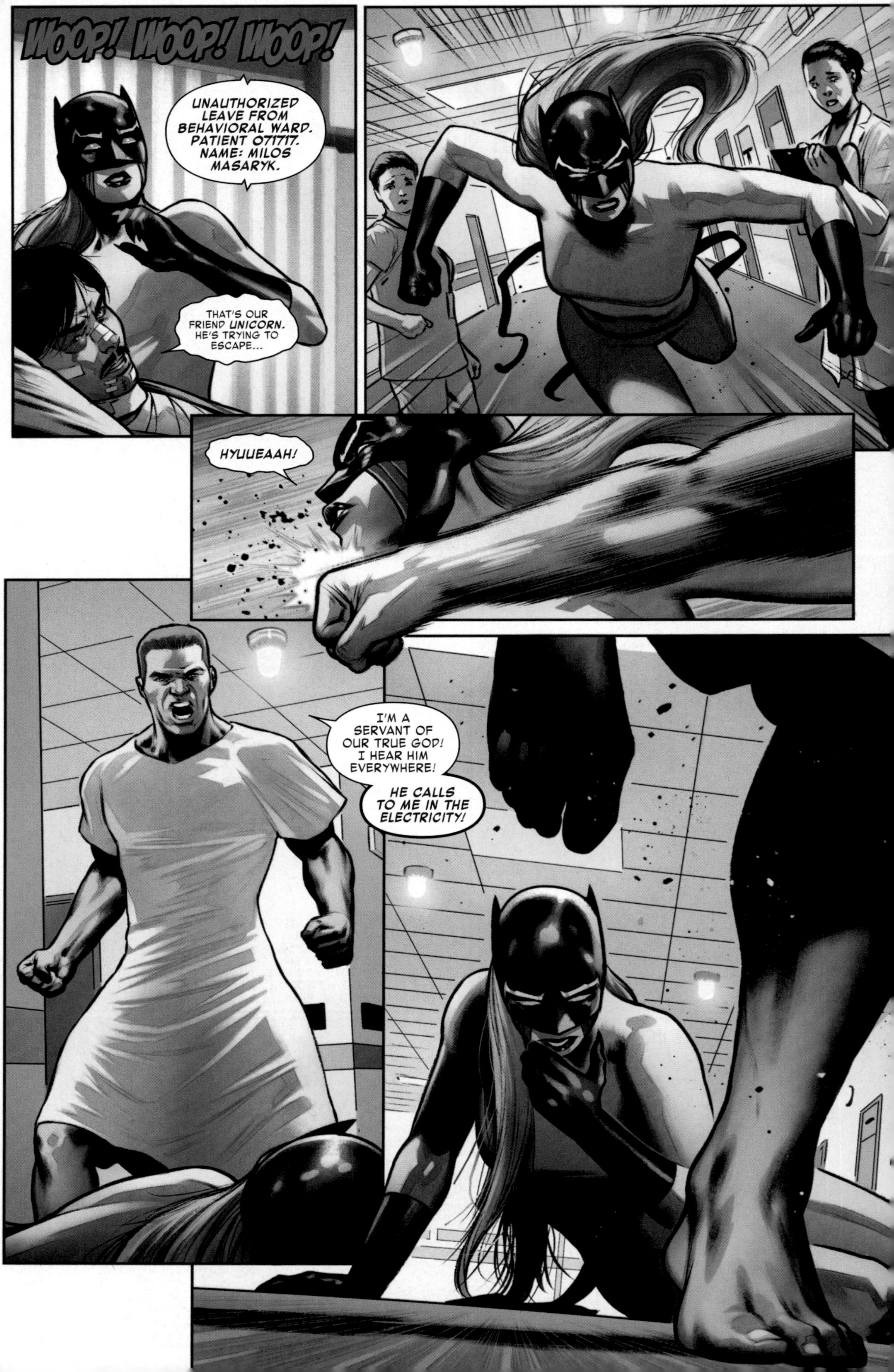
WOOP! WOOP! WOOP!
UNAUTHORIZED LEAVE FROM BEHAVIORAL WARD. PATIENT 071717. NAME: MILOS MASARYK.
THAT'S OUR FRIEND UNICORN. HE'S TRYING TO ESCAPE...
HYUUEAAH!
I'M A SERVANT OF OUR TRUE GOD! I HEAR HIM EVERYWHERE!
HE CALLS TO ME IN THE ELECTRICITY!

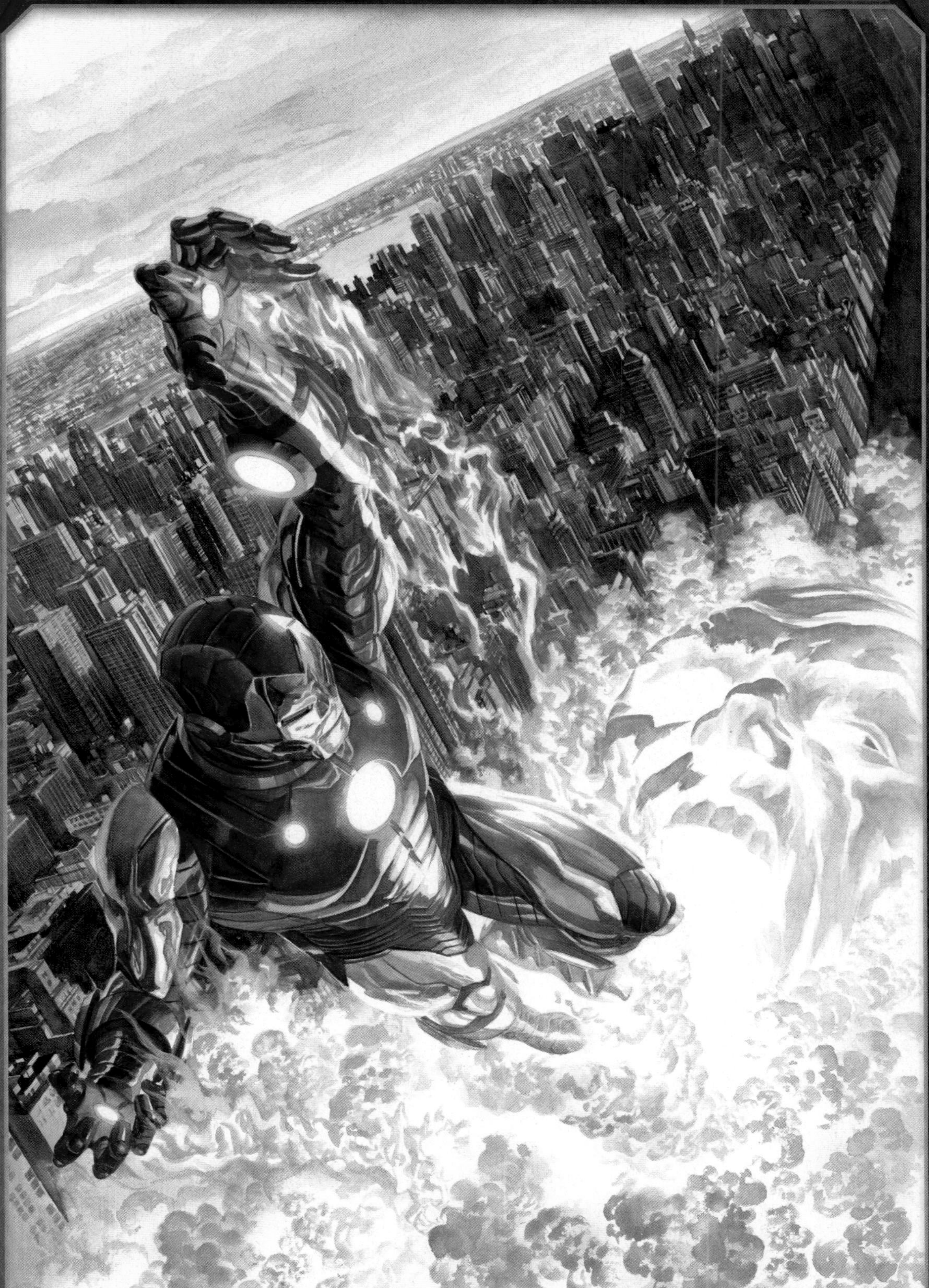

3

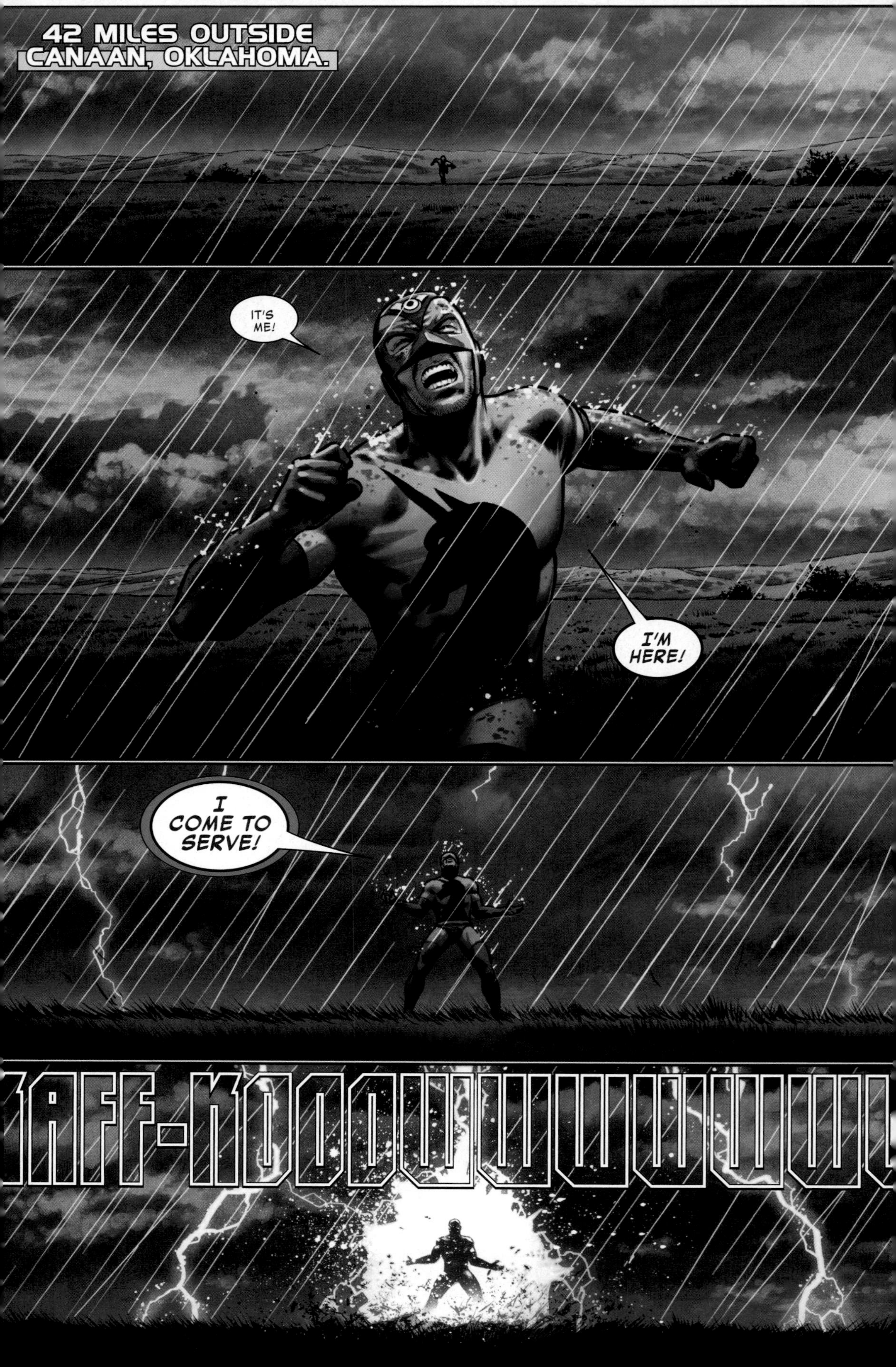
42 MILES OUTSIDE CANAAN, OKLAHOMA.
IT'S ME!
I'M HERE!
I COME TO SERVE!
AFF-KOOOWWWWWW

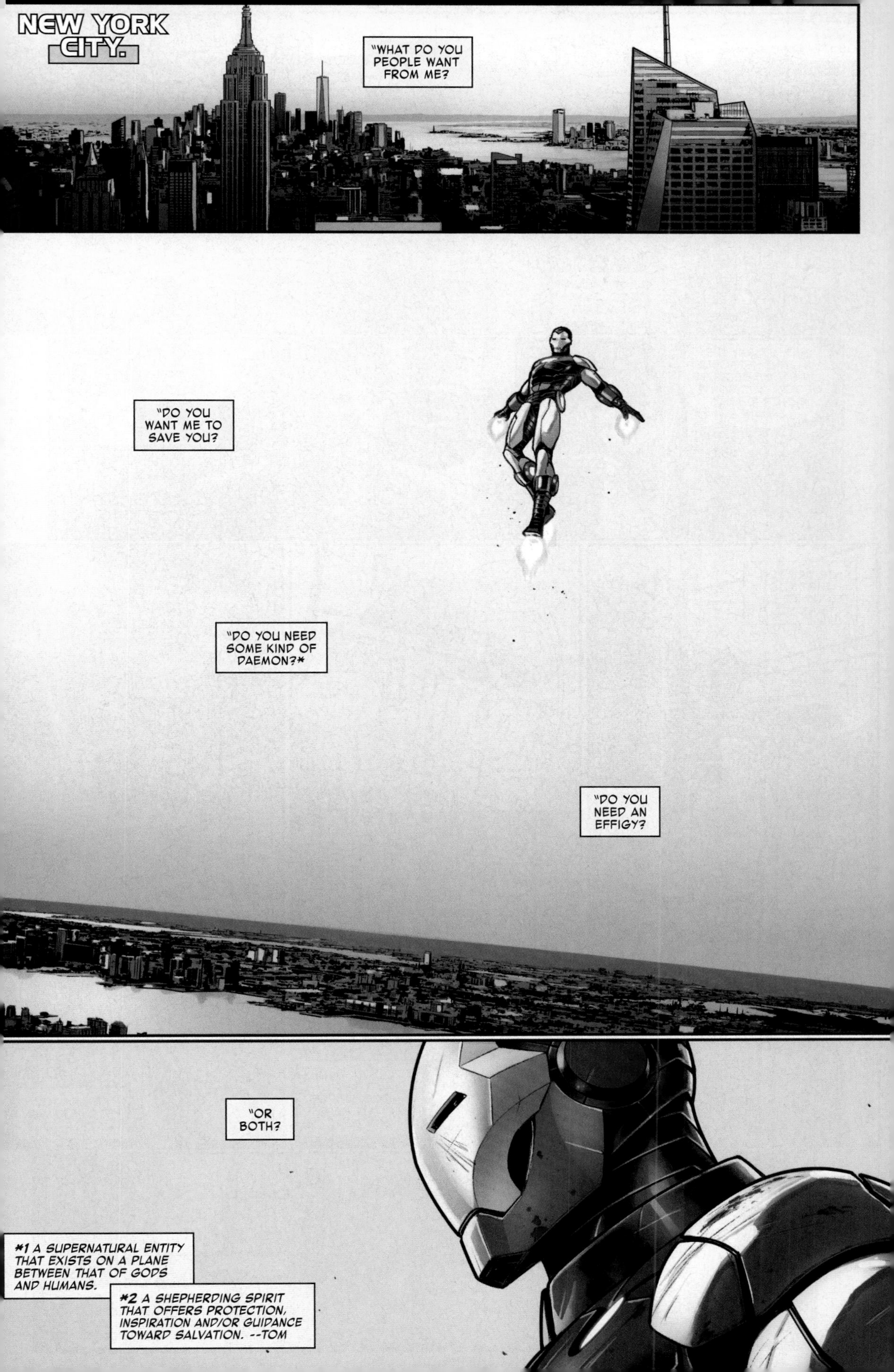
NEW YORK CITY.
"WHAT DO YOU PEOPLE WANT FROM ME?
"DO YOU WANT ME TO SAVE YOU?
"DO YOU NEED SOME KIND OF DAEMON?*
"DO YOU NEED AN EFFIGY?
"OR BOTH?
*1 A SUPERNATURAL ENTITY THAT EXISTS ON A PLANE BETWEEN THAT OF GODS AND HUMANS.
*2 A SHEPHERDING SPIRIT THAT OFFERS PROTECTION, INSPIRATION AND/OR GUIDANCE TOWARD SALVATION. --TOM

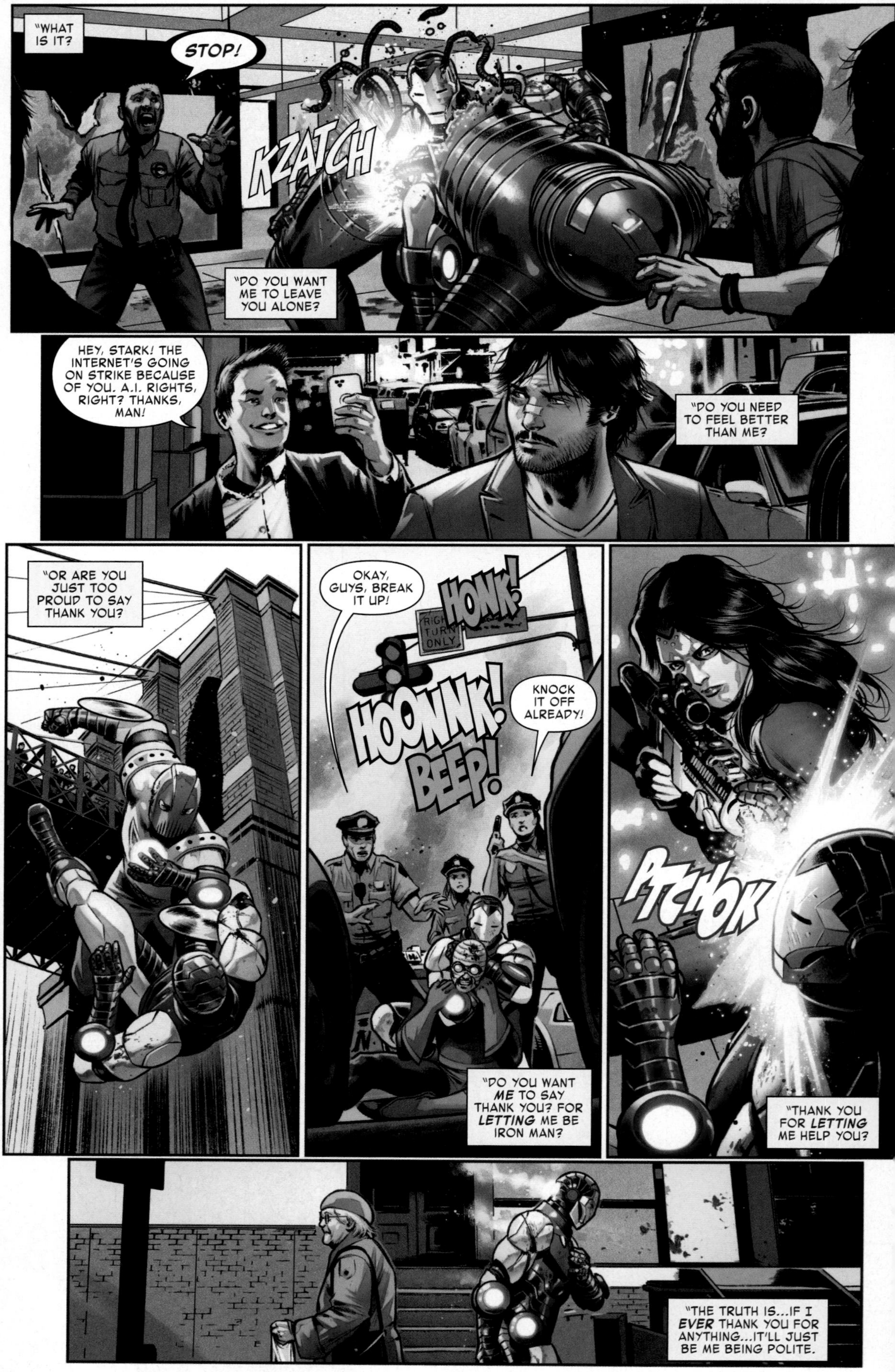
"WHAT IS IT?
STOP!
KZATCH
"DO YOU WANT ME TO LEAVE YOU ALONE?
HEY, STARK! THE INTERNET'S GOING ON STRIKE BECAUSE OF YOU. A.I. RIGHTS, RIGHT? THANKS, MAN!
"DO YOU NEED TO FEEL BETTER THAN ME?
"OR ARE YOU JUST TOO PROUD TO SAY THANK YOU?
OKAY, GUYS, BREAK IT UP!
HONK!
RIGHT TURN ONLY
HOONNK!
BEEP!
KNOCK IT OFF ALREADY!
"DO YOU WANT ME TO SAY THANK YOU? FOR LETTING ME BE IRON MAN?
PTCHOK
"THANK YOU FOR LETTING ME HELP YOU?
"THE TRUTH IS...IF I EVER THANK YOU FOR ANYTHING...IT'LL JUST BE ME BEING POLITE.

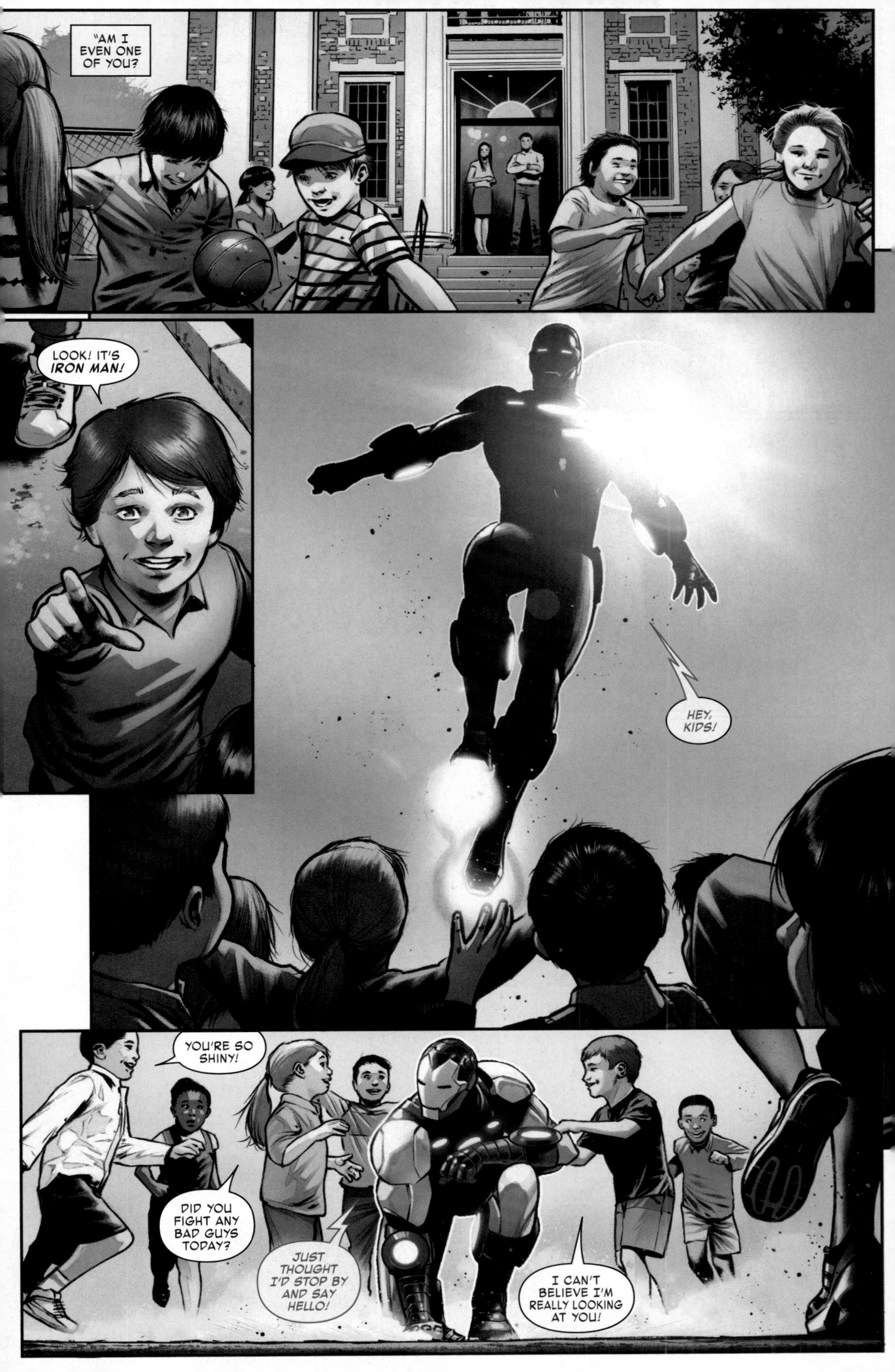
"AM I EVEN ONE OF YOU?
LOOK! IT'S IRON MAN!
HEY, KIDS!
YOU'RE SO SHINY!
DID YOU FIGHT ANY BAD GUYS TODAY?
JUST THOUGHT I'D STOP BY AND SAY HELLO!
I CAN'T BELIEVE I'M REALLY LOOKING AT YOU!

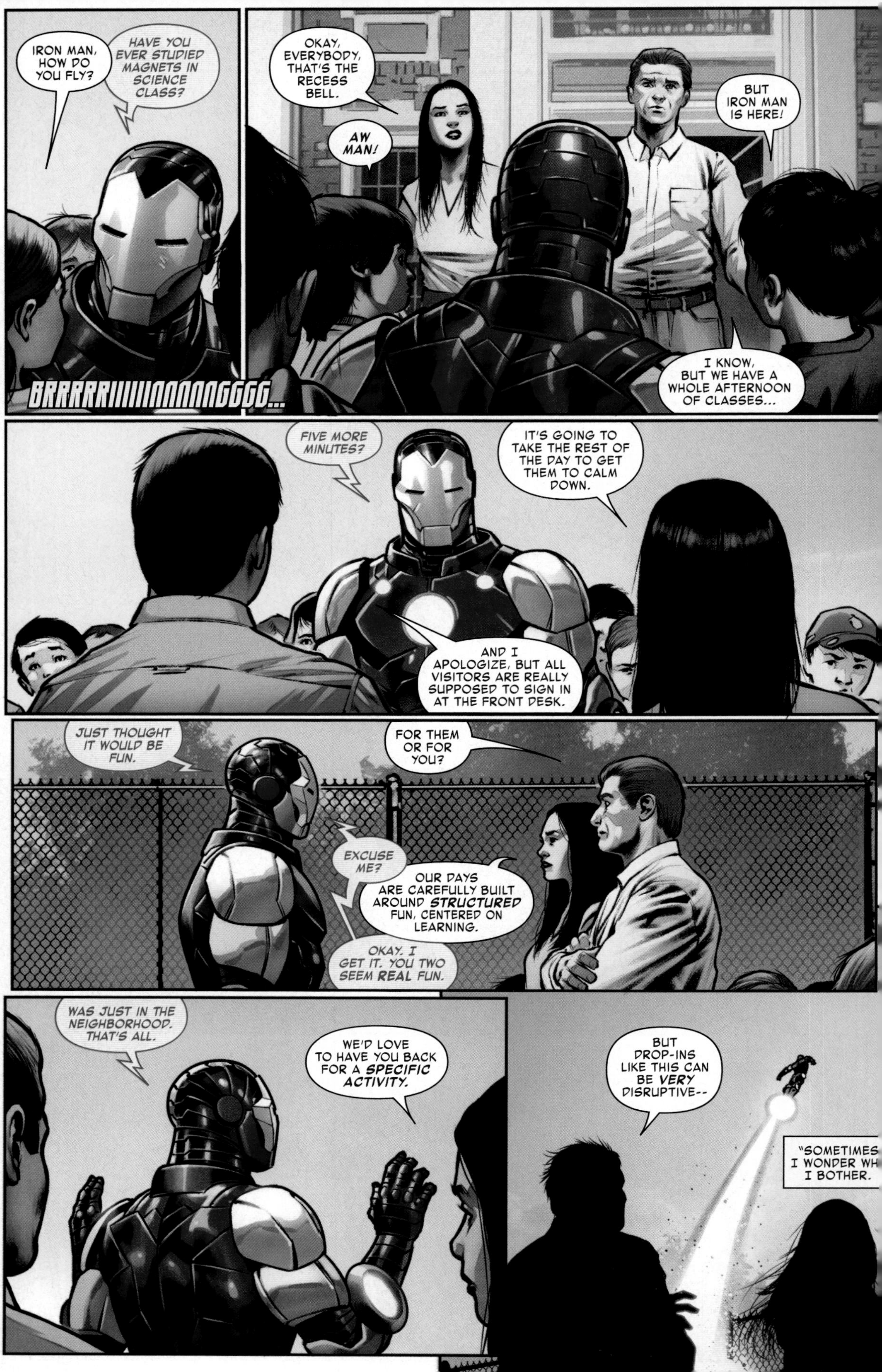

IRON MAN, HOW DO YOU FLY?
HAVE YOU EVER STUDIED MAGNETS IN SCIENCE CLASS?
BRRRRRIIIIIINNNNNGGGG...
OKAY, EVERYBODY, THAT'S THE RECESS BELL.
AW MAN!
BUT IRON MAN IS HERE!
I KNOW, BUT WE HAVE A WHOLE AFTERNOON OF CLASSES...
FIVE MORE MINUTES?
IT'S GOING TO TAKE THE REST OF THE DAY TO GET THEM TO CALM DOWN.
AND I APOLOGIZE, BUT ALL VISITORS ARE REALLY SUPPOSED TO SIGN IN AT THE FRONT DESK.
JUST THOUGHT IT WOULD BE FUN.
FOR THEM OR FOR YOU?
EXCUSE ME?
OUR DAYS ARE CAREFULLY BUILT AROUND **STRUCTURED** FUN, CENTERED ON LEARNING.
OKAY. I GET IT. YOU TWO SEEM **REAL** FUN.
WAS JUST IN THE NEIGHBORHOOD. THAT'S ALL.
WE'D LOVE TO HAVE YOU BACK FOR A **SPECIFIC ACTIVITY.**
BUT DROP-INS LIKE THIS CAN BE **VERY** DISRUPTIVE--
"SOMETIMES I WONDER WH I BOTHER.

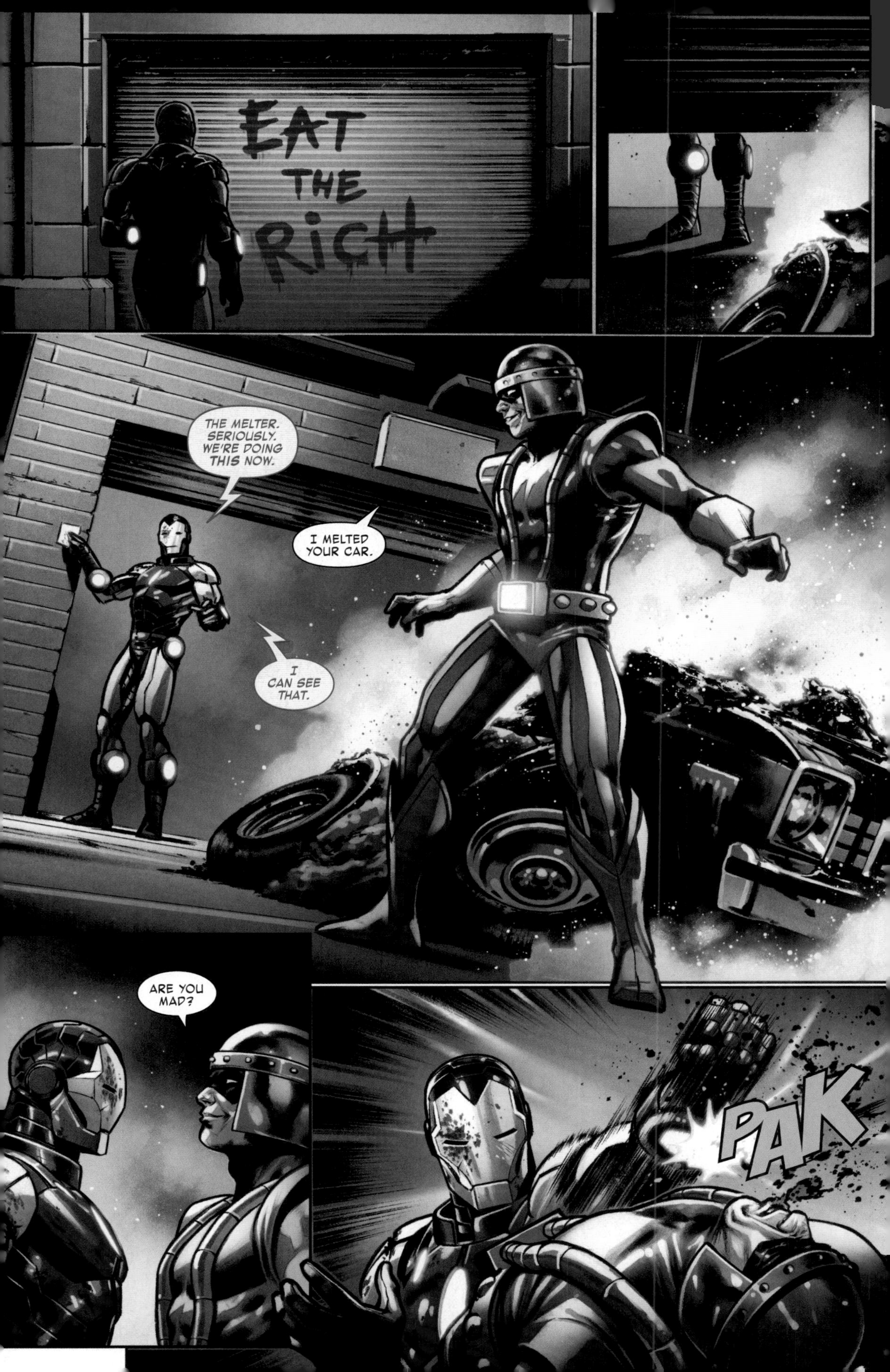
EAT THE RICH
THE MELTER. SERIOUSLY. WE'RE DOING THIS NOW.
I MELTED YOUR CAR.
I CAN SEE THAT.
ARE YOU MAD?
PAK

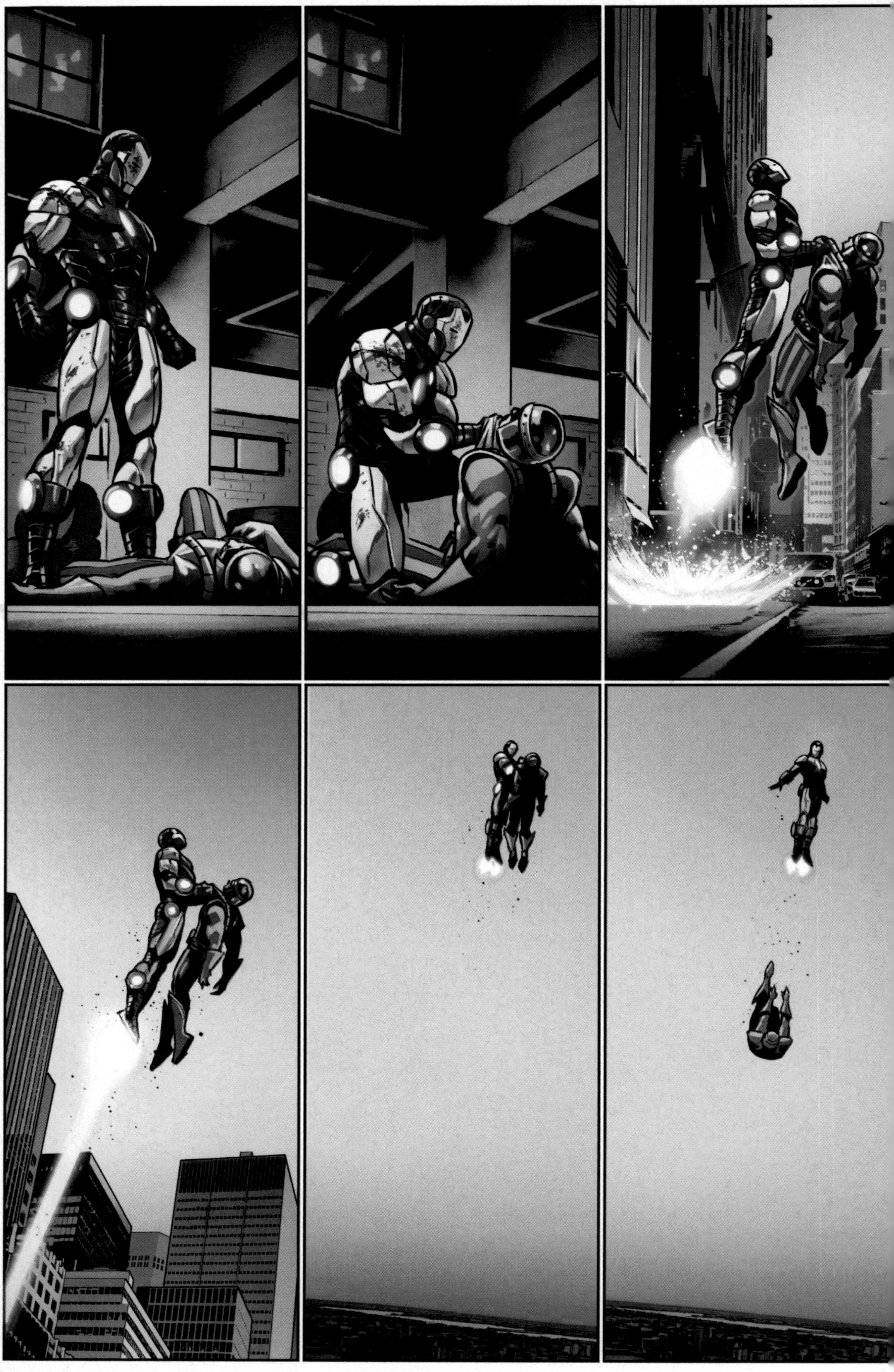

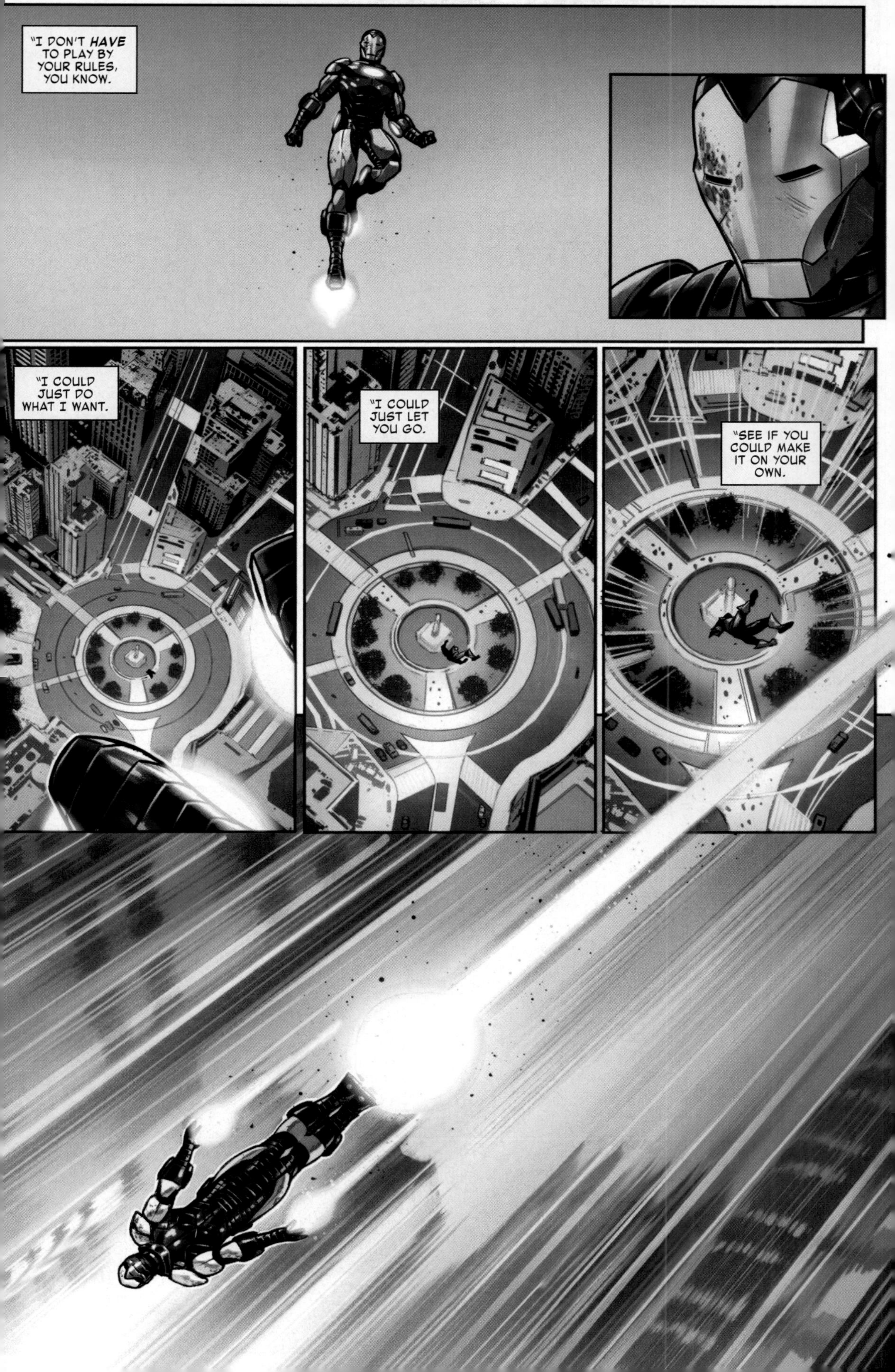
"I DON'T *HAVE* TO PLAY BY YOUR RULES, YOU KNOW.
"I COULD JUST DO WHAT I WANT.
"I COULD JUST LET YOU GO.
"SEE IF YOU COULD MAKE IT ON YOUR OWN.

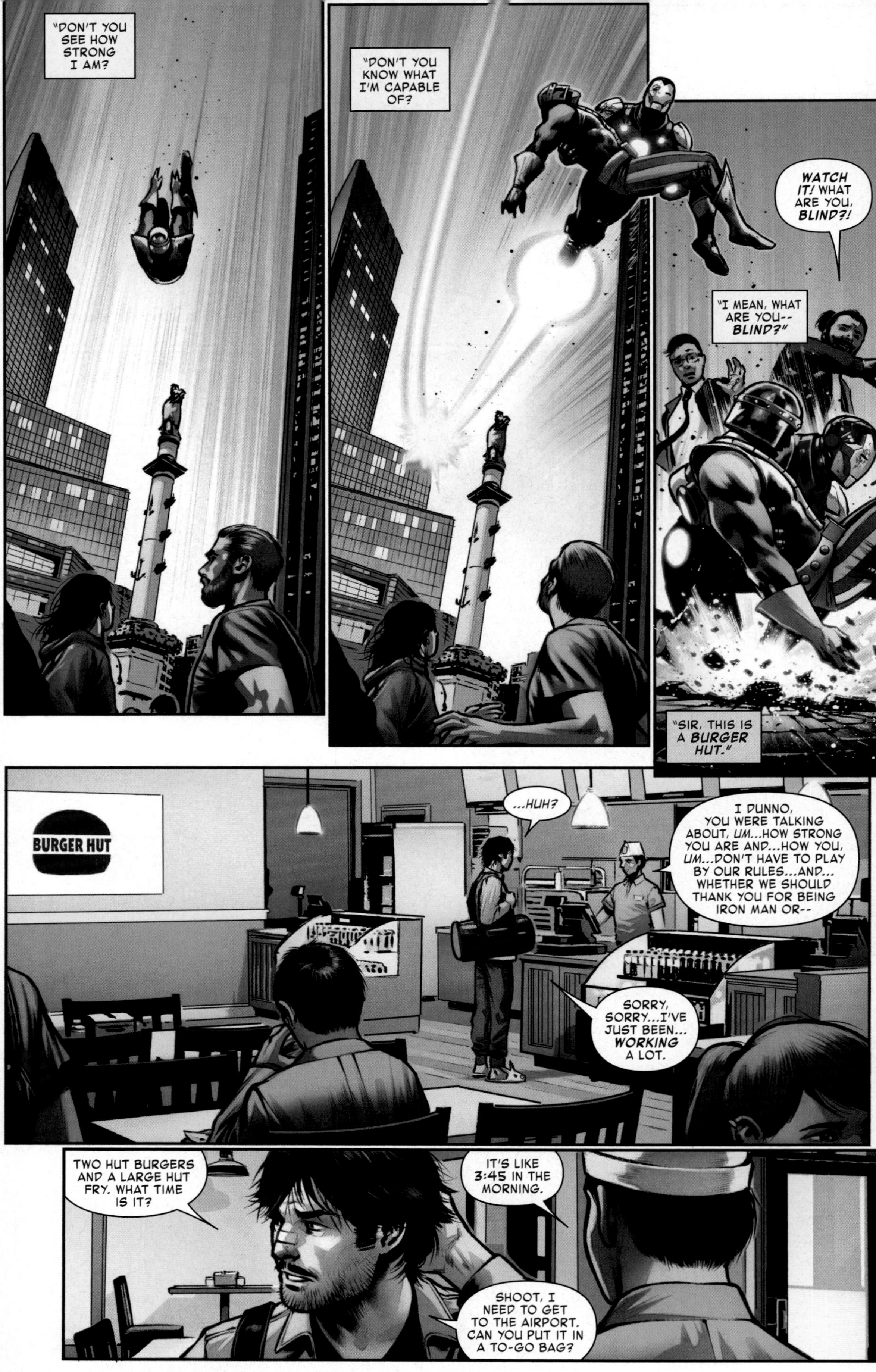
"DON'T YOU SEE HOW STRONG I AM?
"DON'T YOU KNOW WHAT I'M CAPABLE OF?
WATCH IT! WHAT ARE YOU, BLIND?!
"I MEAN, WHAT ARE YOU-- BLIND?"
"SIR, THIS IS A BURGER HUT."
BURGER HUT
...HUH?
I DUNNO, YOU WERE TALKING ABOUT, UM...HOW STRONG YOU ARE AND...HOW YOU, UM...DON'T HAVE TO PLAY BY OUR RULES...AND... WHETHER WE SHOULD THANK YOU FOR BEING IRON MAN OR--
SORRY, SORRY...I'VE JUST BEEN... WORKING A LOT.
TWO HUT BURGERS AND A LARGE HUT FRY. WHAT TIME IS IT?
IT'S LIKE 3:45 IN THE MORNING.
SHOOT, I NEED TO GET TO THE AIRPORT. CAN YOU PUT IT IN A TO-GO BAG?

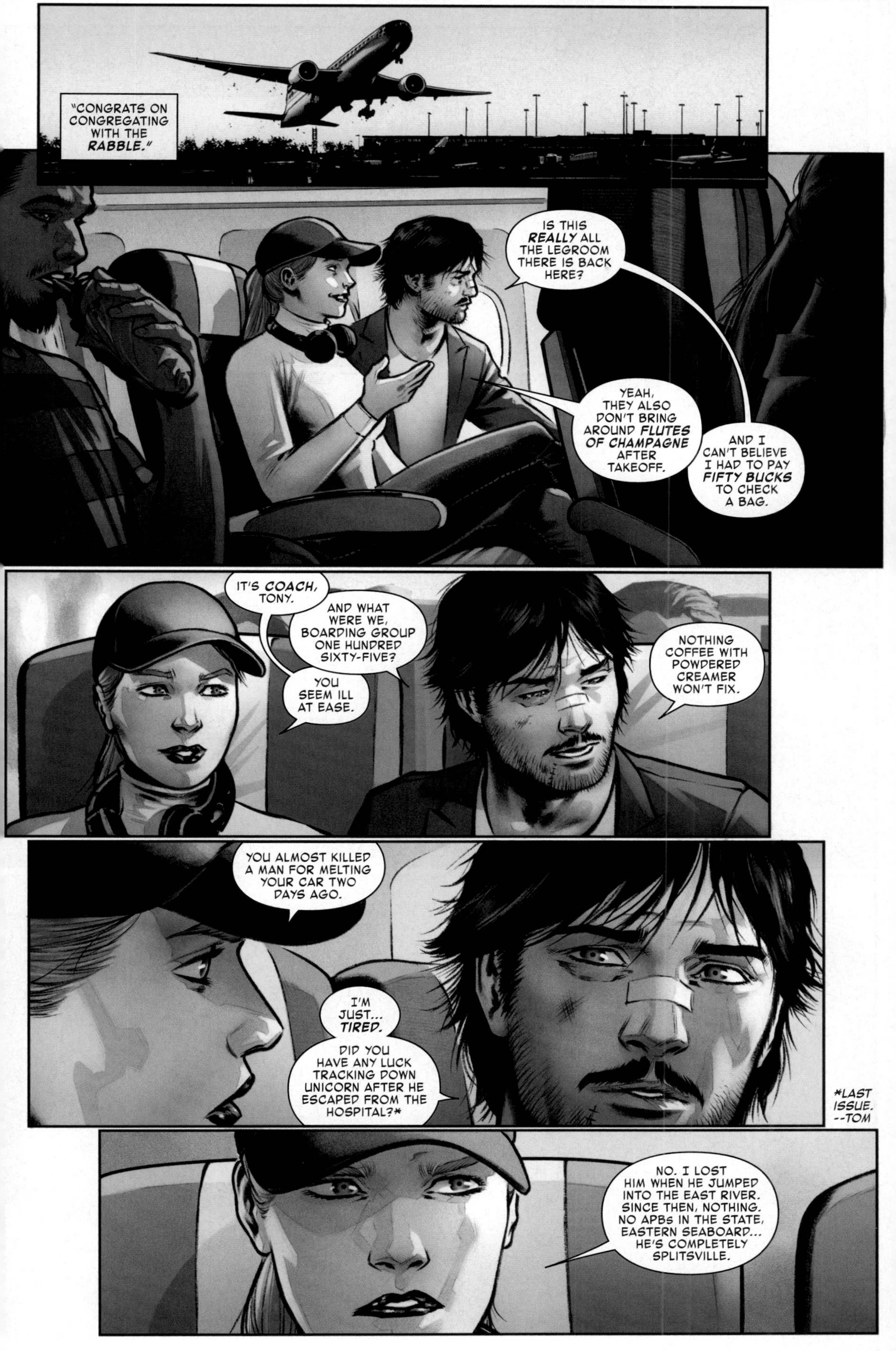

"CONGRATS ON CONGREGATING WITH THE RABBLE."
IS THIS REALLY ALL THE LEGROOM THERE IS BACK HERE?
YEAH, THEY ALSO DON'T BRING AROUND FLUTES OF CHAMPAGNE AFTER TAKEOFF.
AND I CAN'T BELIEVE I HAD TO PAY FIFTY BUCKS TO CHECK A BAG.
IT'S COACH, TONY.
AND WHAT WERE WE, BOARDING GROUP ONE HUNDRED SIXTY-FIVE?
YOU SEEM ILL AT EASE.
NOTHING COFFEE WITH POWDERED CREAMER WON'T FIX.
YOU ALMOST KILLED A MAN FOR MELTING YOUR CAR TWO DAYS AGO.
I'M JUST... TIRED.
DID YOU HAVE ANY LUCK TRACKING DOWN UNICORN AFTER HE ESCAPED FROM THE HOSPITAL?*
*LAST ISSUE. --TOM
NO. I LOST HIM WHEN HE JUMPED INTO THE EAST RIVER. SINCE THEN, NOTHING. NO APBs IN THE STATE, EASTERN SEABOARD... HE'S COMPLETELY SPLITSVILLE.

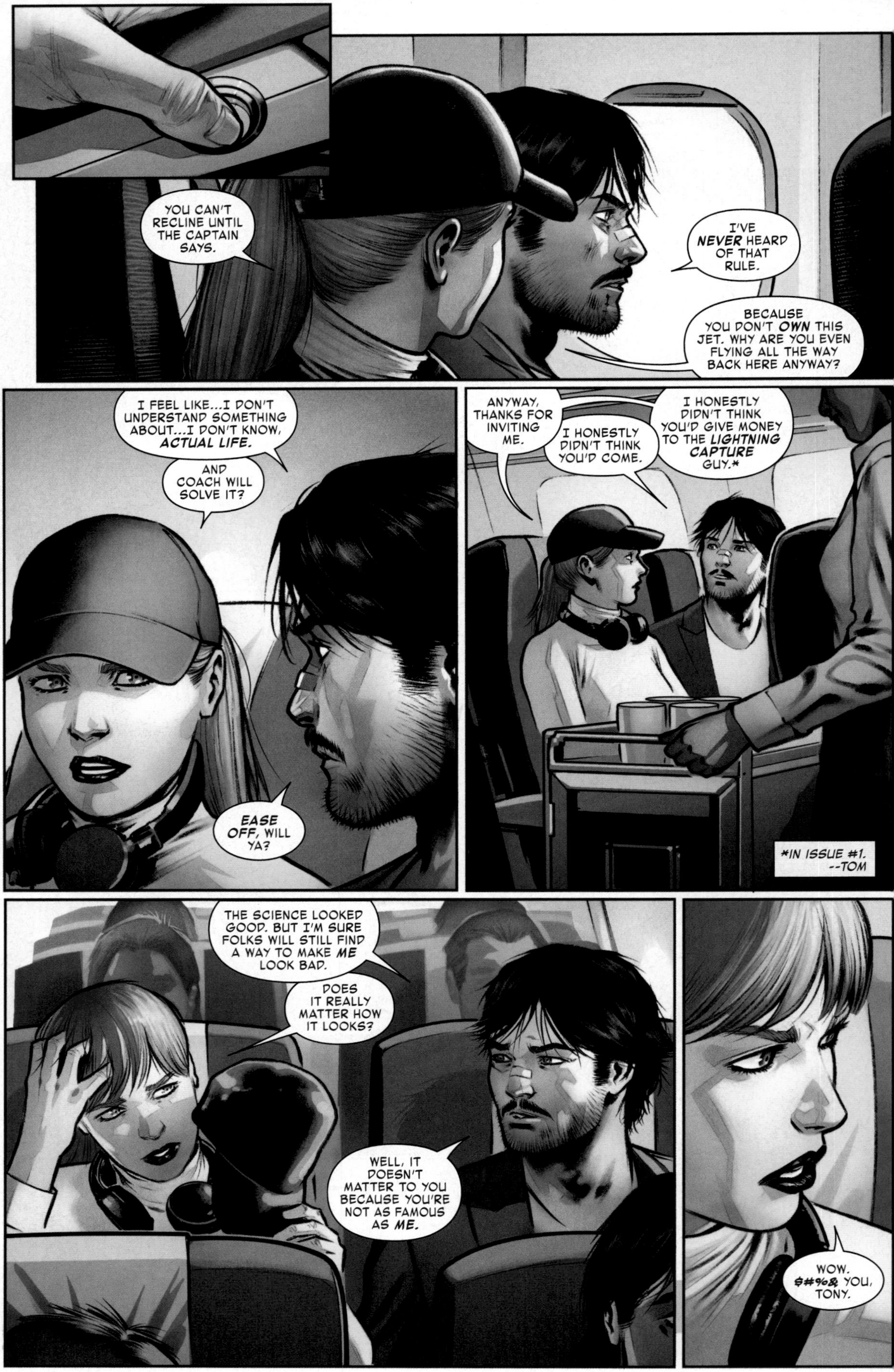
YOU CAN'T RECLINE UNTIL THE CAPTAIN SAYS.
I'VE NEVER HEARD OF THAT RULE.
BECAUSE YOU DON'T OWN THIS JET. WHY ARE YOU EVEN FLYING ALL THE WAY BACK HERE ANYWAY?
I FEEL LIKE...I DON'T UNDERSTAND SOMETHING ABOUT...I DON'T KNOW, ACTUAL LIFE.
AND COACH WILL SOLVE IT?
EASE OFF, WILL YA?
ANYWAY, THANKS FOR INVITING ME.
I HONESTLY DIDN'T THINK YOU'D COME.
I HONESTLY DIDN'T THINK YOU'D GIVE MONEY TO THE LIGHTNING CAPTURE GUY.*
*IN ISSUE #1. --TOM
THE SCIENCE LOOKED GOOD. BUT I'M SURE FOLKS WILL STILL FIND A WAY TO MAKE ME LOOK BAD.
DOES IT REALLY MATTER HOW IT LOOKS?
WELL, IT DOESN'T MATTER TO YOU BECAUSE YOU'RE NOT AS FAMOUS AS ME.
WOW. $#%& YOU, TONY.

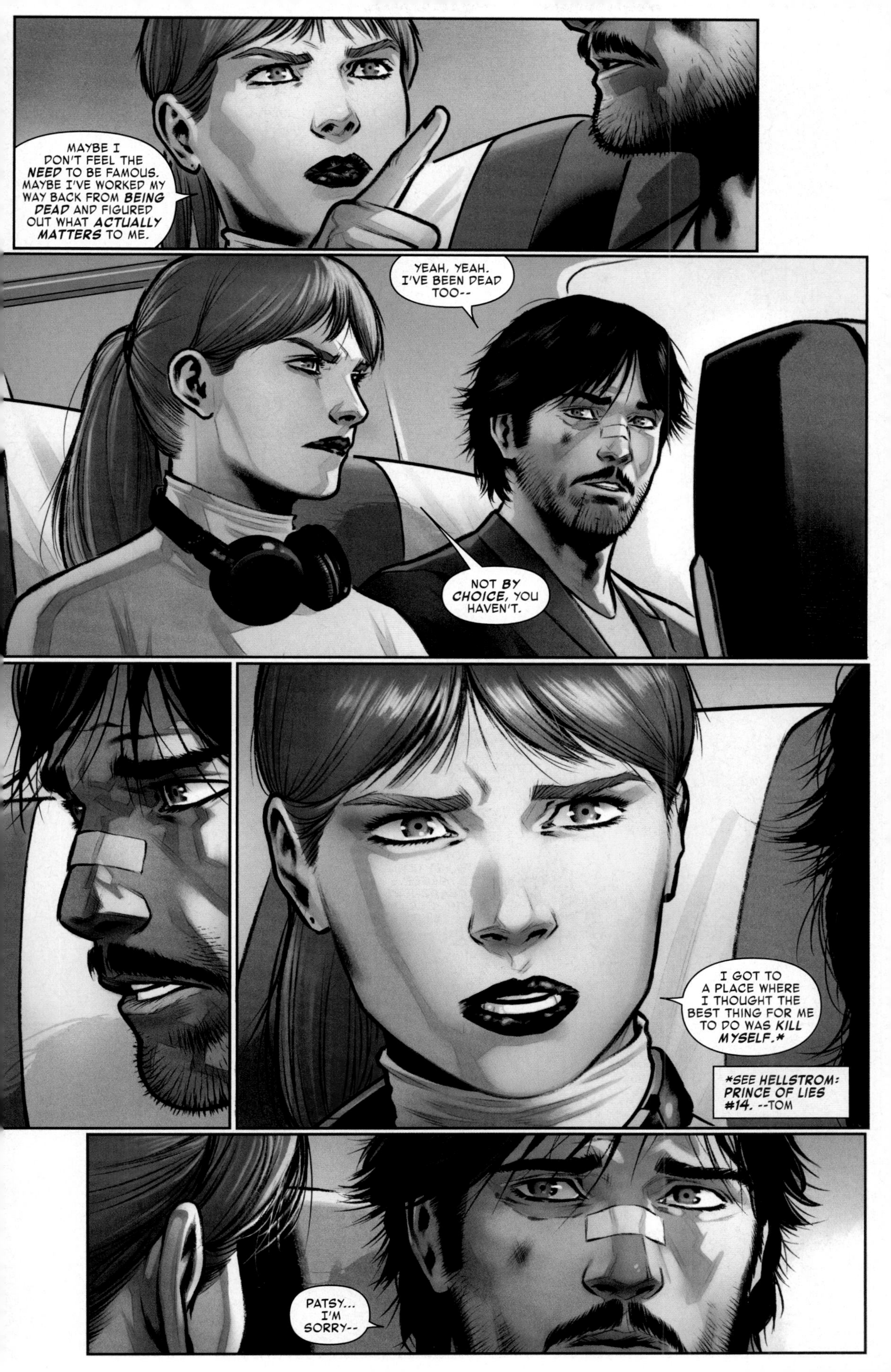
MAYBE I DON'T FEEL THE NEED TO BE FAMOUS. MAYBE I'VE WORKED MY WAY BACK FROM BEING DEAD AND FIGURED OUT WHAT ACTUALLY MATTERS TO ME.
YEAH, YEAH. I'VE BEEN DEAD TOO--
NOT BY CHOICE, YOU HAVEN'T.
I GOT TO A PLACE WHERE I THOUGHT THE BEST THING FOR ME TO DO WAS KILL MYSELF.*
*SEE HELLSTROM: PRINCE OF LIES #14. --TOM
PATSY... I'M SORRY--

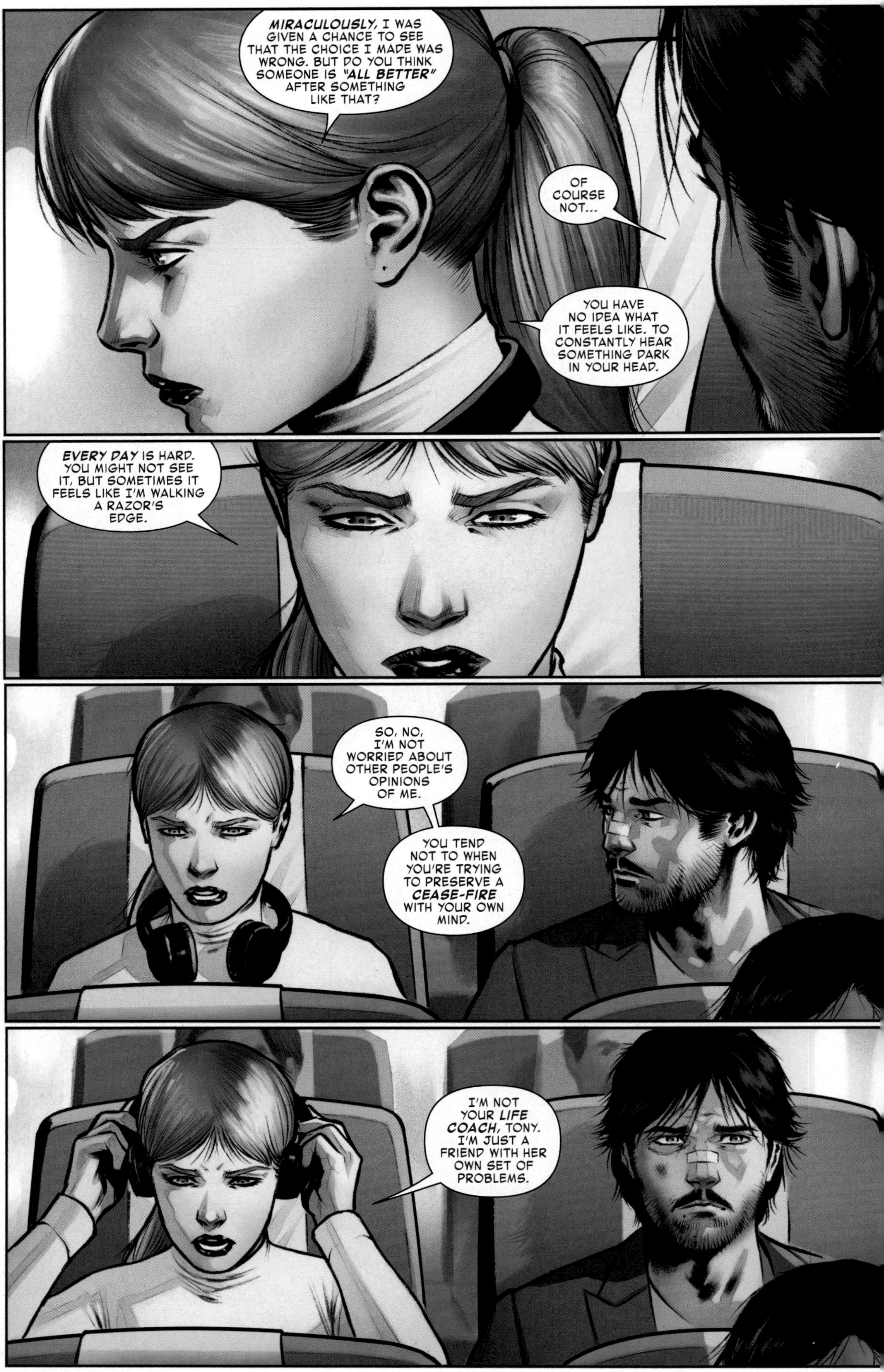
MIRACULOUSLY, I WAS GIVEN A CHANCE TO SEE THAT THE CHOICE I MADE WAS WRONG. BUT DO YOU THINK SOMEONE IS "ALL BETTER" AFTER SOMETHING LIKE THAT?
OF COURSE NOT...
YOU HAVE NO IDEA WHAT IT FEELS LIKE. TO CONSTANTLY HEAR SOMETHING DARK IN YOUR HEAD.
EVERY DAY IS HARD. YOU MIGHT NOT SEE IT, BUT SOMETIMES IT FEELS LIKE I'M WALKING A RAZOR'S EDGE.
SO, NO, I'M NOT WORRIED ABOUT OTHER PEOPLE'S OPINIONS OF ME.
YOU TEND NOT TO WHEN YOU'RE TRYING TO PRESERVE A CEASE-FIRE WITH YOUR OWN MIND.
I'M NOT YOUR LIFE COACH, TONY. I'M JUST A FRIEND WITH HER OWN SET OF PROBLEMS.

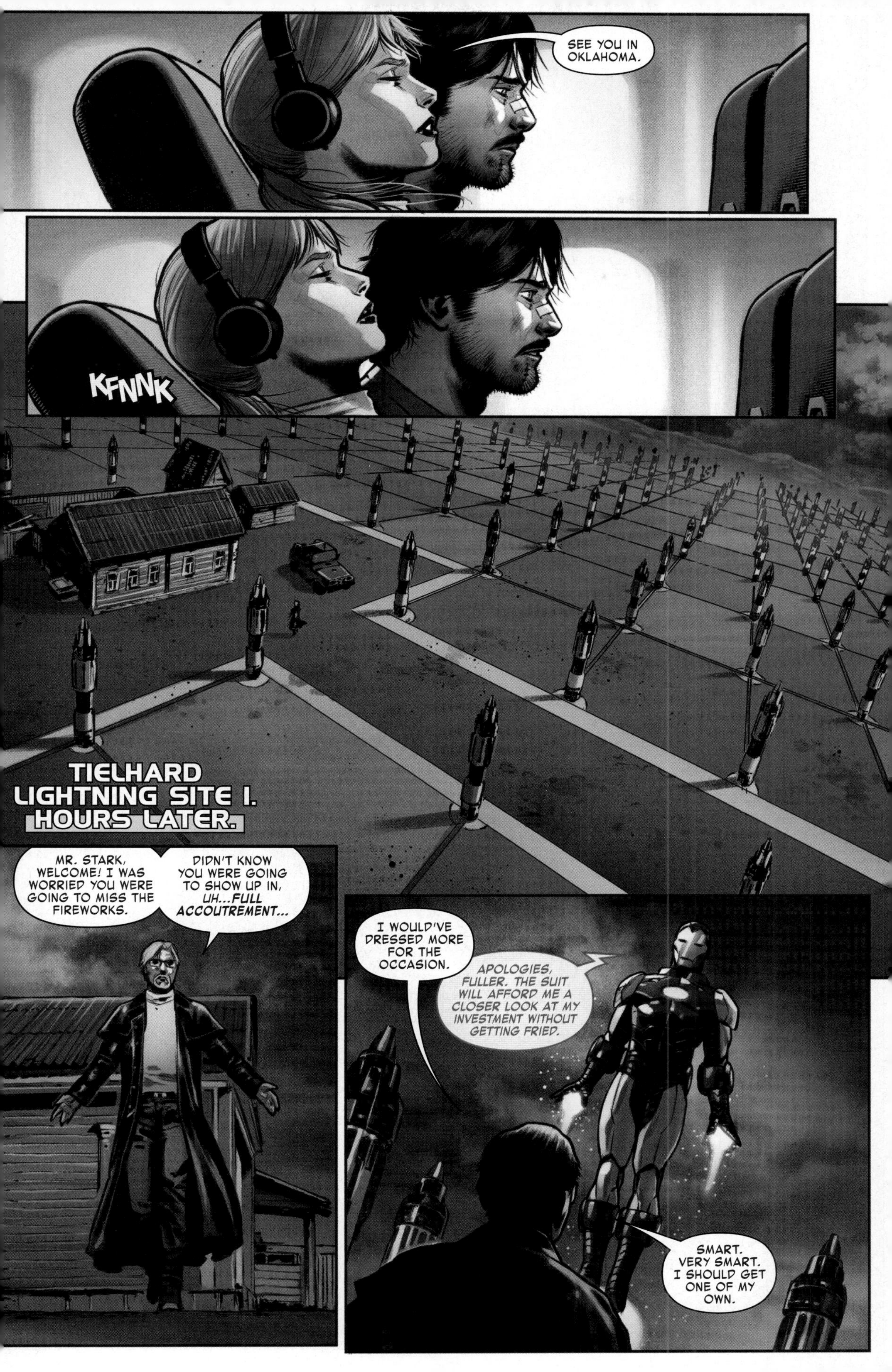

SEE YOU IN OKLAHOMA.
KFNNK
TIELHARD LIGHTNING SITE I. HOURS LATER.
MR. STARK, WELCOME! I WAS WORRIED YOU WERE GOING TO MISS THE FIREWORKS.
DIDN'T KNOW YOU WERE GOING TO SHOW UP IN, UH...FULL ACCOUTREMENT...
I WOULD'VE DRESSED MORE FOR THE OCCASION.
APOLOGIES, FULLER. THE SUIT WILL AFFORD ME A CLOSER LOOK AT MY INVESTMENT WITHOUT GETTING FRIED.
SMART. VERY SMART. I SHOULD GET ONE OF MY OWN.

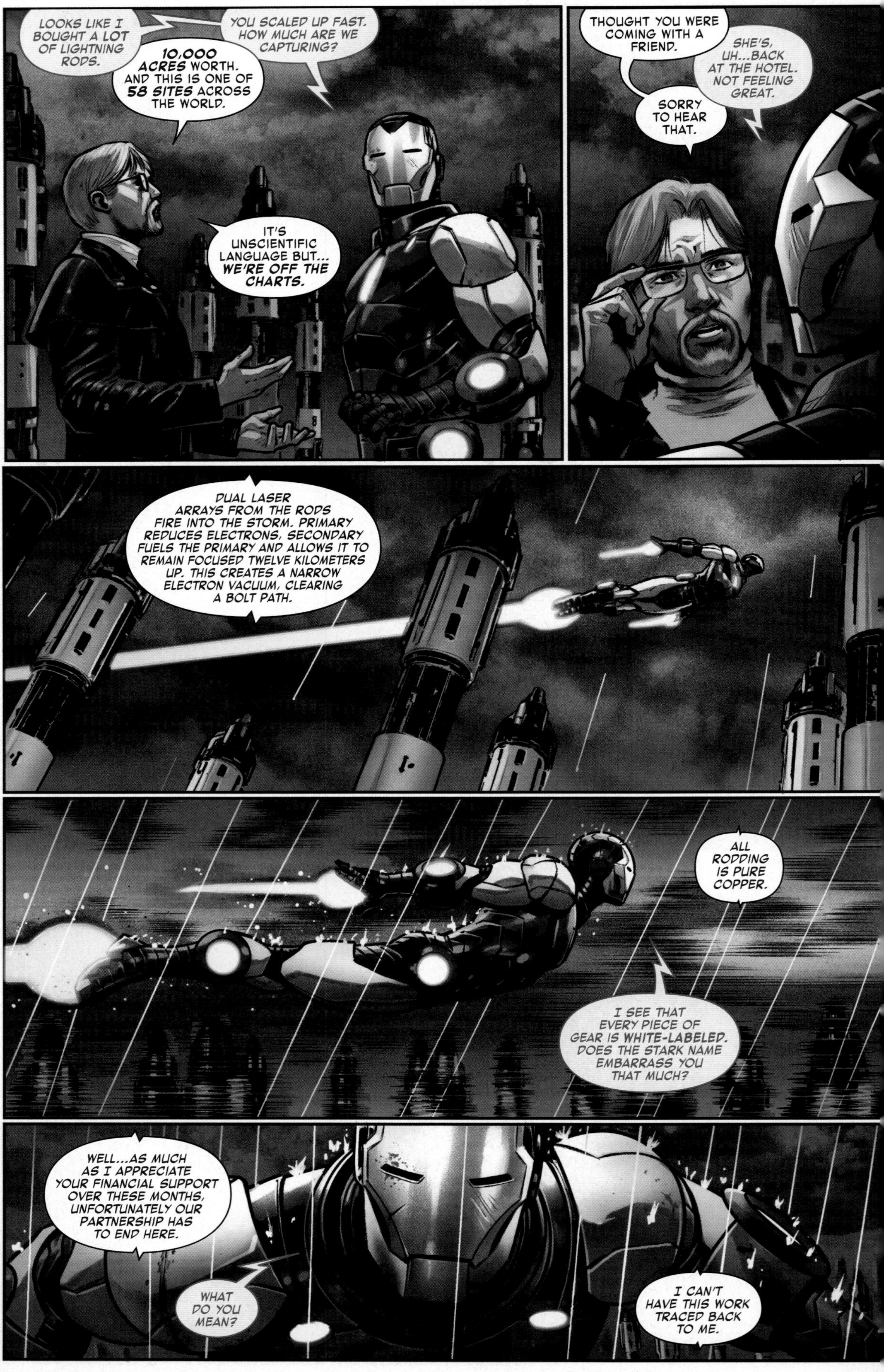
LOOKS LIKE I BOUGHT A LOT OF LIGHTNING RODS.
YOU SCALED UP FAST. HOW MUCH ARE WE CAPTURING?
10,000 ACRES WORTH. AND THIS IS ONE OF 58 SITES ACROSS THE WORLD.
IT'S UNSCIENTIFIC LANGUAGE BUT... WE'RE OFF THE CHARTS.
THOUGHT YOU WERE COMING WITH A FRIEND.
SHE'S, UH...BACK AT THE HOTEL. NOT FEELING GREAT.
SORRY TO HEAR THAT.
DUAL LASER ARRAYS FROM THE RODS FIRE INTO THE STORM. PRIMARY REDUCES ELECTRONS, SECONDARY FUELS THE PRIMARY AND ALLOWS IT TO REMAIN FOCUSED TWELVE KILOMETERS UP. THIS CREATES A NARROW ELECTRON VACUUM, CLEARING A BOLT PATH.
ALL RODDING IS PURE COPPER.
I SEE THAT EVERY PIECE OF GEAR IS WHITE-LABELED. DOES THE STARK NAME EMBARRASS YOU THAT MUCH?
WELL...AS MUCH AS I APPRECIATE YOUR FINANCIAL SUPPORT OVER THESE MONTHS, UNFORTUNATELY OUR PARTNERSHIP HAS TO END HERE.
WHAT DO YOU MEAN?
I CAN'T HAVE THIS WORK TRACED BACK TO ME.

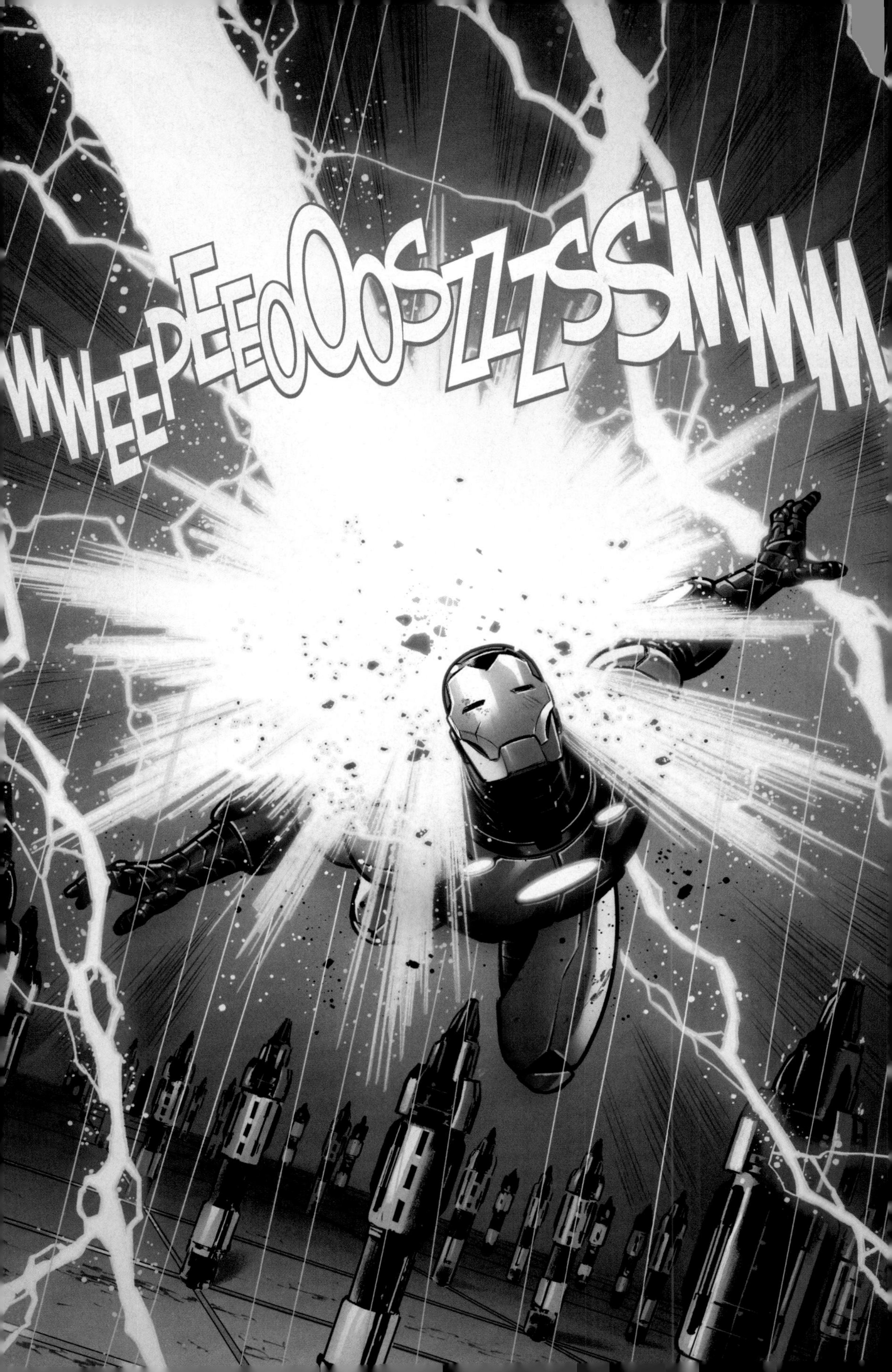
WWEEPEEEOOOSZZZSSMMMM

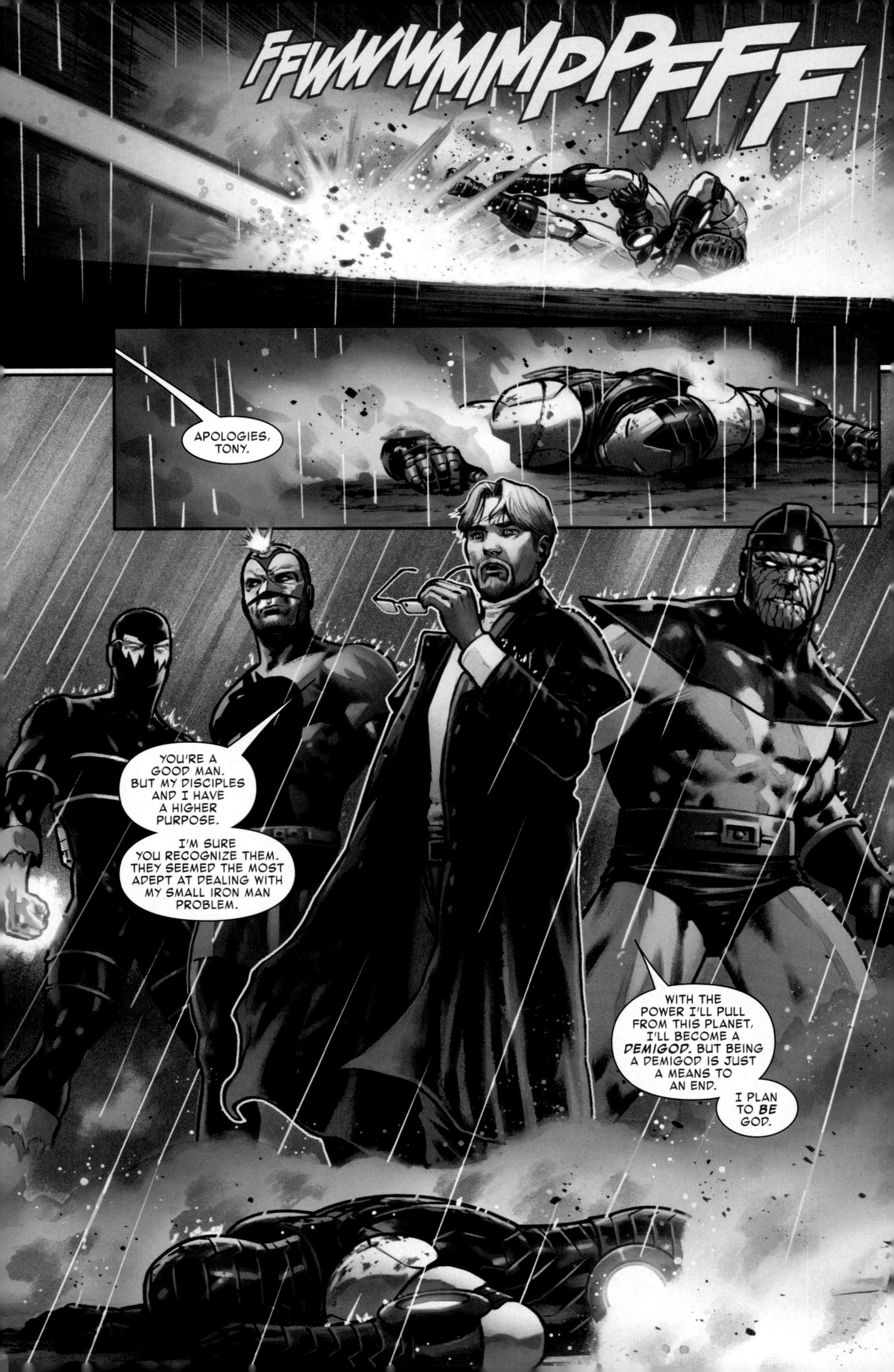
FFWWWMMPPFFF
APOLOGIES, TONY.
YOU'RE A GOOD MAN. BUT MY DISCIPLES AND I HAVE A HIGHER PURPOSE.
I'M SURE YOU RECOGNIZE THEM. THEY SEEMED THE MOST ADEPT AT DEALING WITH MY SMALL IRON MAN PROBLEM.
WITH THE POWER I'LL PULL FROM THIS PLANET, I'LL BECOME A *DEMIGOD.* BUT BEING A DEMIGOD IS JUST A MEANS TO AN END.
I PLAN TO *BE* GOD.

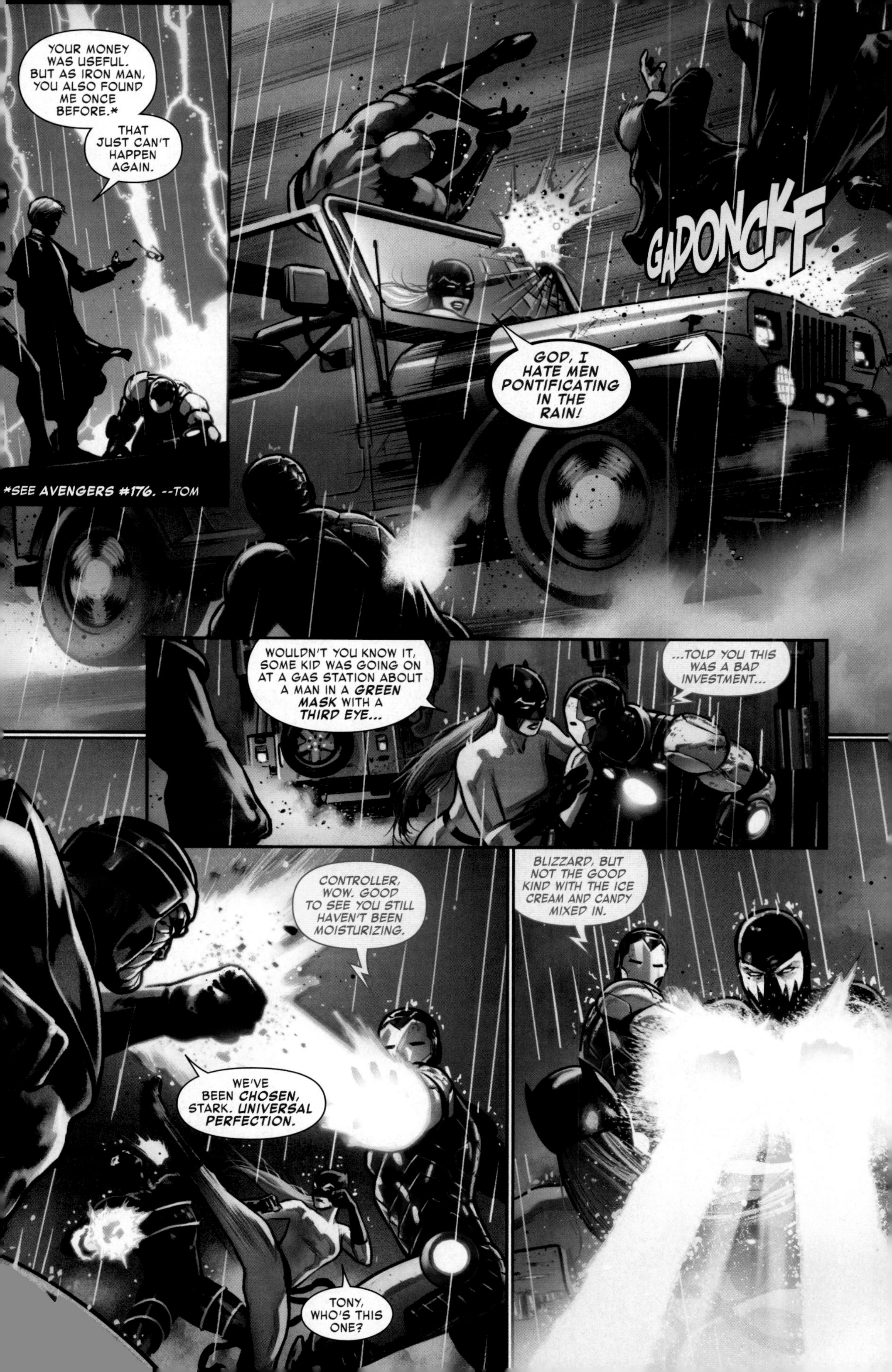
YOUR MONEY WAS USEFUL. BUT AS IRON MAN, YOU ALSO FOUND ME ONCE BEFORE.*
THAT JUST CAN'T HAPPEN AGAIN.
*SEE AVENGERS #176. --TOM
GADONCKF
GOD, I HATE MEN PONTIFICATING IN THE RAIN!
WOULDN'T YOU KNOW IT, SOME KID WAS GOING ON AT A GAS STATION ABOUT A MAN IN A GREEN MASK WITH A THIRD EYE...
...TOLD YOU THIS WAS A BAD INVESTMENT...
CONTROLLER, WOW. GOOD TO SEE YOU STILL HAVEN'T BEEN MOISTURIZING.
WE'VE BEEN CHOSEN, STARK. UNIVERSAL PERFECTION.
TONY, WHO'S THIS ONE?
BLIZZARD, BUT NOT THE GOOD KIND WITH THE ICE CREAM AND CANDY MIXED IN.

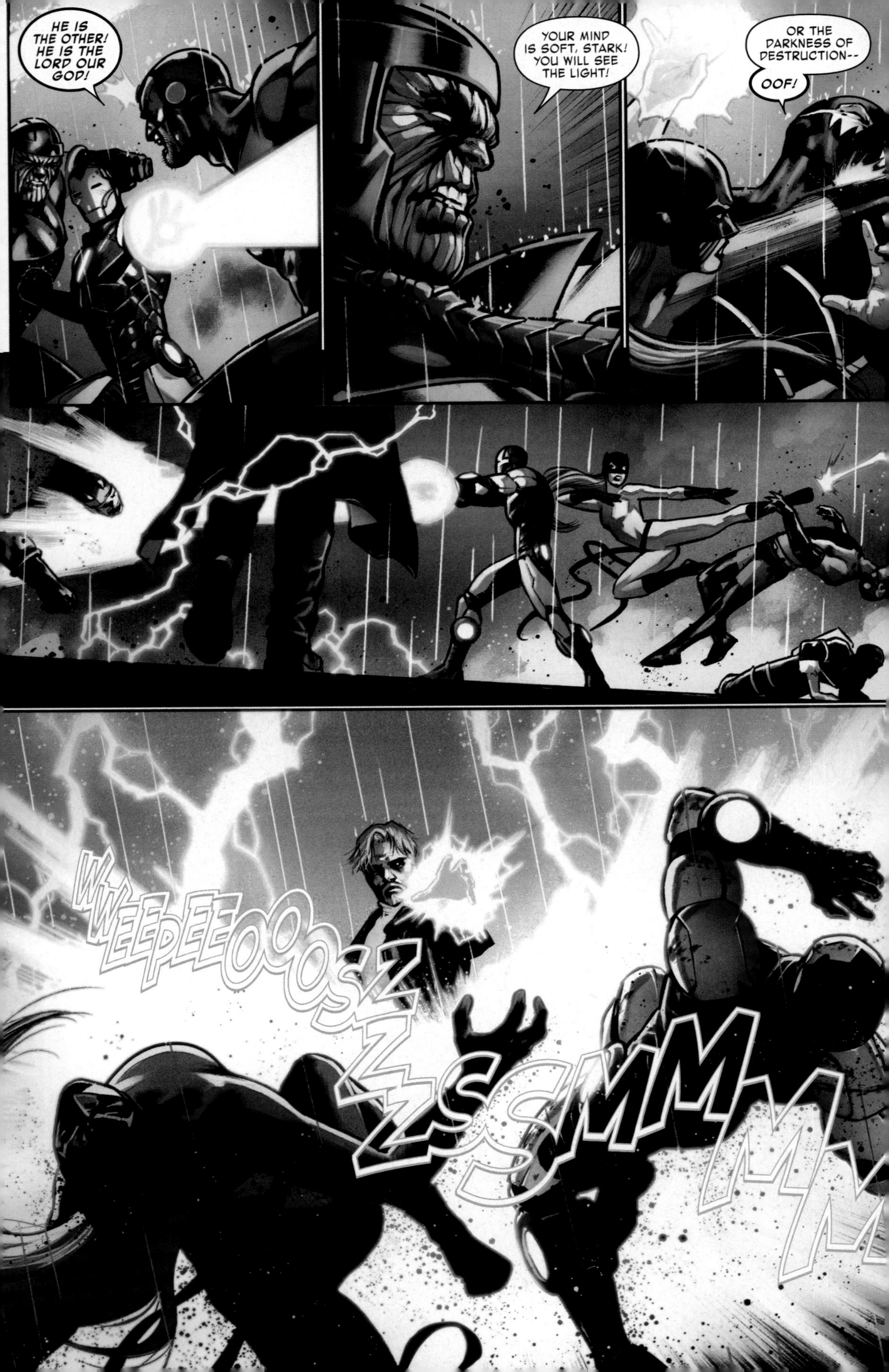
HE IS THE OTHER! HE IS THE LORD OUR GOD!
YOUR MIND IS SOFT, STARK! YOU WILL SEE THE LIGHT!
OR THE DARKNESS OF DESTRUCTION--
OOF!
WWEEPEEOOOSZZ
ZSSMMMMM

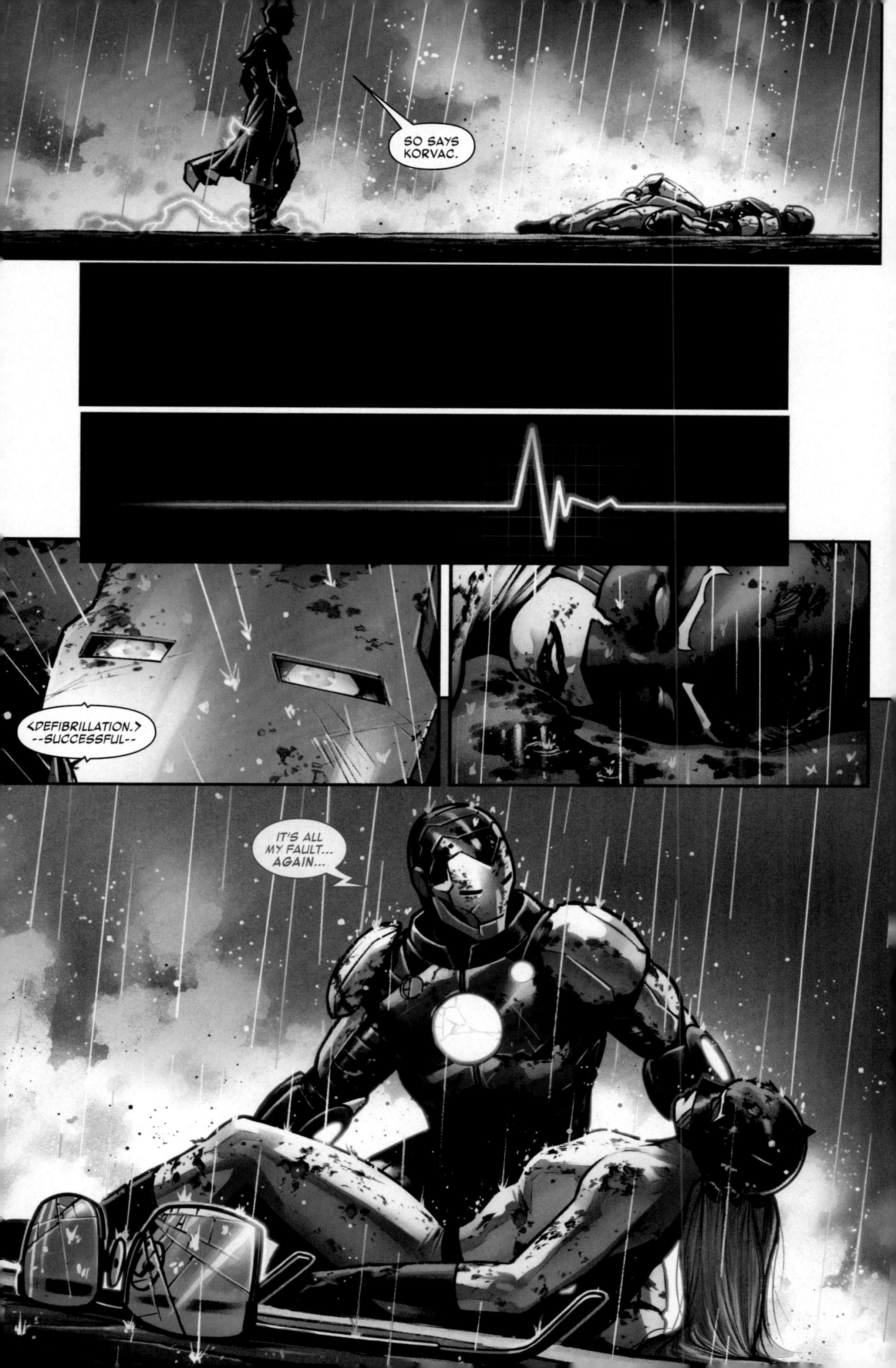
SO SAYS KORVAC.
<DEFIBRILLATION.> --SUCCESSFUL--
IT'S ALL MY FAULT... AGAIN...

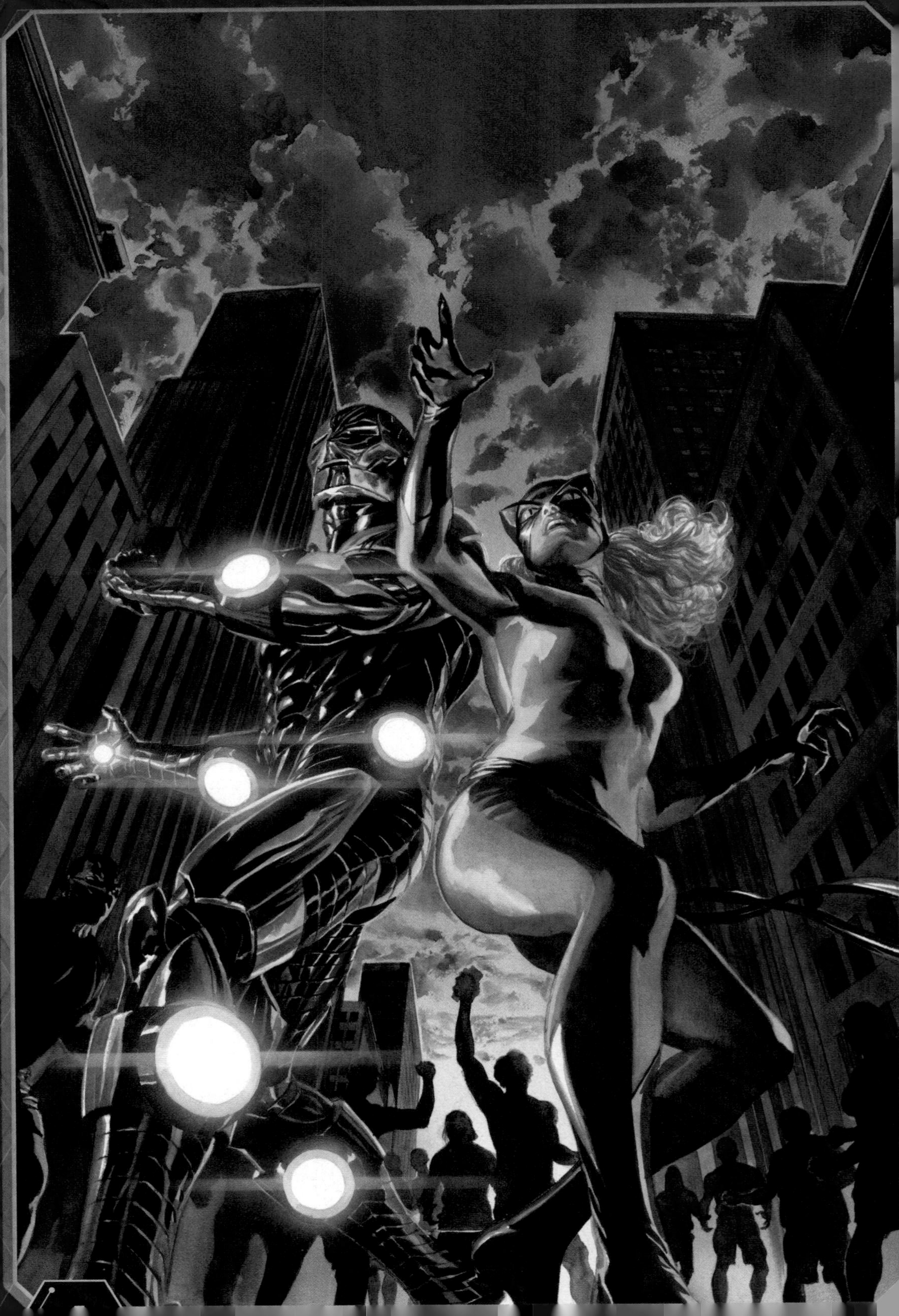

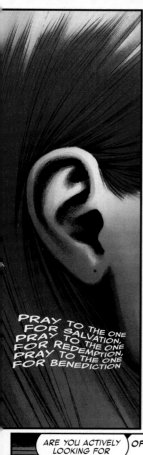

PRAY TO THE ONE FOR SALVATION, PRAY TO THE ONE FOR REDEMPTION, PRAY TO THE ONE FOR BENEDICTION

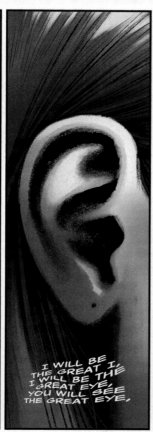

I WILL BE THE GREAT I, I WILL BE THE GREAT EYE, YOU WILL SEE THE GREAT EYE,

YOU WILL SEE FOR THE GREAT EYE, YOU WILL SEE WITH THE GREAT EYE

ORDER, PEACE, HARMONY, PERFECT SINGULAR TRUTH

ARE YOU ACTIVELY LOOKING FOR HIM?

OF COURSE, HE'S MY FRIEND--

AS IRON MAN? WHAT OTHER RESOURCES ARE YOU USING? STARK UNLIMITED?

I'M LETTING THE AUTHORITIES TAKE THE LEAD--

JAMES RHODES MISSING

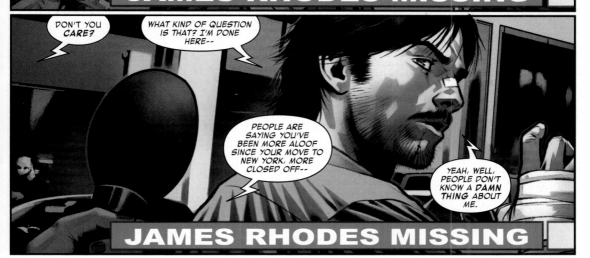

DON'T YOU *CARE?*

WHAT KIND OF QUESTION IS THAT? I'M DONE HERE--

PEOPLE ARE SAYING YOU'VE BEEN MORE ALOOF SINCE YOUR MOVE TO NEW YORK, MORE CLOSED OFF--

YEAH, WELL, PEOPLE DON'T KNOW A *DAMN* THING ABOUT ME.

JAMES RHODES MISSING

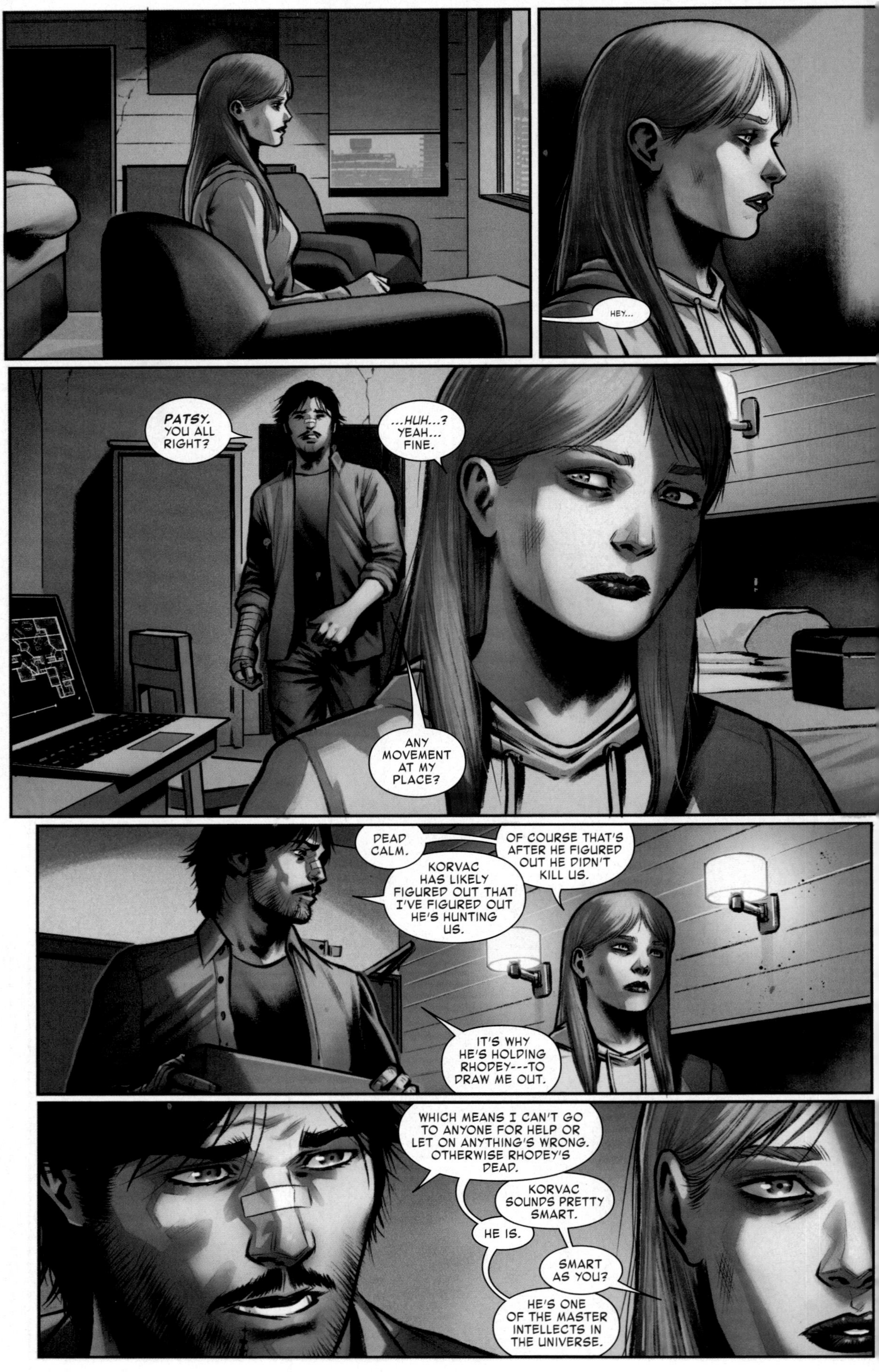
HEY...
PATSY. YOU ALL RIGHT?
...HUH...? YEAH... FINE.
ANY MOVEMENT AT MY PLACE?
DEAD CALM.
KORVAC HAS LIKELY FIGURED OUT THAT I'VE FIGURED OUT HE'S HUNTING US.
OF COURSE THAT'S AFTER HE FIGURED OUT HE DIDN'T KILL US.
IT'S WHY HE'S HOLDING RHODEY---TO DRAW ME OUT.
WHICH MEANS I CAN'T GO TO ANYONE FOR HELP OR LET ON ANYTHING'S WRONG. OTHERWISE RHODEY'S DEAD.
KORVAC SOUNDS PRETTY SMART.
HE IS.
SMART AS YOU?
HE'S ONE OF THE MASTER INTELLECTS IN THE UNIVERSE.

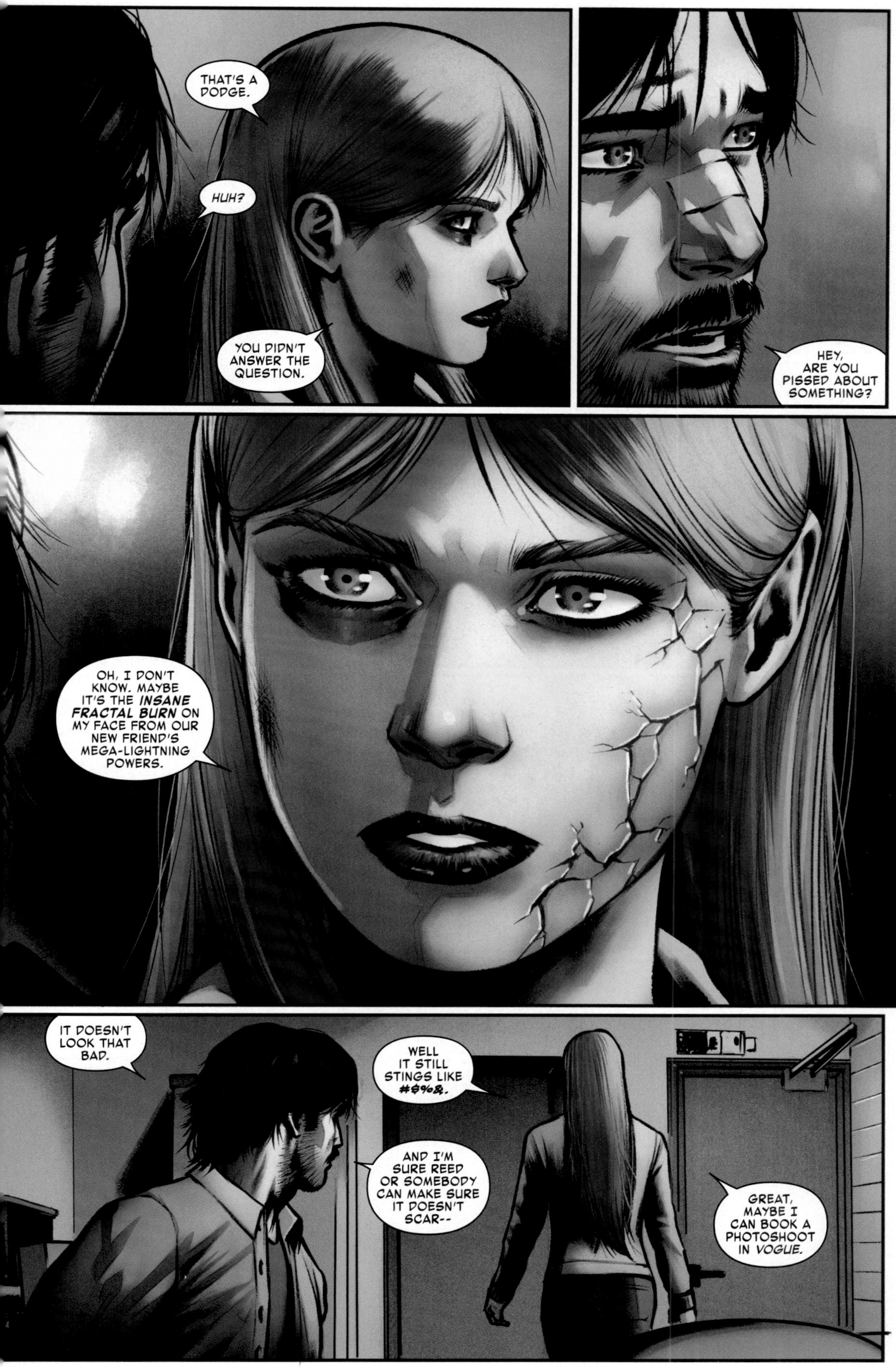
THAT'S A DODGE.
HUH?
YOU DIDN'T ANSWER THE QUESTION.
HEY, ARE YOU PISSED ABOUT SOMETHING?
OH, I DON'T KNOW. MAYBE IT'S THE *INSANE FRACTAL BURN* ON MY FACE FROM OUR NEW FRIEND'S MEGA-LIGHTNING POWERS.
IT DOESN'T LOOK THAT BAD.
WELL IT STILL STINGS LIKE #$%&.
AND I'M SURE REED OR SOMEBODY CAN MAKE SURE IT DOESN'T SCAR--
GREAT, MAYBE I CAN BOOK A PHOTOSHOOT IN *VOGUE*.

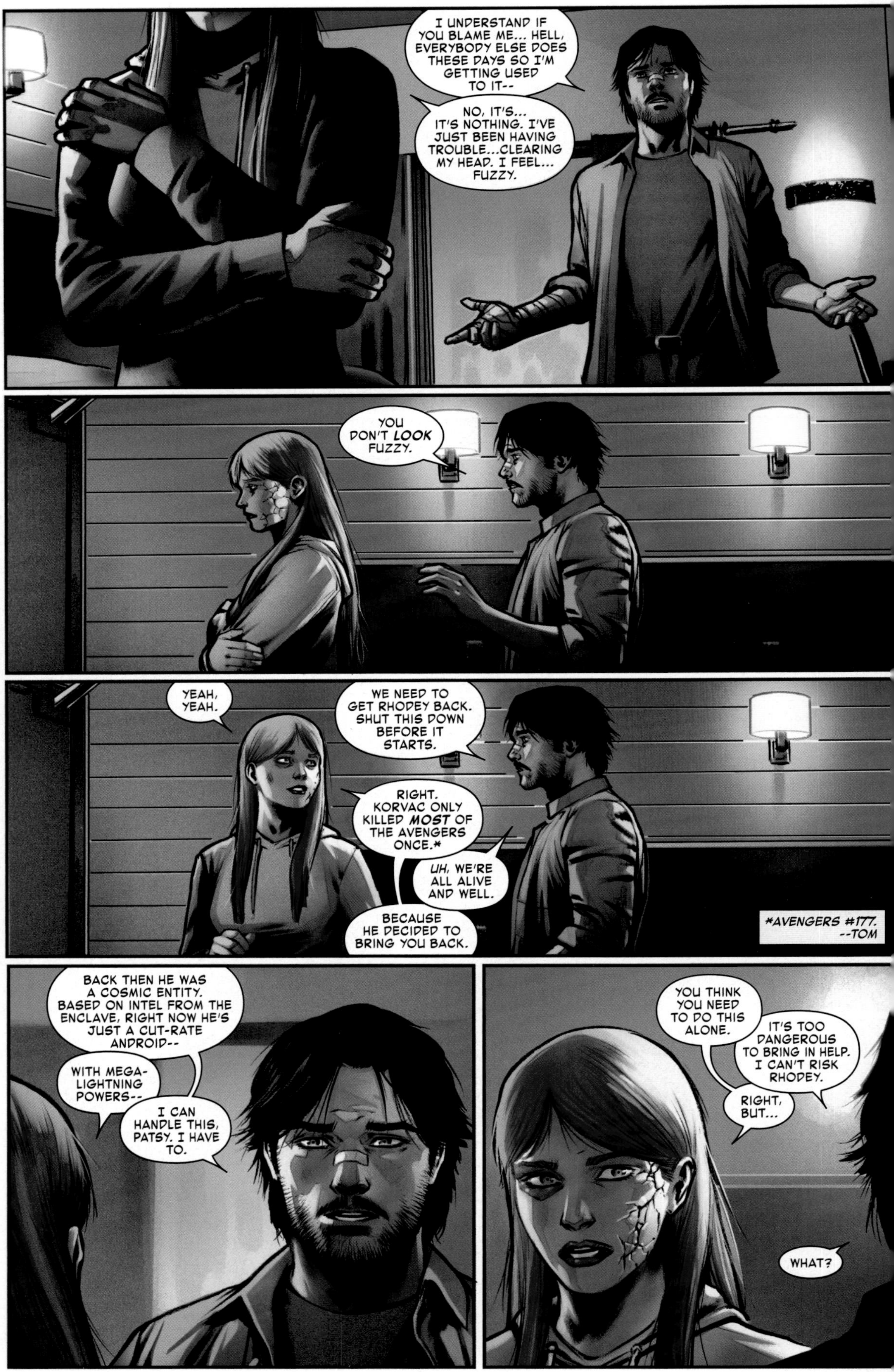

I UNDERSTAND IF YOU BLAME ME... HELL, EVERYBODY ELSE DOES THESE DAYS SO I'M GETTING USED TO IT--
NO, IT'S... IT'S NOTHING. I'VE JUST BEEN HAVING TROUBLE...CLEARING MY HEAD. I FEEL... FUZZY.
YOU DON'T **LOOK** FUZZY.
YEAH, YEAH.
WE NEED TO GET RHODEY BACK. SHUT THIS DOWN BEFORE IT STARTS.
RIGHT. KORVAC ONLY KILLED ***MOST*** OF THE AVENGERS ONCE.*
UH, WE'RE ALL ALIVE AND WELL.
BECAUSE HE DECIDED TO BRING YOU BACK.
*AVENGERS #177. --TOM
BACK THEN HE WAS A COSMIC ENTITY. BASED ON INTEL FROM THE ENCLAVE, RIGHT NOW HE'S JUST A CUT-RATE ANDROID--
WITH MEGA-LIGHTNING POWERS--
I CAN HANDLE THIS, PATSY. I HAVE TO.
YOU THINK YOU NEED TO DO THIS ALONE.
IT'S TOO DANGEROUS TO BRING IN HELP. I CAN'T RISK RHODEY.
RIGHT, BUT...
WHAT?

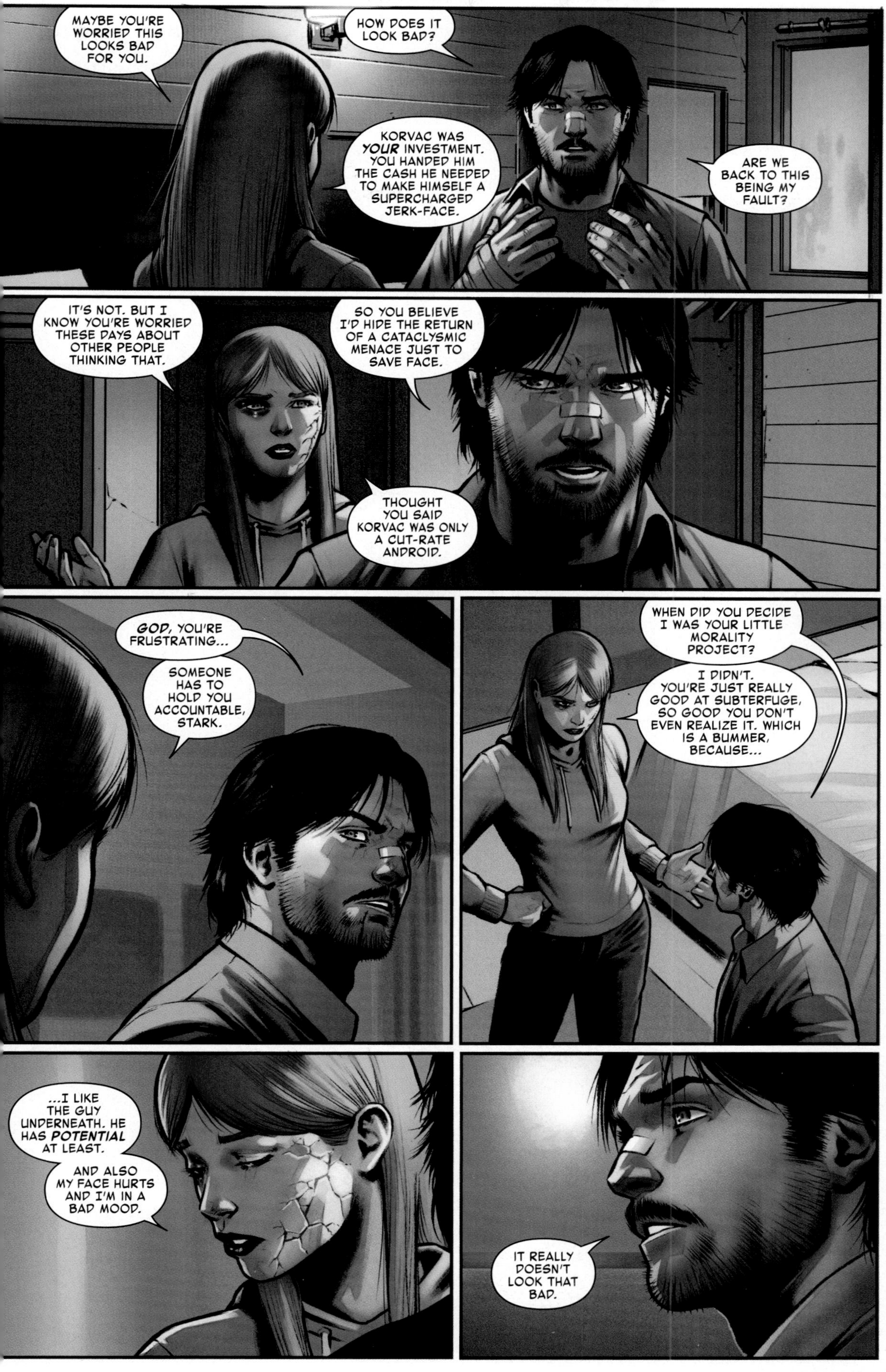
MAYBE YOU'RE WORRIED THIS LOOKS BAD FOR YOU.
HOW DOES IT LOOK BAD?
KORVAC WAS *YOUR* INVESTMENT. YOU HANDED HIM THE CASH HE NEEDED TO MAKE HIMSELF A SUPERCHARGED JERK-FACE.
ARE WE BACK TO THIS BEING MY FAULT?
IT'S NOT. BUT I KNOW YOU'RE WORRIED THESE DAYS ABOUT OTHER PEOPLE THINKING THAT.
SO YOU BELIEVE I'D HIDE THE RETURN OF A CATACLYSMIC MENACE JUST TO SAVE FACE.
THOUGHT YOU SAID KORVAC WAS ONLY A CUT-RATE ANDROID.
GOD, YOU'RE FRUSTRATING...
SOMEONE HAS TO HOLD YOU ACCOUNTABLE, STARK.
WHEN DID YOU DECIDE I WAS YOUR LITTLE MORALITY PROJECT?
I DIDN'T. YOU'RE JUST REALLY GOOD AT SUBTERFUGE, SO GOOD YOU DON'T EVEN REALIZE IT. WHICH IS A BUMMER, BECAUSE...
...I LIKE THE GUY UNDERNEATH. HE HAS *POTENTIAL* AT LEAST.
AND ALSO MY FACE HURTS AND I'M IN A BAD MOOD.
IT REALLY DOESN'T LOOK THAT BAD.

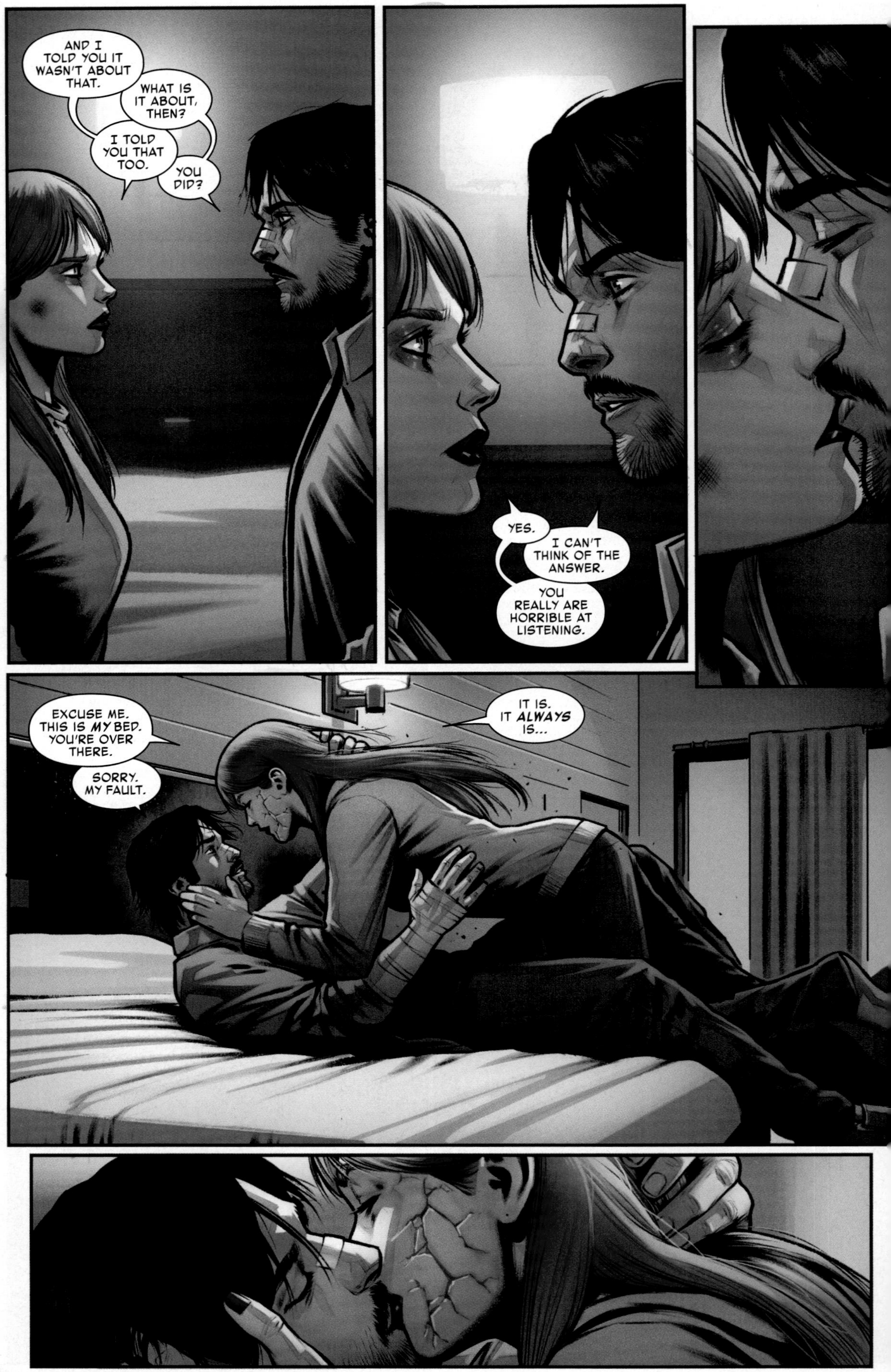
AND I TOLD YOU IT WASN'T ABOUT THAT.
WHAT IS IT ABOUT, THEN?
I TOLD YOU THAT TOO.
YOU DID?
YES.
I CAN'T THINK OF THE ANSWER.
YOU REALLY ARE HORRIBLE AT LISTENING.
EXCUSE ME. THIS IS *MY* BED. YOU'RE OVER THERE.
SORRY. MY FAULT.
IT IS. IT *ALWAYS* IS...

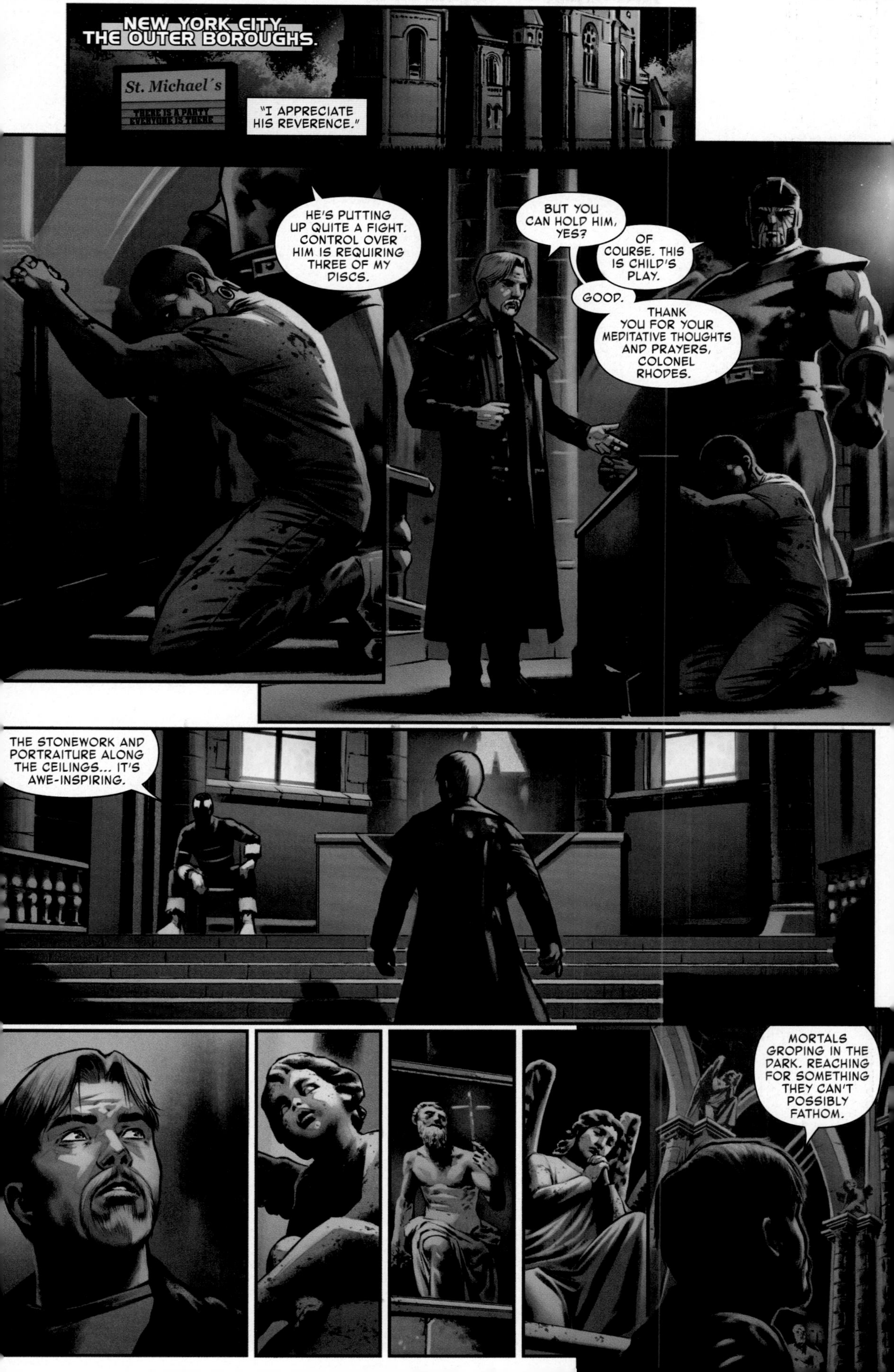
NEW YORK CITY. THE OUTER BOROUGHS.
St. Michael´s
THERE IS A PARTY
EVERYONE IS THERE
"I APPRECIATE HIS REVERENCE."
HE'S PUTTING UP QUITE A FIGHT. CONTROL OVER HIM IS REQUIRING THREE OF MY DISCS.
BUT YOU CAN HOLD HIM, YES?
OF COURSE. THIS IS CHILD'S PLAY.
GOOD.
THANK YOU FOR YOUR MEDITATIVE THOUGHTS AND PRAYERS, COLONEL RHODES.
THE STONEWORK AND PORTRAITURE ALONG THE CEILINGS... IT'S AWE-INSPIRING.
MORTALS GROPING IN THE DARK. REACHING FOR SOMETHING THEY CAN'T POSSIBLY FATHOM.

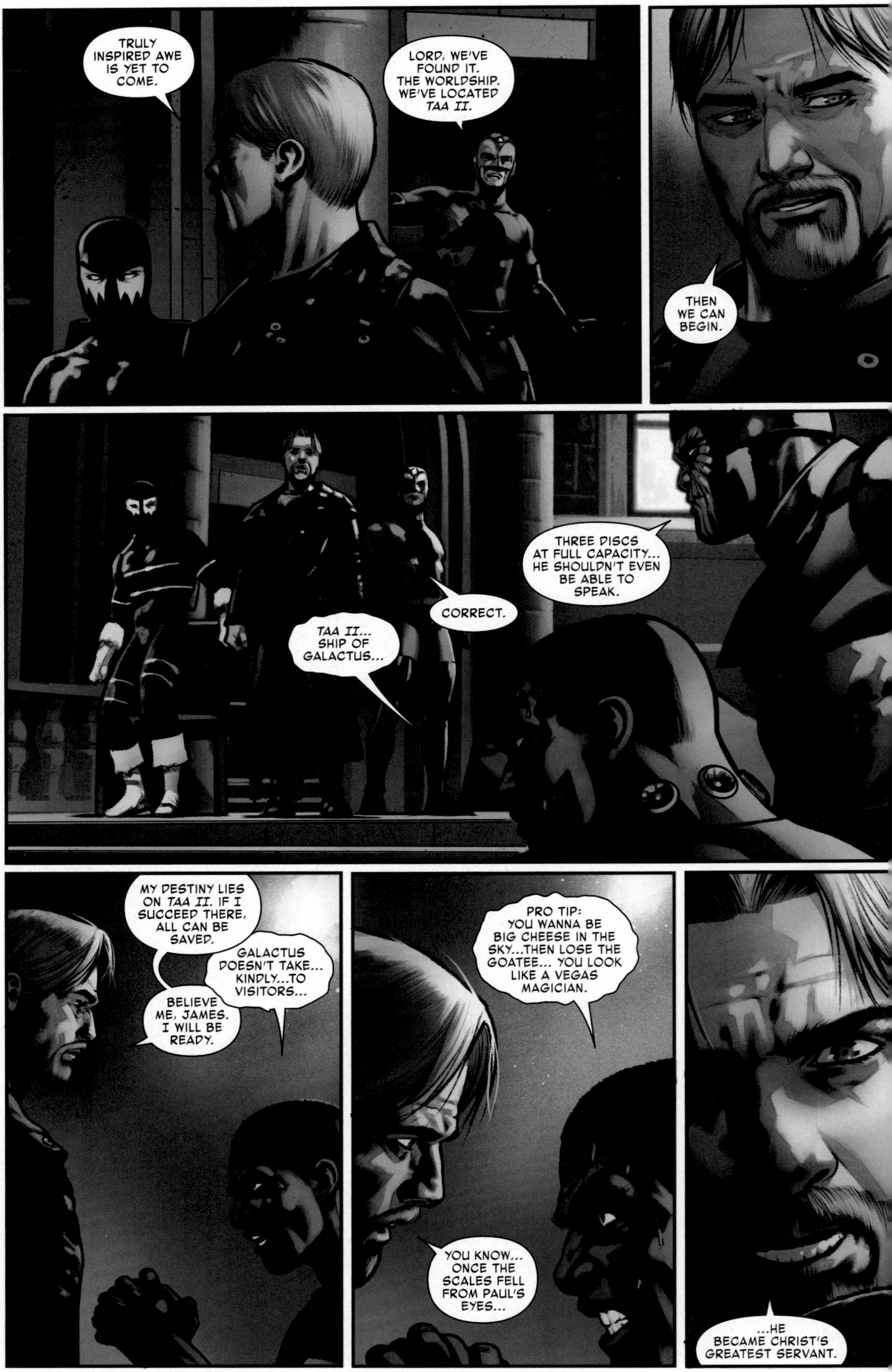
TRULY INSPIRED AWE IS YET TO COME.
LORD, WE'VE FOUND IT. THE WORLDSHIP. WE'VE LOCATED *TAA II.*
THEN WE CAN BEGIN.
THREE DISCS AT FULL CAPACITY... HE SHOULDN'T EVEN BE ABLE TO SPEAK.
CORRECT.
TAA II... SHIP OF GALACTUS...
MY DESTINY LIES ON *TAA II.* IF I SUCCEED THERE, ALL CAN BE SAVED.
GALACTUS DOESN'T TAKE... KINDLY...TO VISITORS...
BELIEVE ME, JAMES. I WILL BE READY.
PRO TIP: YOU WANNA BE BIG CHEESE IN THE SKY...THEN LOSE THE GOATEE... YOU LOOK LIKE A VEGAS MAGICIAN.
YOU KNOW... ONCE THE SCALES FELL FROM PAUL'S EYES...
...HE BECAME CHRIST'S GREATEST SERVANT.

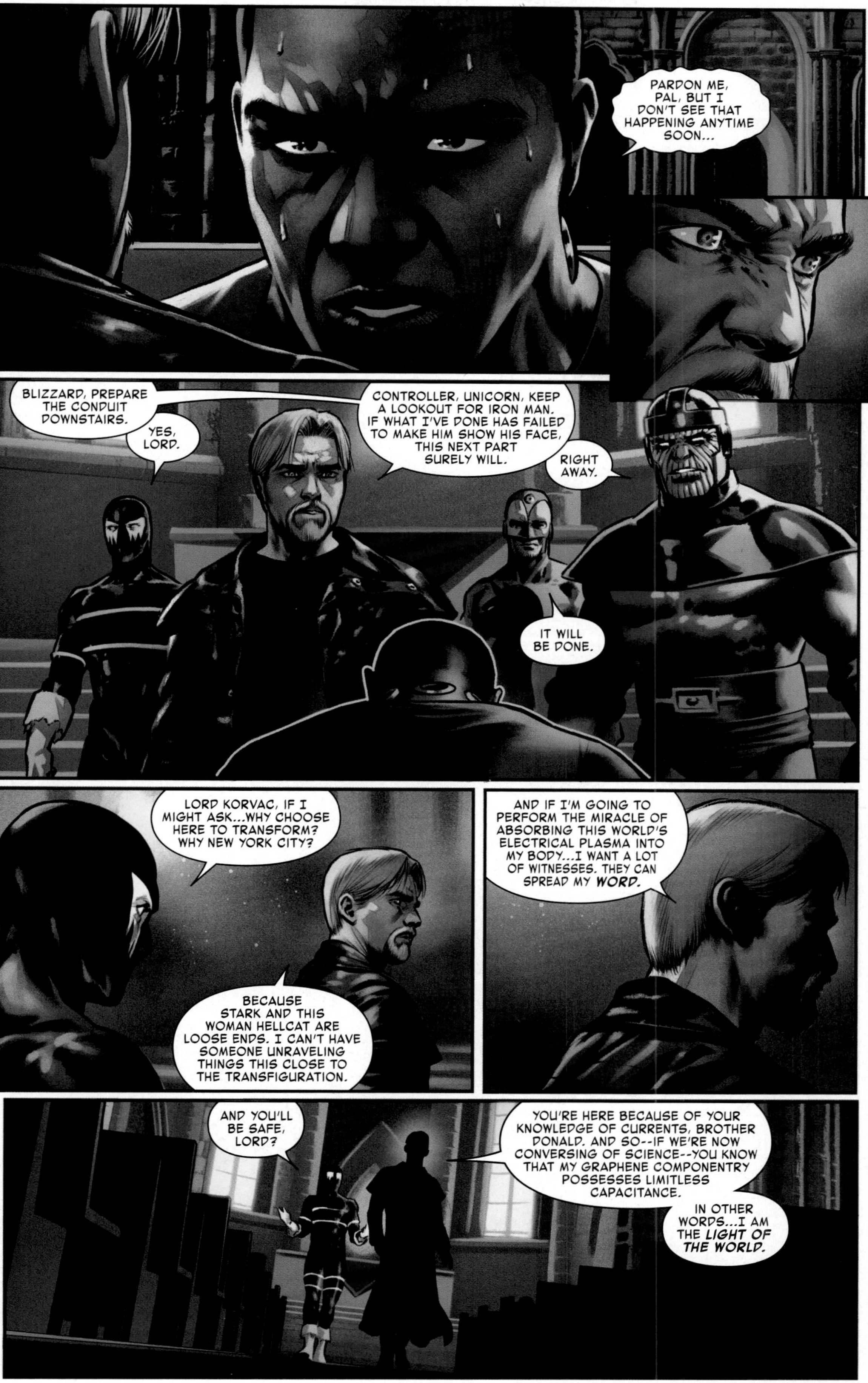
PARDON ME, PAL, BUT I DON'T SEE THAT HAPPENING ANYTIME SOON...
BLIZZARD, PREPARE THE CONDUIT DOWNSTAIRS.
YES, LORD.
CONTROLLER, UNICORN, KEEP A LOOKOUT FOR IRON MAN. IF WHAT I'VE DONE HAS FAILED TO MAKE HIM SHOW HIS FACE, THIS NEXT PART SURELY WILL.
RIGHT AWAY.
IT WILL BE DONE.
LORD KORVAC, IF I MIGHT ASK...WHY CHOOSE HERE TO TRANSFORM? WHY NEW YORK CITY?
BECAUSE STARK AND THIS WOMAN HELLCAT ARE LOOSE ENDS. I CAN'T HAVE SOMEONE UNRAVELING THINGS THIS CLOSE TO THE TRANSFIGURATION.
AND IF I'M GOING TO PERFORM THE MIRACLE OF ABSORBING THIS WORLD'S ELECTRICAL PLASMA INTO MY BODY...I WANT A LOT OF WITNESSES. THEY CAN SPREAD MY *WORD.*
AND YOU'LL BE SAFE, LORD?
YOU'RE HERE BECAUSE OF YOUR KNOWLEDGE OF CURRENTS, BROTHER DONALD. AND SO--IF WE'RE NOW CONVERSING OF SCIENCE--YOU KNOW THAT MY GRAPHENE COMPONENTRY POSSESSES LIMITLESS CAPACITANCE.
IN OTHER WORDS...I AM THE *LIGHT OF THE WORLD.*

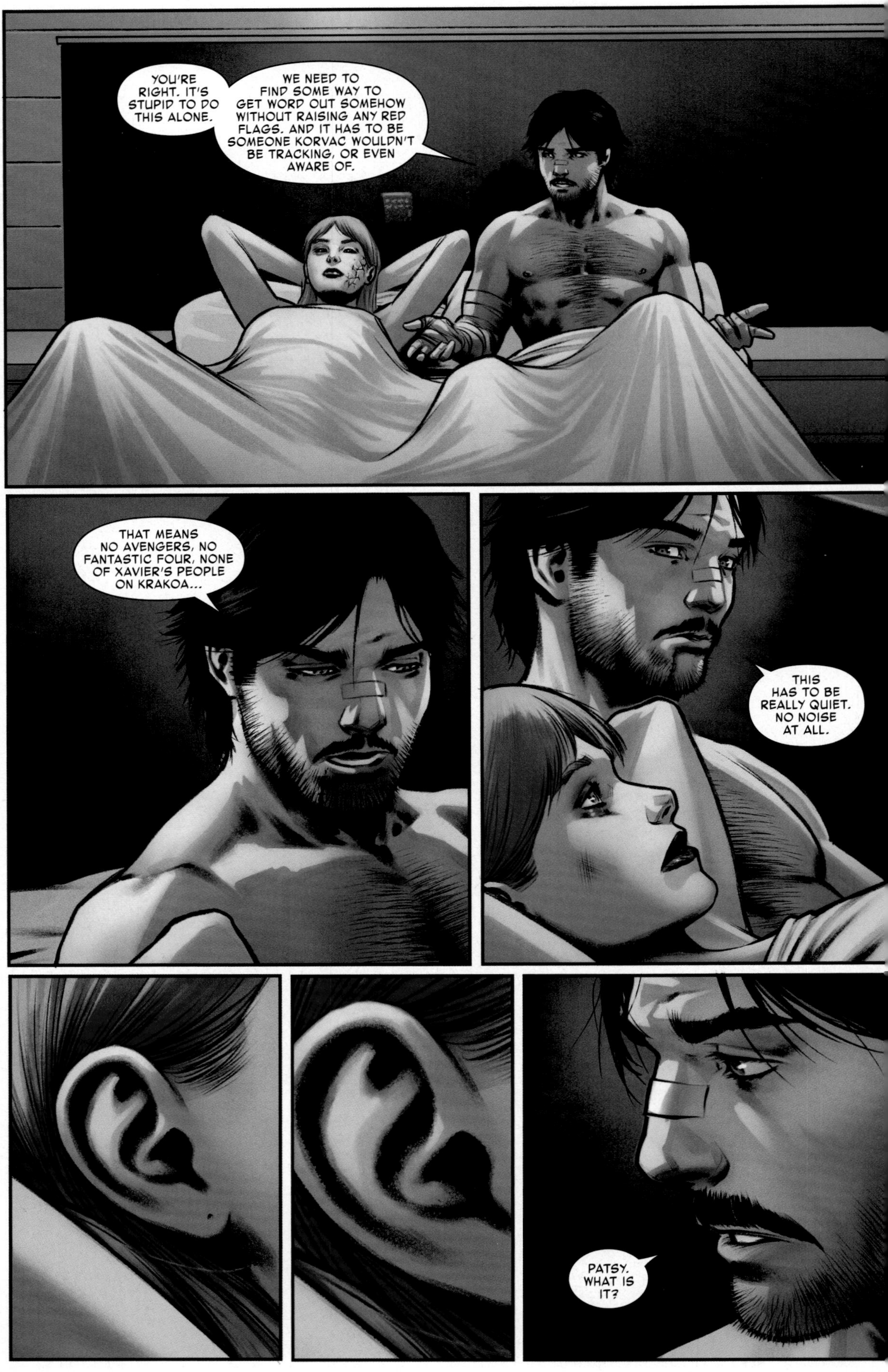

YOU'RE RIGHT. IT'S STUPID TO DO THIS ALONE.
WE NEED TO FIND SOME WAY TO GET WORD OUT SOMEHOW WITHOUT RAISING ANY RED FLAGS. AND IT HAS TO BE SOMEONE KORVAC WOULDN'T BE TRACKING, OR EVEN AWARE OF.
THAT MEANS NO AVENGERS, NO FANTASTIC FOUR, NONE OF XAVIER'S PEOPLE ON KRAKOA...
THIS HAS TO BE REALLY QUIET. NO NOISE AT ALL.
PATSY. WHAT IS IT?

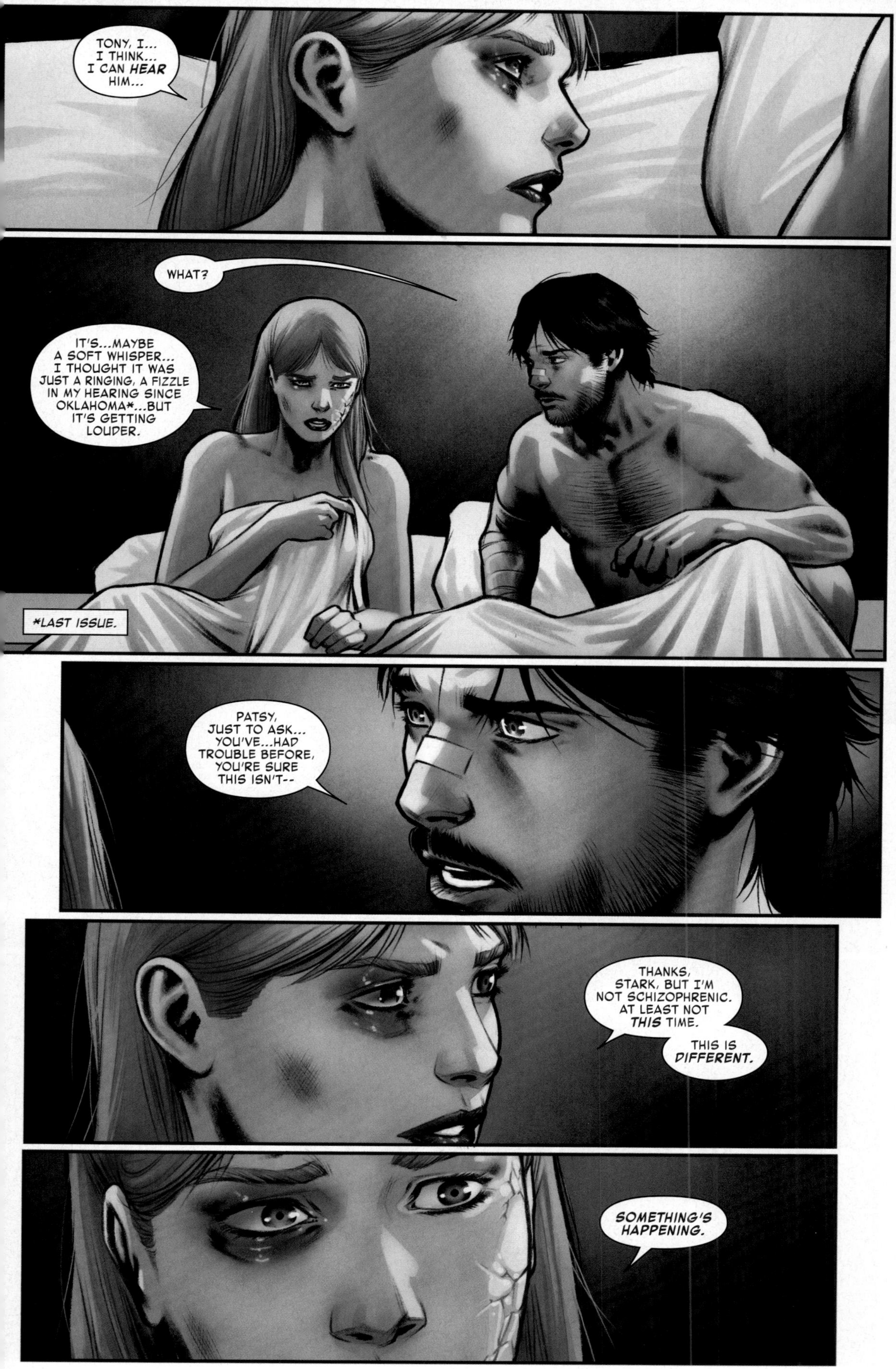

TONY, I... I THINK... I CAN *HEAR* HIM...
WHAT?
IT'S...MAYBE A SOFT WHISPER... I THOUGHT IT WAS JUST A RINGING, A FIZZLE IN MY HEARING SINCE OKLAHOMA*...BUT IT'S GETTING LOUDER.
*LAST ISSUE.
PATSY, JUST TO ASK... YOU'VE...HAD TROUBLE BEFORE, YOU'RE SURE THIS ISN'T--
THANKS, STARK, BUT I'M NOT SCHIZOPHRENIC. AT LEAST NOT *THIS* TIME.
THIS IS *DIFFERENT.*
SOMETHING'S HAPPENING.

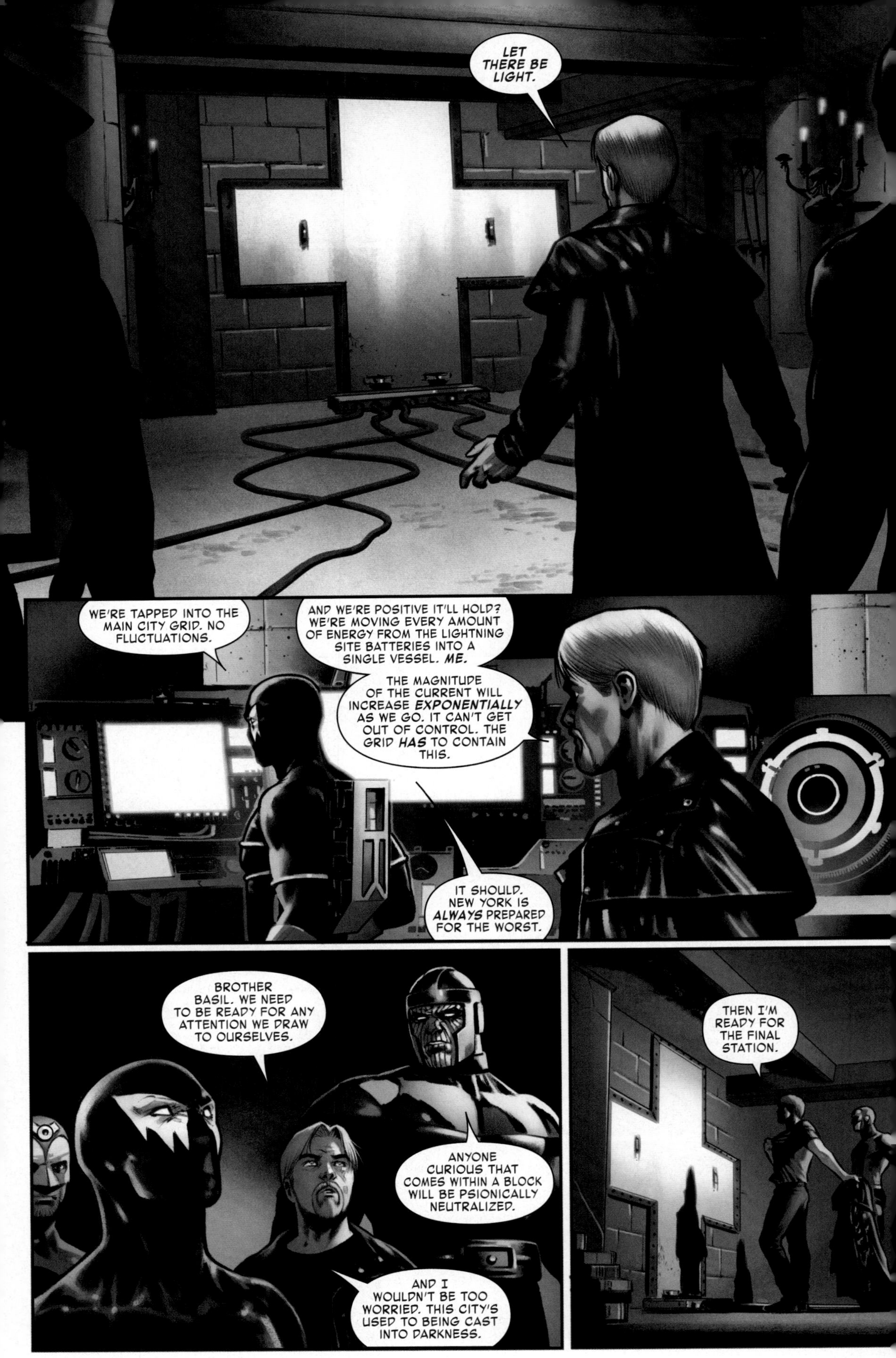
LET THERE BE LIGHT.
WE'RE TAPPED INTO THE MAIN CITY GRID. NO FLUCTUATIONS.
AND WE'RE POSITIVE IT'LL HOLD? WE'RE MOVING EVERY AMOUNT OF ENERGY FROM THE LIGHTNING SITE BATTERIES INTO A SINGLE VESSEL. ME.
THE MAGNITUDE OF THE CURRENT WILL INCREASE EXPONENTIALLY AS WE GO. IT CAN'T GET OUT OF CONTROL. THE GRID HAS TO CONTAIN THIS.
IT SHOULD. NEW YORK IS ALWAYS PREPARED FOR THE WORST.
BROTHER BASIL. WE NEED TO BE READY FOR ANY ATTENTION WE DRAW TO OURSELVES.
ANYONE CURIOUS THAT COMES WITHIN A BLOCK WILL BE PSIONICALLY NEUTRALIZED.
AND I WOULDN'T BE TOO WORRIED. THIS CITY'S USED TO BEING CAST INTO DARKNESS.
THEN I'M READY FOR THE FINAL STATION.

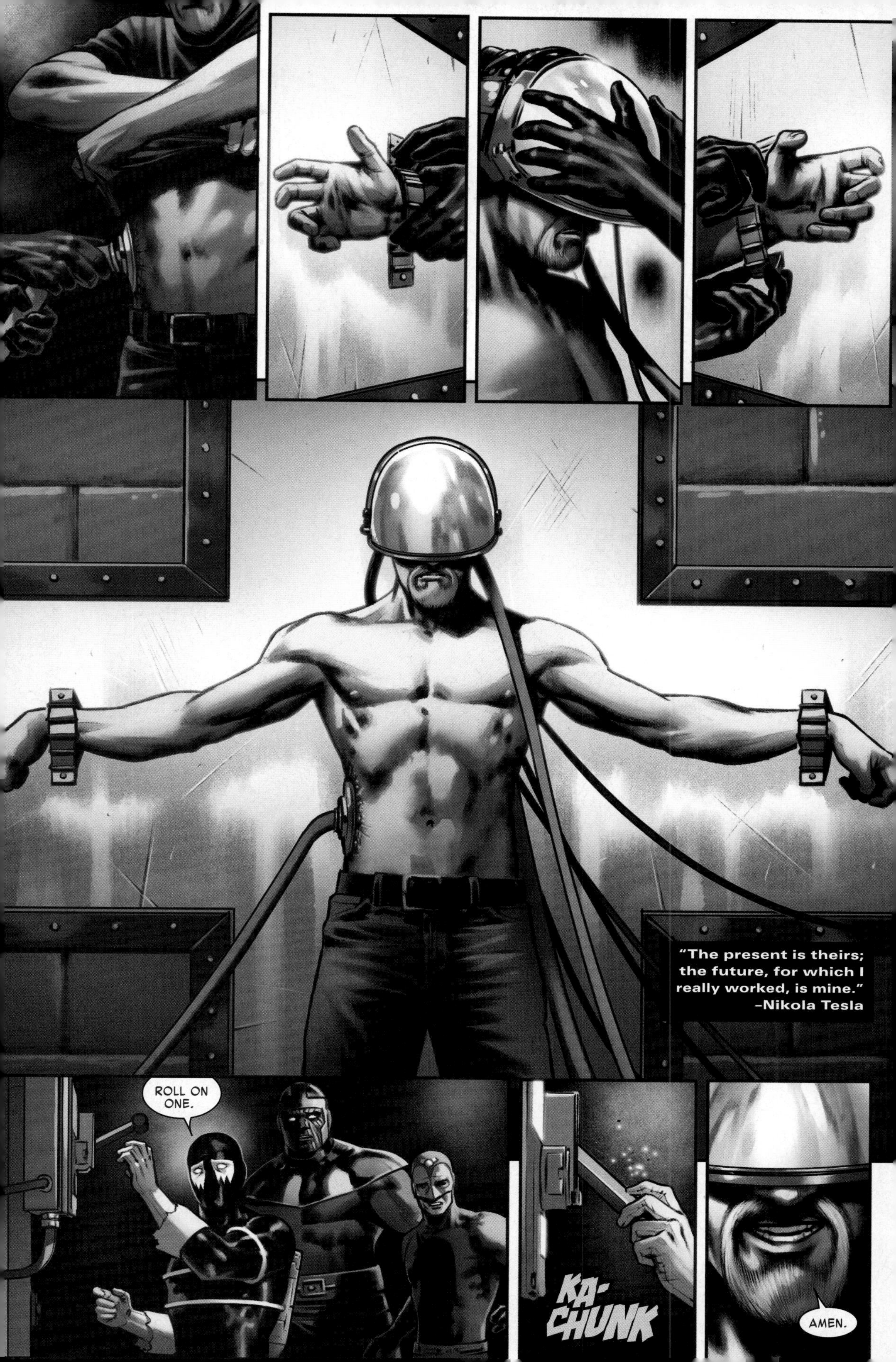
"The present is theirs; the future, for which I really worked, is mine."
–Nikola Tesla
ROLL ON ONE.
KA-CHUNK
AMEN.

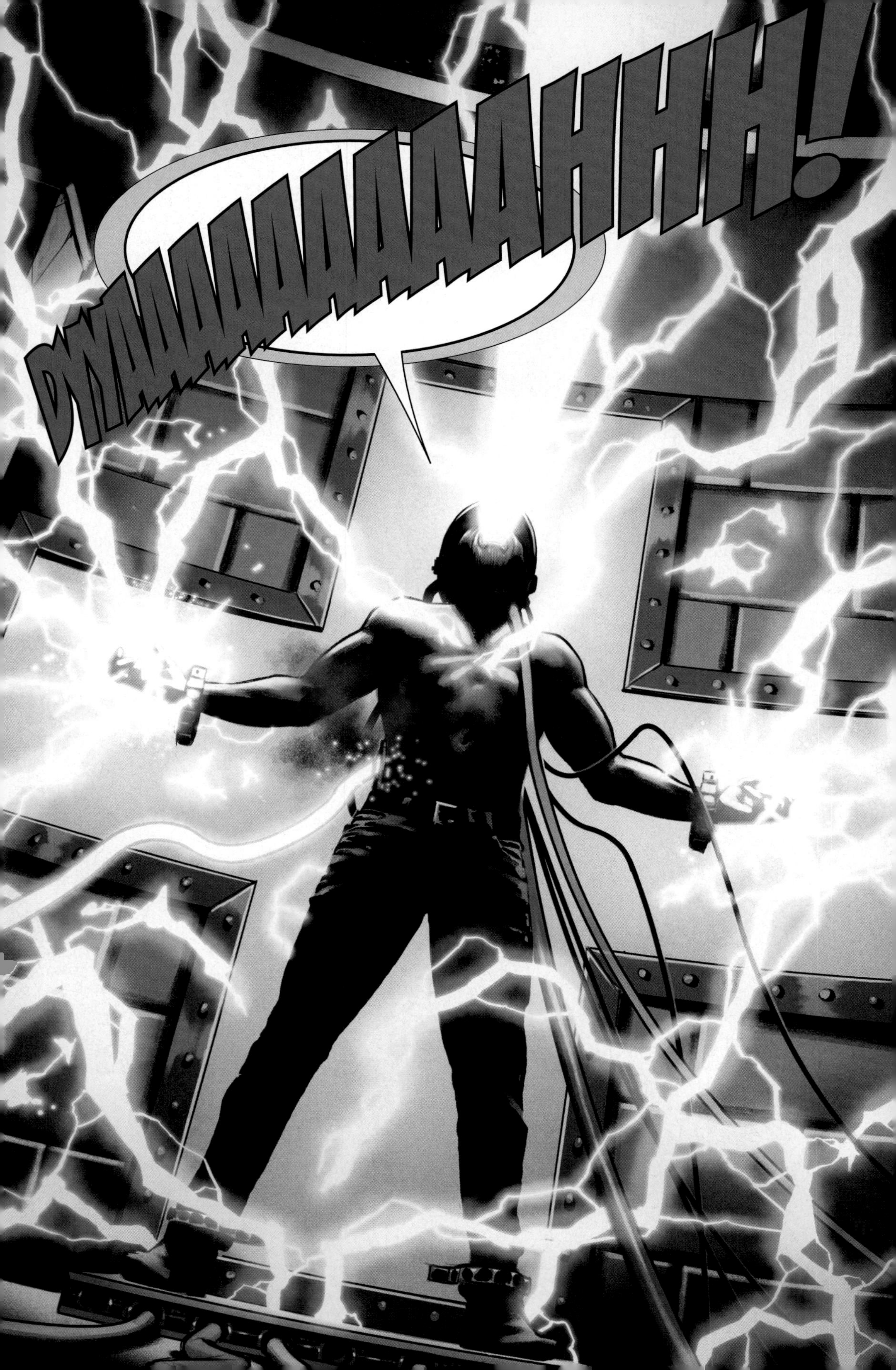
DYAAAAAAAAAAAHHH!

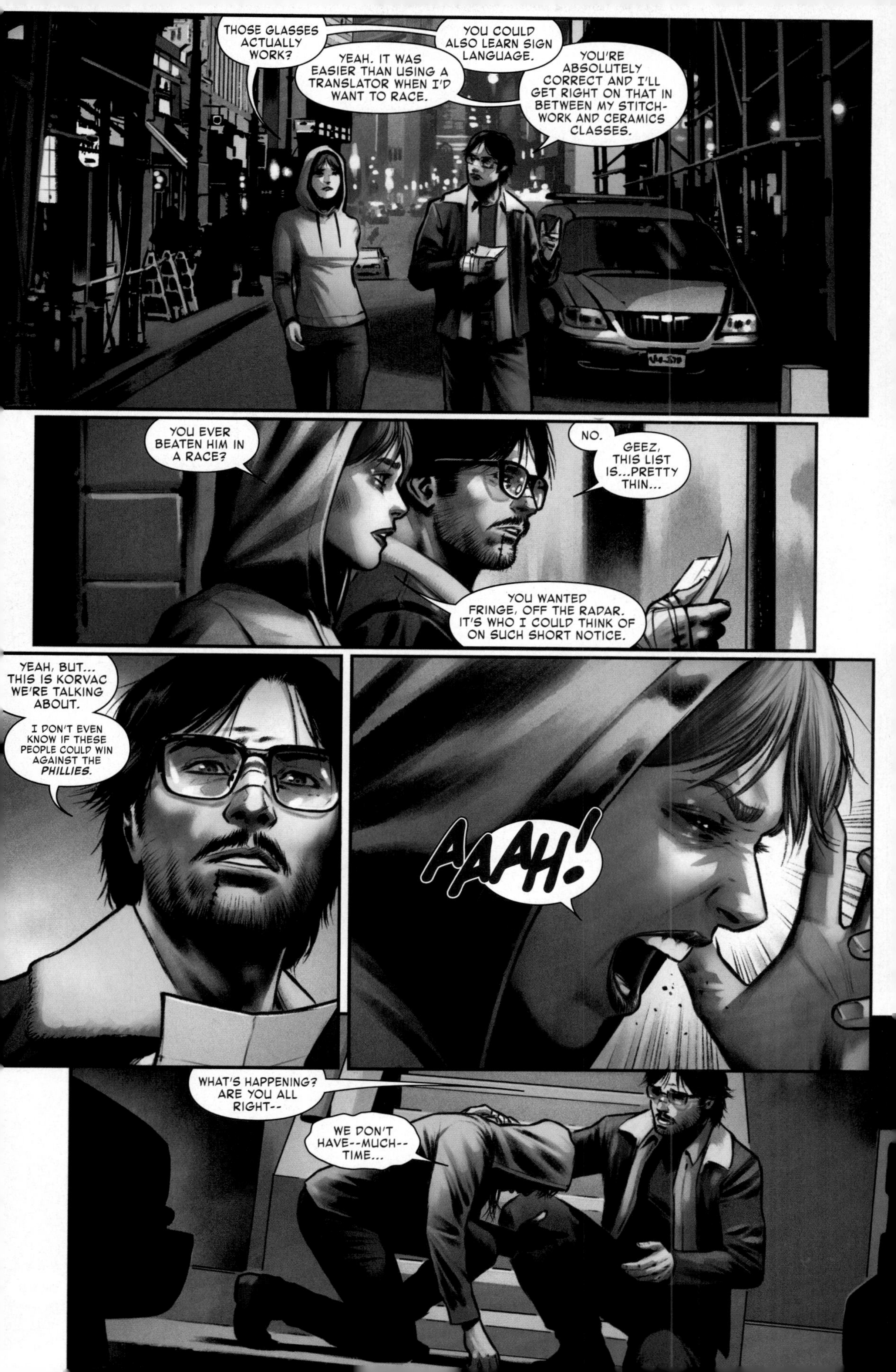
THOSE GLASSES ACTUALLY WORK?
YEAH. IT WAS EASIER THAN USING A TRANSLATOR WHEN I'D WANT TO RACE.
YOU COULD ALSO LEARN SIGN LANGUAGE.
YOU'RE ABSOLUTELY CORRECT AND I'LL GET RIGHT ON THAT IN BETWEEN MY STITCH-WORK AND CERAMICS CLASSES.
YOU EVER BEATEN HIM IN A RACE?
NO.
GEEZ, THIS LIST IS...PRETTY THIN...
YOU WANTED FRINGE, OFF THE RADAR. IT'S WHO I COULD THINK OF ON SUCH SHORT NOTICE.
YEAH, BUT... THIS IS KORVAC WE'RE TALKING ABOUT.
I DON'T EVEN KNOW IF THESE PEOPLE COULD WIN AGAINST THE *PHILLIES.*
AAAH!
WHAT'S HAPPENING? ARE YOU ALL RIGHT--
WE DON'T HAVE--MUCH--TIME...

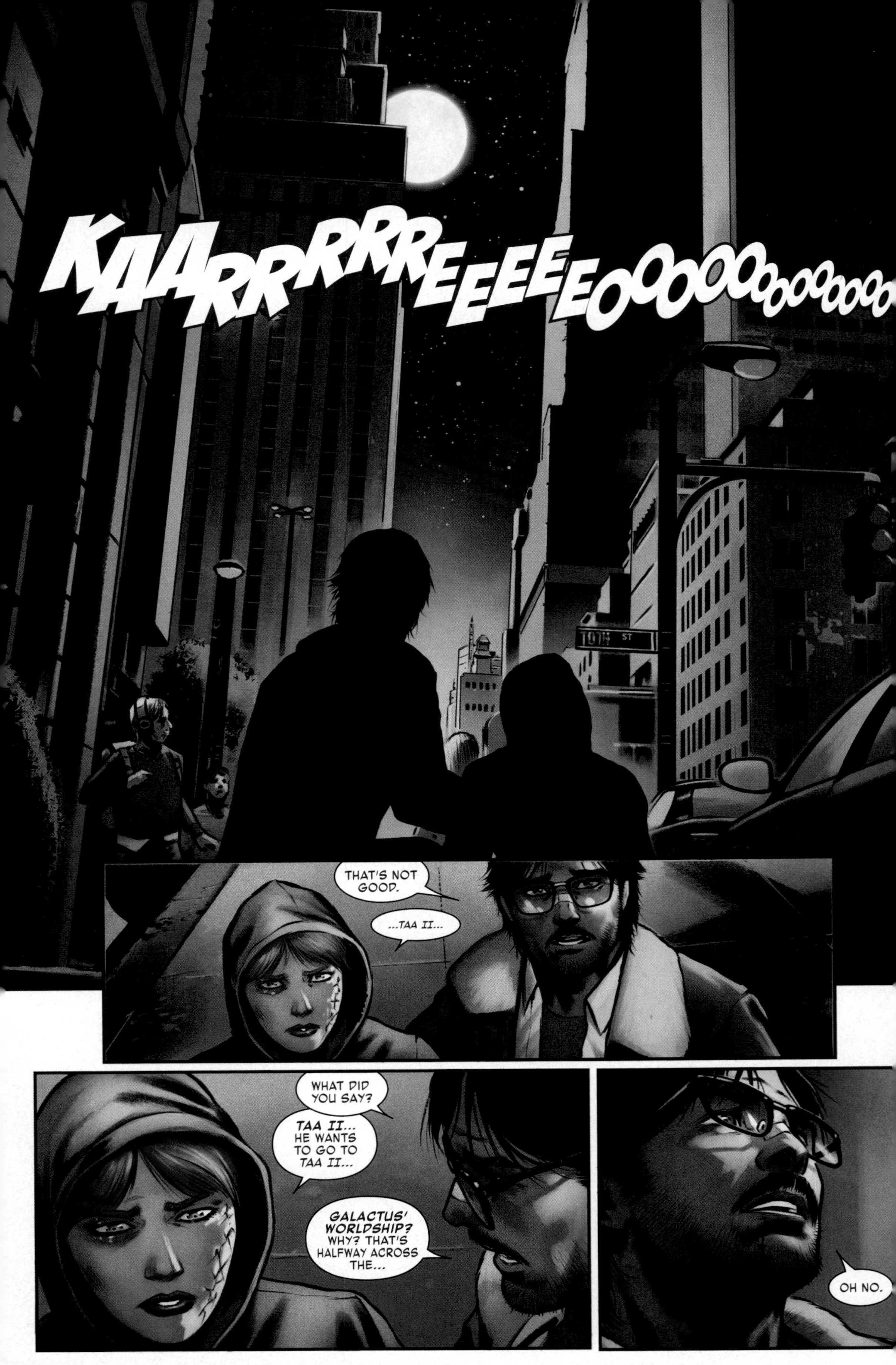

KAARRRRREEEEEOOOOOOOOOO
10TH ST
THAT'S NOT GOOD.
...TAA II...
WHAT DID YOU SAY?
TAA II... HE WANTS TO GO TO TAA II...
GALACTUS' WORLDSHIP? WHY? THAT'S HALFWAY ACROSS THE...
OH NO.

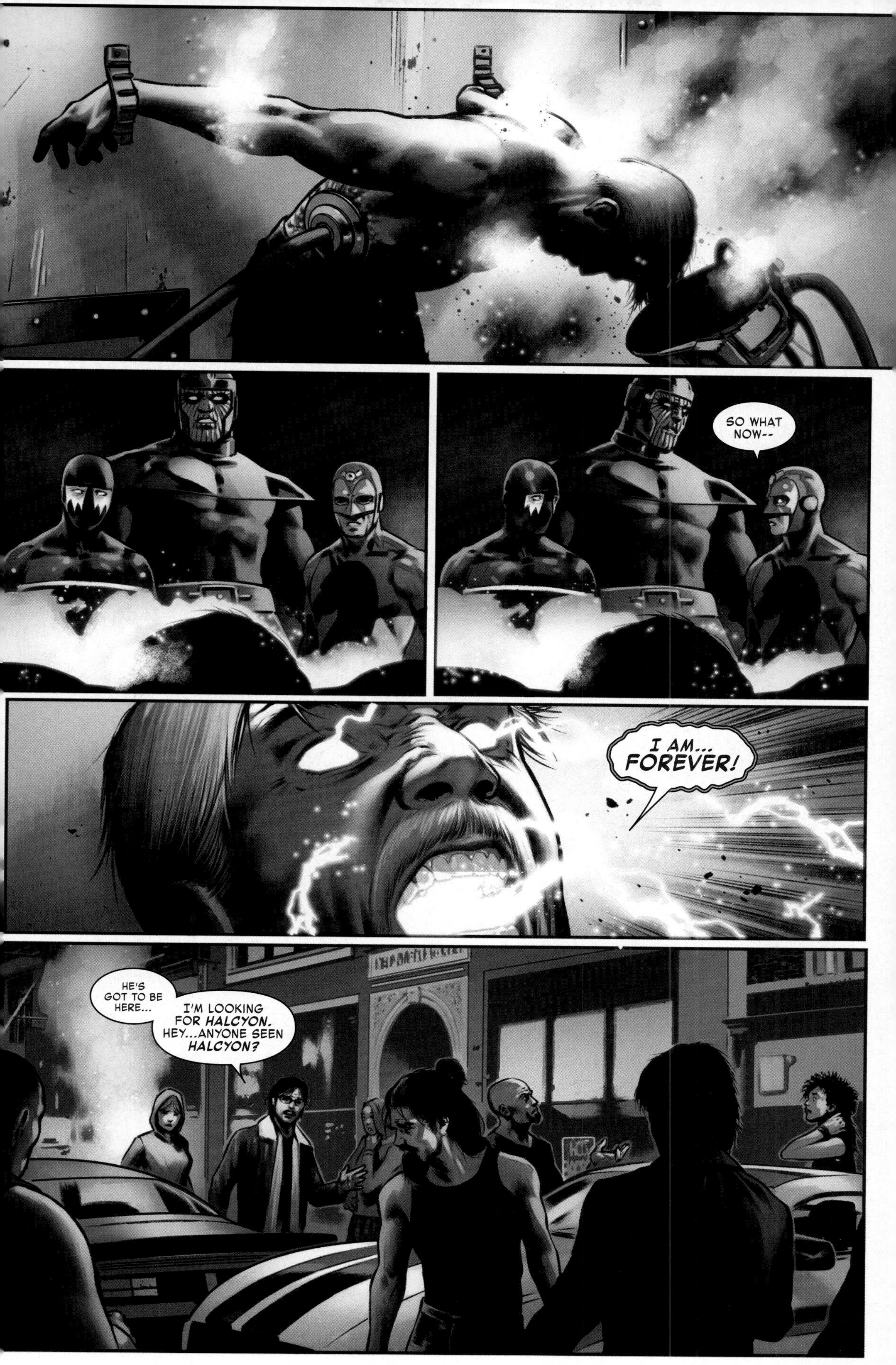
SO WHAT NOW--
I AM... FOREVER!
HE'S GOT TO BE HERE...
I'M LOOKING FOR HALCYON. HEY...ANYONE SEEN HALCYON?

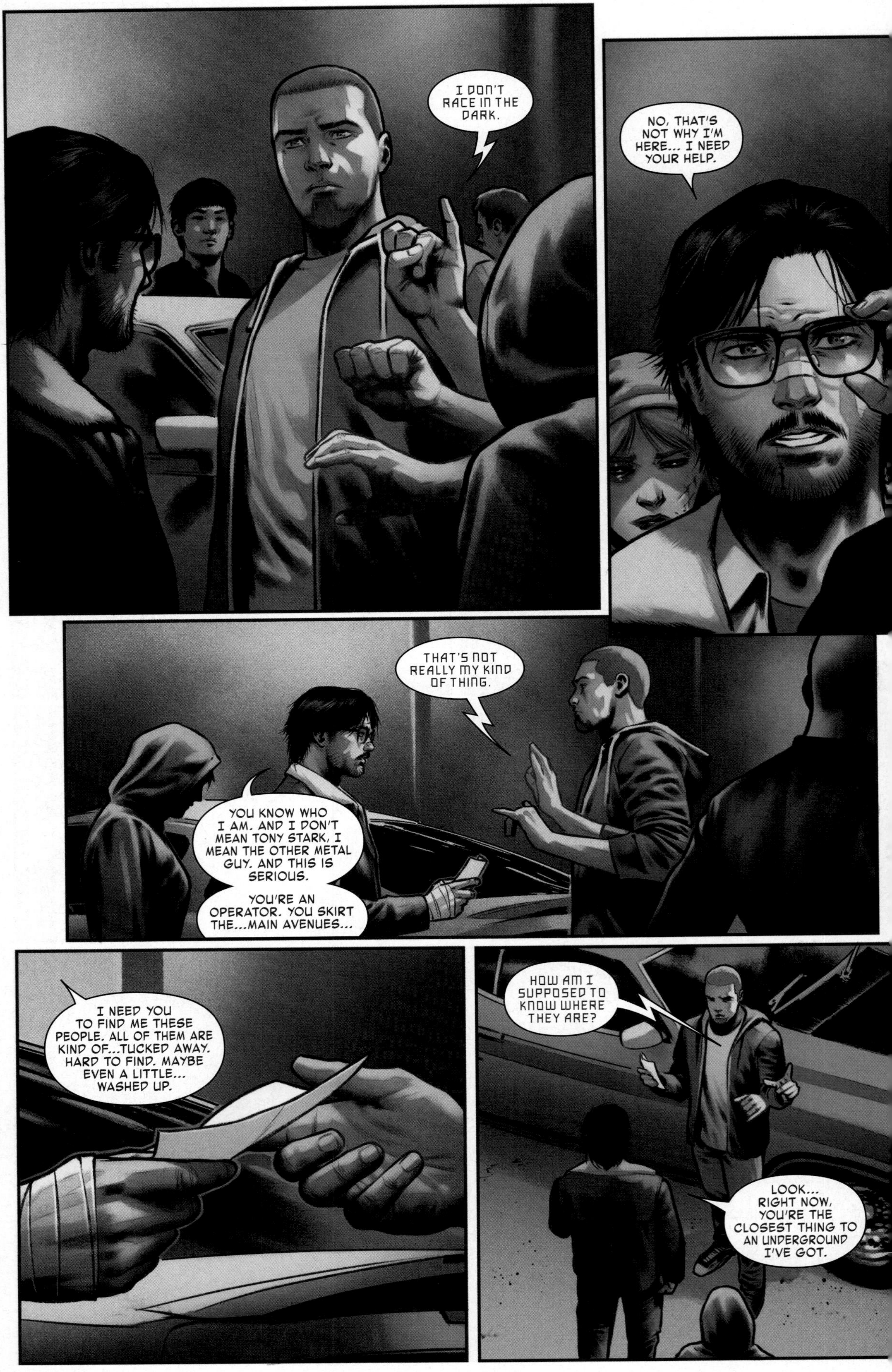
I DON'T RACE IN THE DARK.
NO, THAT'S NOT WHY I'M HERE... I NEED YOUR HELP.
THAT'S NOT REALLY MY KIND OF THING.
YOU KNOW WHO I AM. AND I DON'T MEAN TONY STARK, I MEAN THE OTHER METAL GUY. AND THIS IS SERIOUS.
YOU'RE AN OPERATOR. YOU SKIRT THE...MAIN AVENUES...
I NEED YOU TO FIND ME THESE PEOPLE. ALL OF THEM ARE KIND OF...TUCKED AWAY. HARD TO FIND. MAYBE EVEN A LITTLE... WASHED UP.
HOW AM I SUPPOSED TO KNOW WHERE THEY ARE?
LOOK... RIGHT NOW, YOU'RE THE CLOSEST THING TO AN UNDERGROUND I'VE GOT.

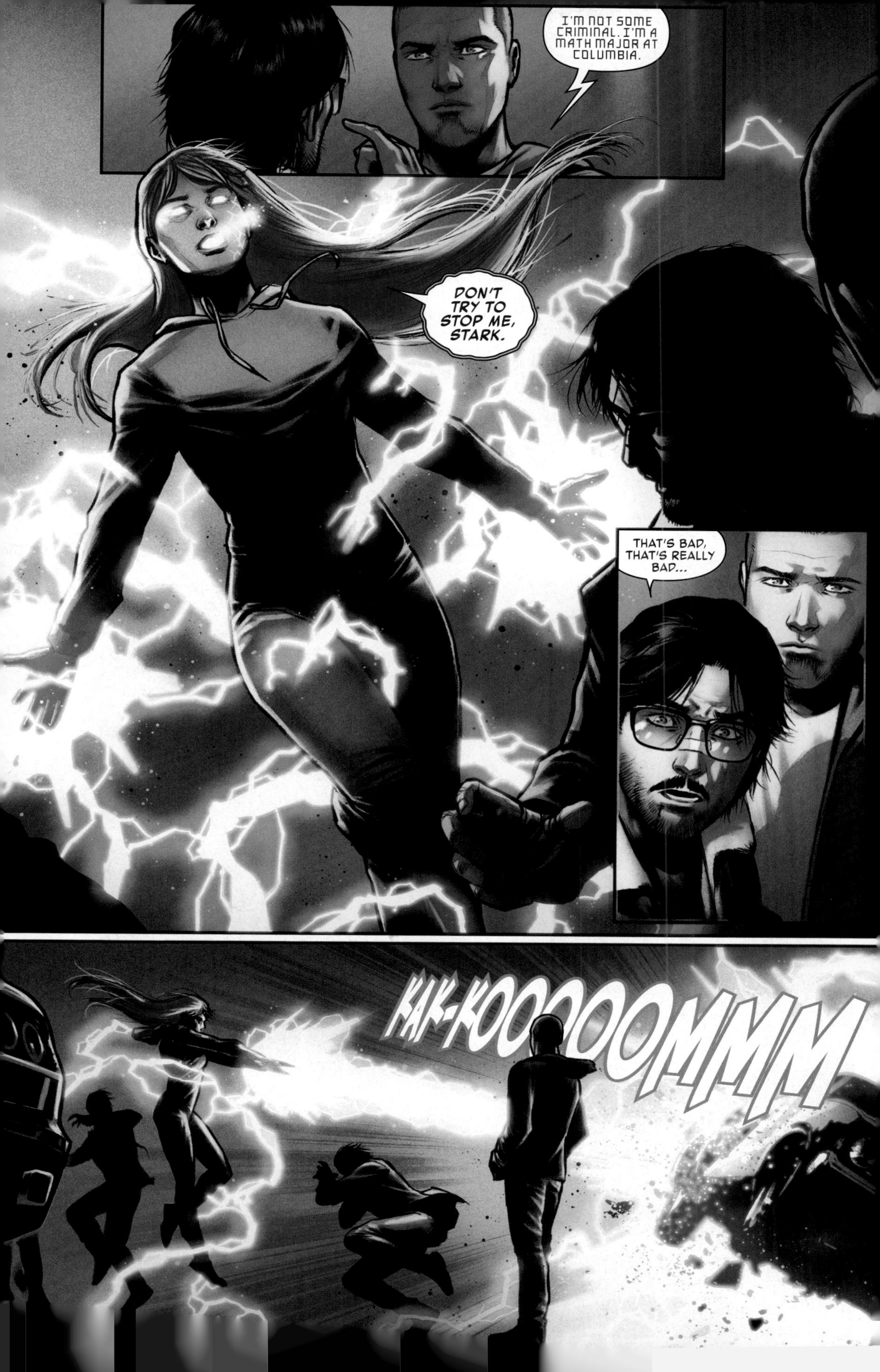
I'M NOT SOME CRIMINAL. I'M A MATH MAJOR AT COLUMBIA.
DON'T TRY TO STOP ME, STARK.
THAT'S BAD, THAT'S REALLY BAD...
KAK-KOOOOOMMMM

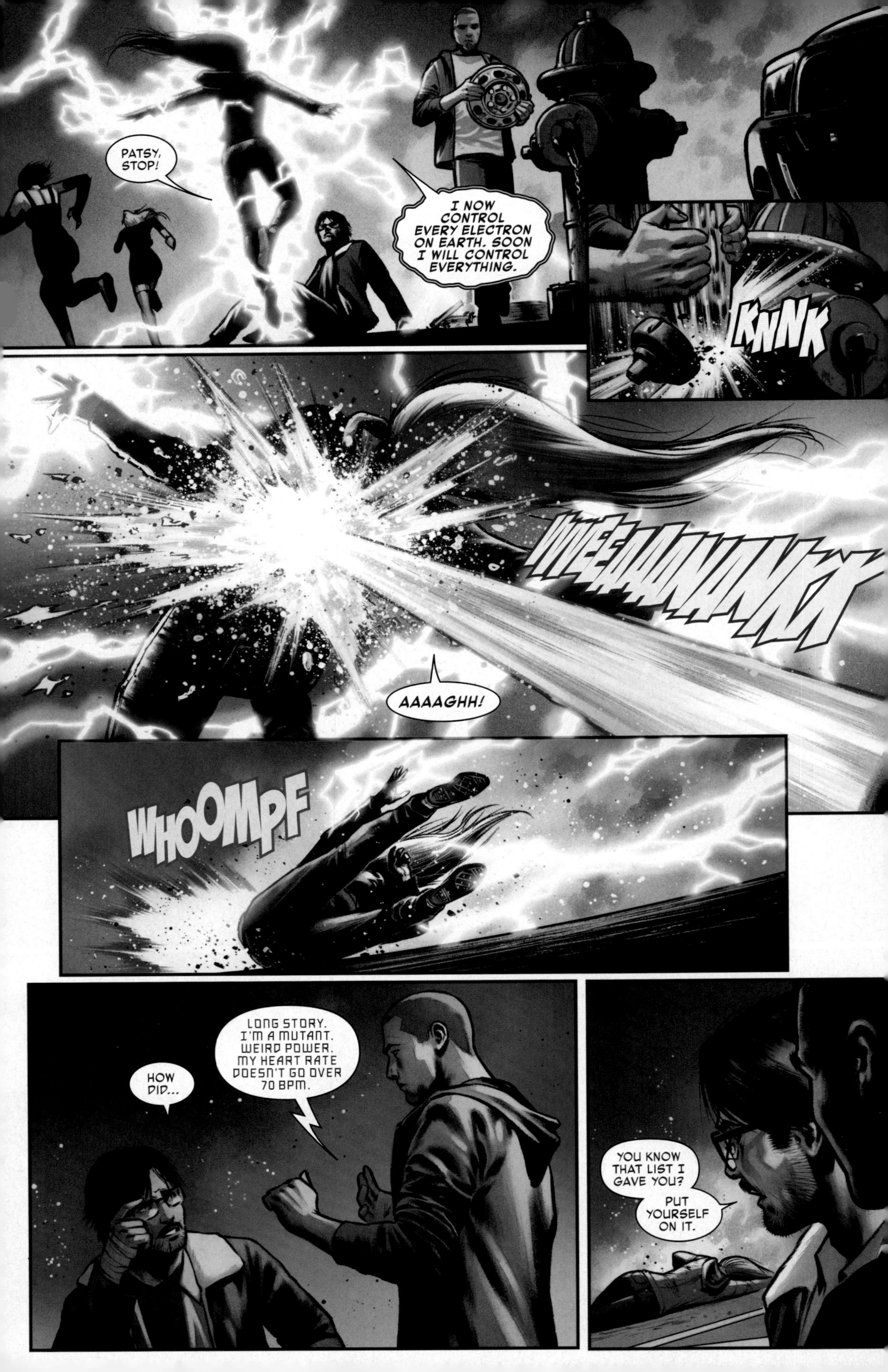
PATSY, STOP!
I NOW CONTROL EVERY ELECTRON ON EARTH. SOON I WILL CONTROL EVERYTHING.
KNNK
VVVEEAAANNNNKK
AAAAGHH!
WHOOMPF
HOW DID...
LONG STORY. I'M A MUTANT. WEIRD POWER. MY HEART RATE DOESN'T GO OVER 70 BPM.
YOU KNOW THAT LIST I GAVE YOU?
PUT YOURSELF ON IT.

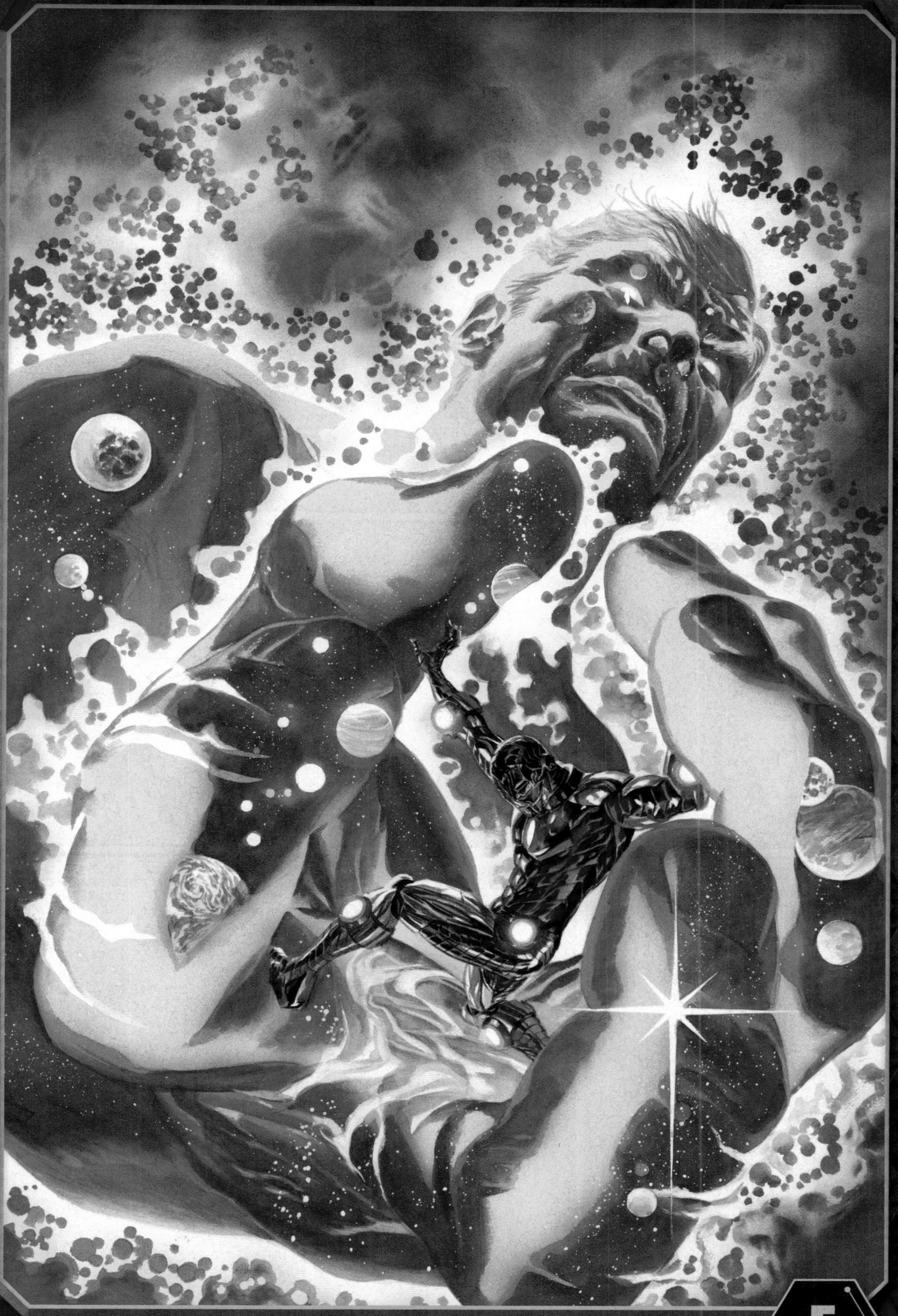

5

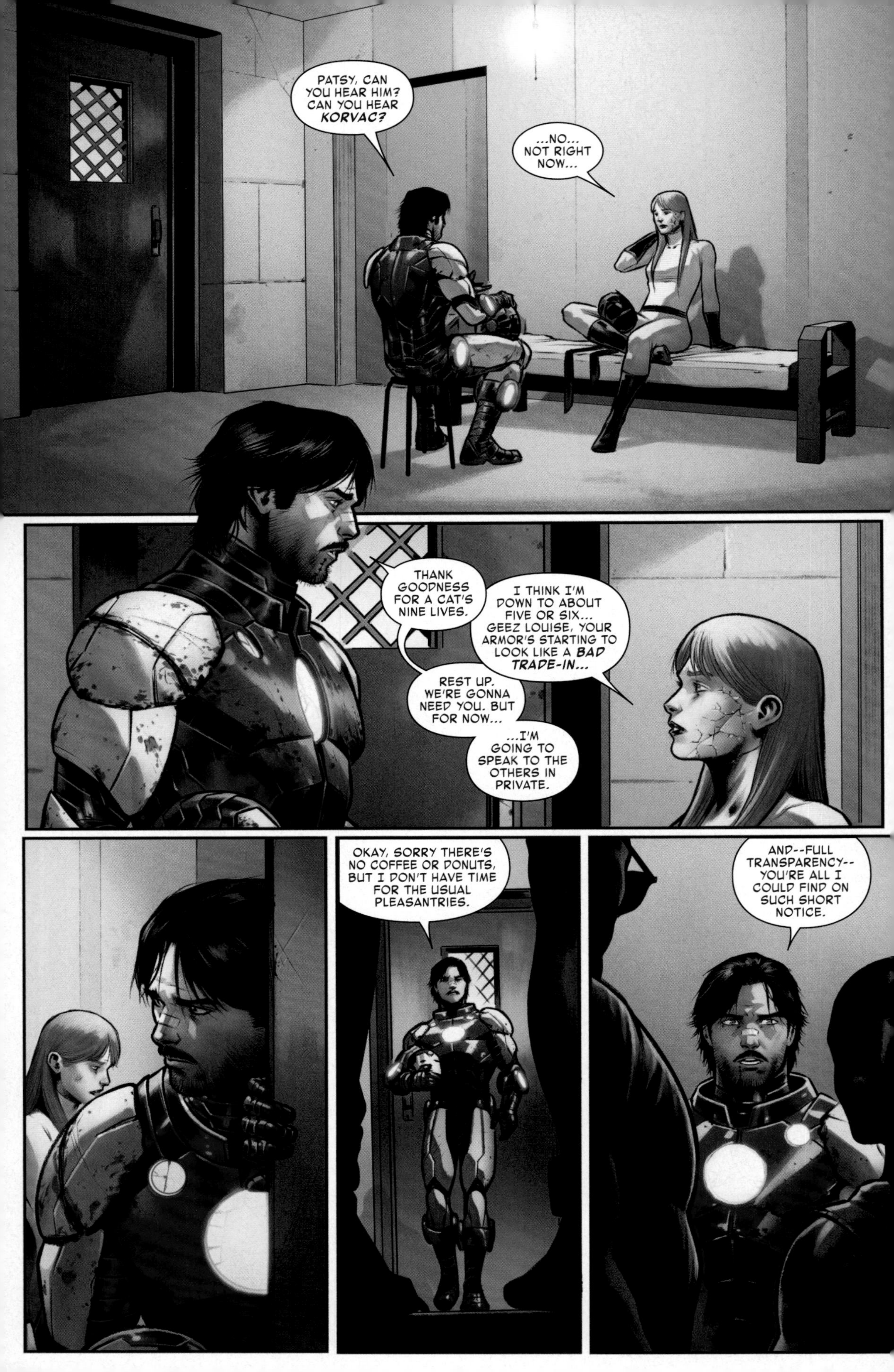
PATSY, CAN YOU HEAR HIM? CAN YOU HEAR KORVAC?
...NO... NOT RIGHT NOW...
THANK GOODNESS FOR A CAT'S NINE LIVES.
I THINK I'M DOWN TO ABOUT FIVE OR SIX... GEEZ LOUISE, YOUR ARMOR'S STARTING TO LOOK LIKE A BAD TRADE-IN...
REST UP. WE'RE GONNA NEED YOU. BUT FOR NOW...
...I'M GOING TO SPEAK TO THE OTHERS IN PRIVATE.
OKAY, SORRY THERE'S NO COFFEE OR DONUTS, BUT I DON'T HAVE TIME FOR THE USUAL PLEASANTRIES.
AND--FULL TRANSPARENCY--YOU'RE ALL I COULD FIND ON SUCH SHORT NOTICE.

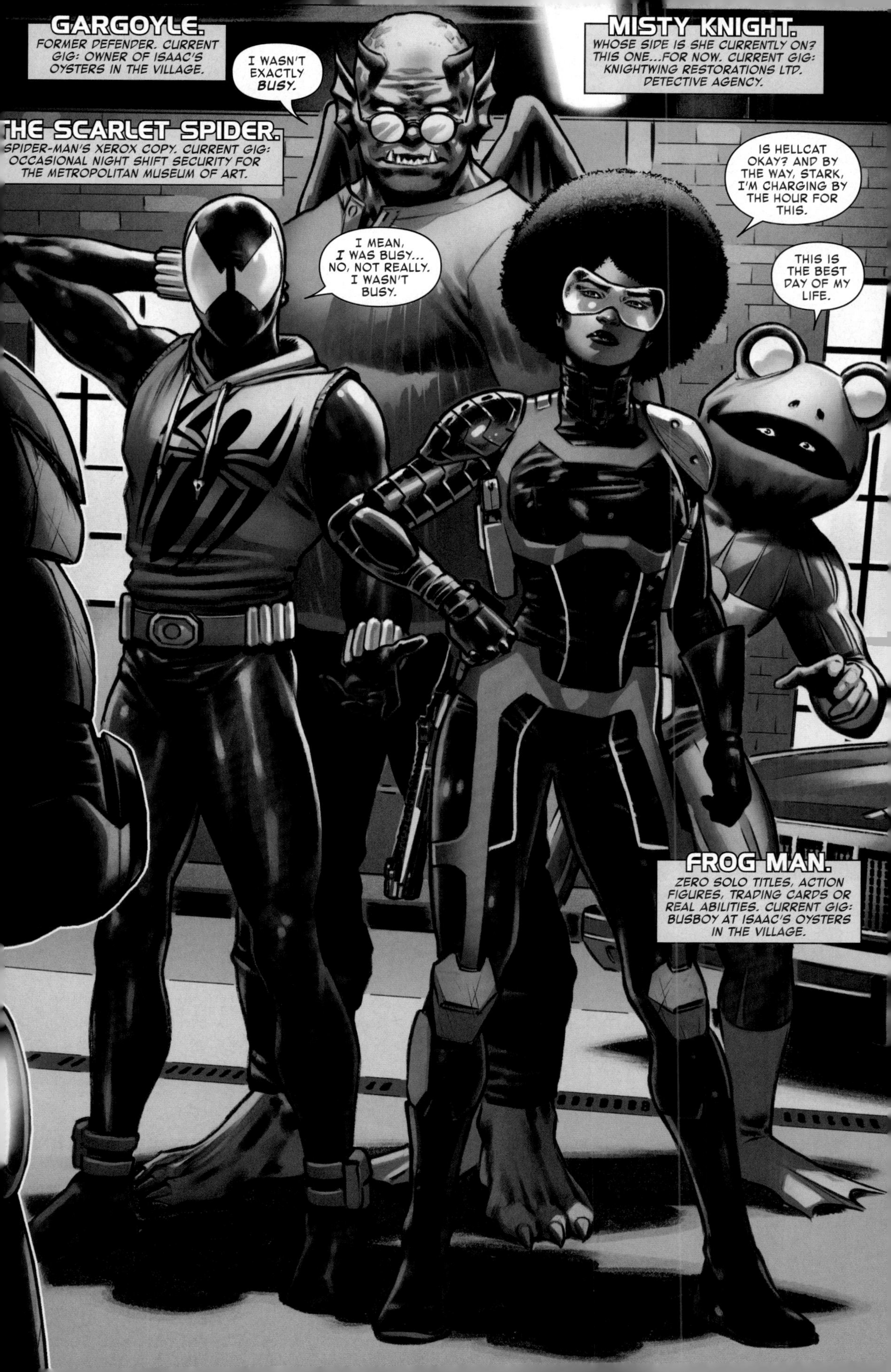
GARGOYLE.
FORMER DEFENDER. CURRENT GIG: OWNER OF ISAAC'S OYSTERS IN THE VILLAGE.
I WASN'T EXACTLY BUSY.
MISTY KNIGHT.
WHOSE SIDE IS SHE CURRENTLY ON? THIS ONE...FOR NOW. CURRENT GIG: KNIGHTWING RESTORATIONS LTD. DETECTIVE AGENCY.
THE SCARLET SPIDER.
SPIDER-MAN'S XEROX COPY. CURRENT GIG: OCCASIONAL NIGHT SHIFT SECURITY FOR THE METROPOLITAN MUSEUM OF ART.
IS HELLCAT OKAY? AND BY THE WAY, STARK, I'M CHARGING BY THE HOUR FOR THIS.
I MEAN, I WAS BUSY... NO, NOT REALLY. I WASN'T BUSY.
THIS IS THE BEST DAY OF MY LIFE.
FROG MAN.
ZERO SOLO TITLES, ACTION FIGURES, TRADING CARDS OR REAL ABILITIES. CURRENT GIG: BUSBOY AT ISAAC'S OYSTERS IN THE VILLAGE.

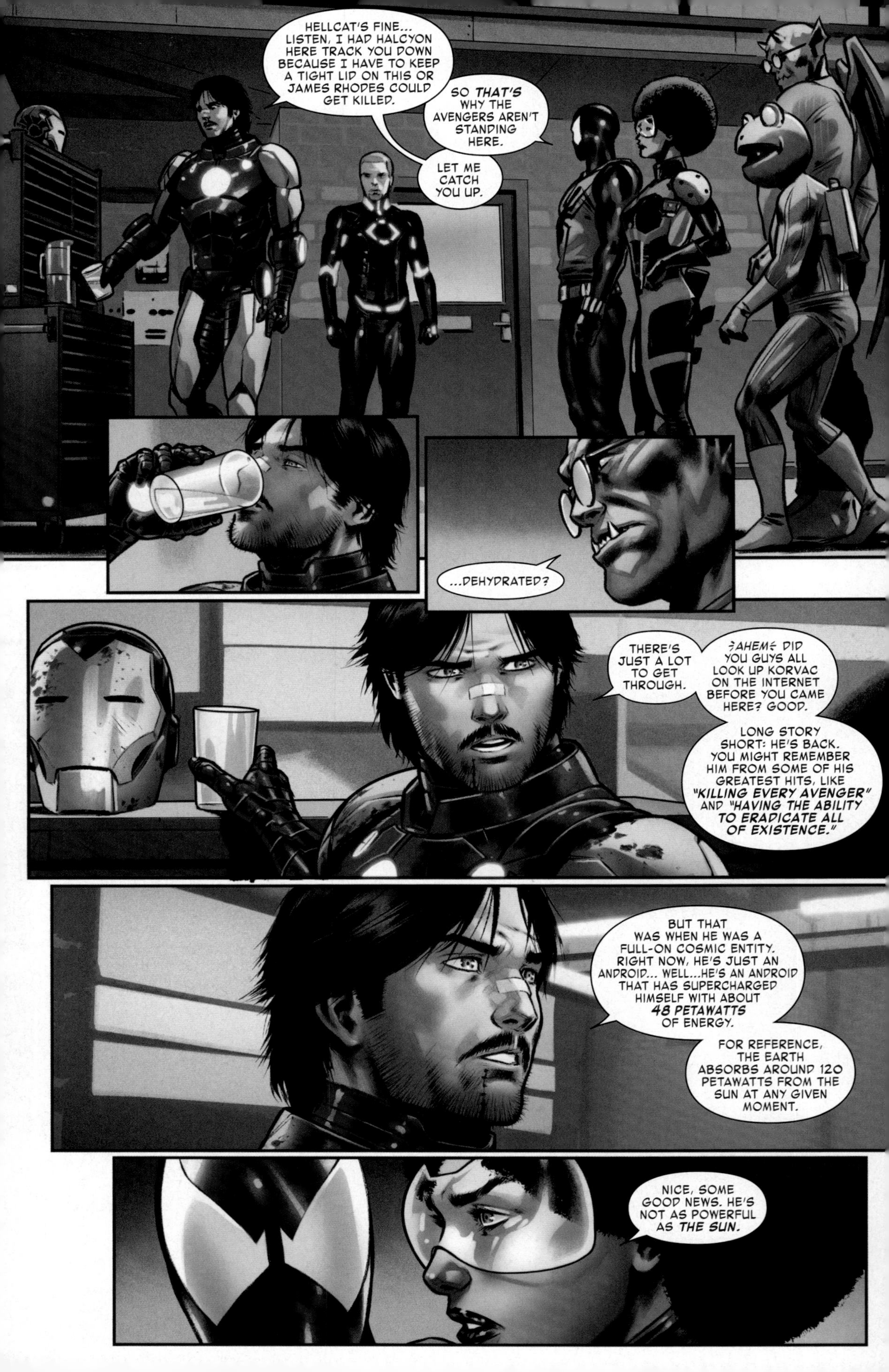
HELLCAT'S FINE... LISTEN, I HAD HALCYON HERE TRACK YOU DOWN BECAUSE I HAVE TO KEEP A TIGHT LID ON THIS OR JAMES RHODES COULD GET KILLED.
SO *THAT'S* WHY THE AVENGERS AREN'T STANDING HERE.
LET ME CATCH YOU UP.
...DEHYDRATED?
THERE'S JUST A LOT TO GET THROUGH.
AHEM DID YOU GUYS ALL LOOK UP KORVAC ON THE INTERNET BEFORE YOU CAME HERE? GOOD.
LONG STORY SHORT: HE'S BACK. YOU MIGHT REMEMBER HIM FROM SOME OF HIS GREATEST HITS, LIKE ***"KILLING EVERY AVENGER"*** AND ***"HAVING THE ABILITY TO ERADICATE ALL OF EXISTENCE."***
BUT THAT WAS WHEN HE WAS A FULL-ON COSMIC ENTITY. RIGHT NOW, HE'S JUST AN ANDROID... WELL...HE'S AN ANDROID THAT HAS SUPERCHARGED HIMSELF WITH ABOUT ***48 PETAWATTS*** OF ENERGY.
FOR REFERENCE, THE EARTH ABSORBS AROUND 120 PETAWATTS FROM THE SUN AT ANY GIVEN MOMENT.
NICE, SOME GOOD NEWS. HE'S NOT AS POWERFUL AS ***THE SUN.***

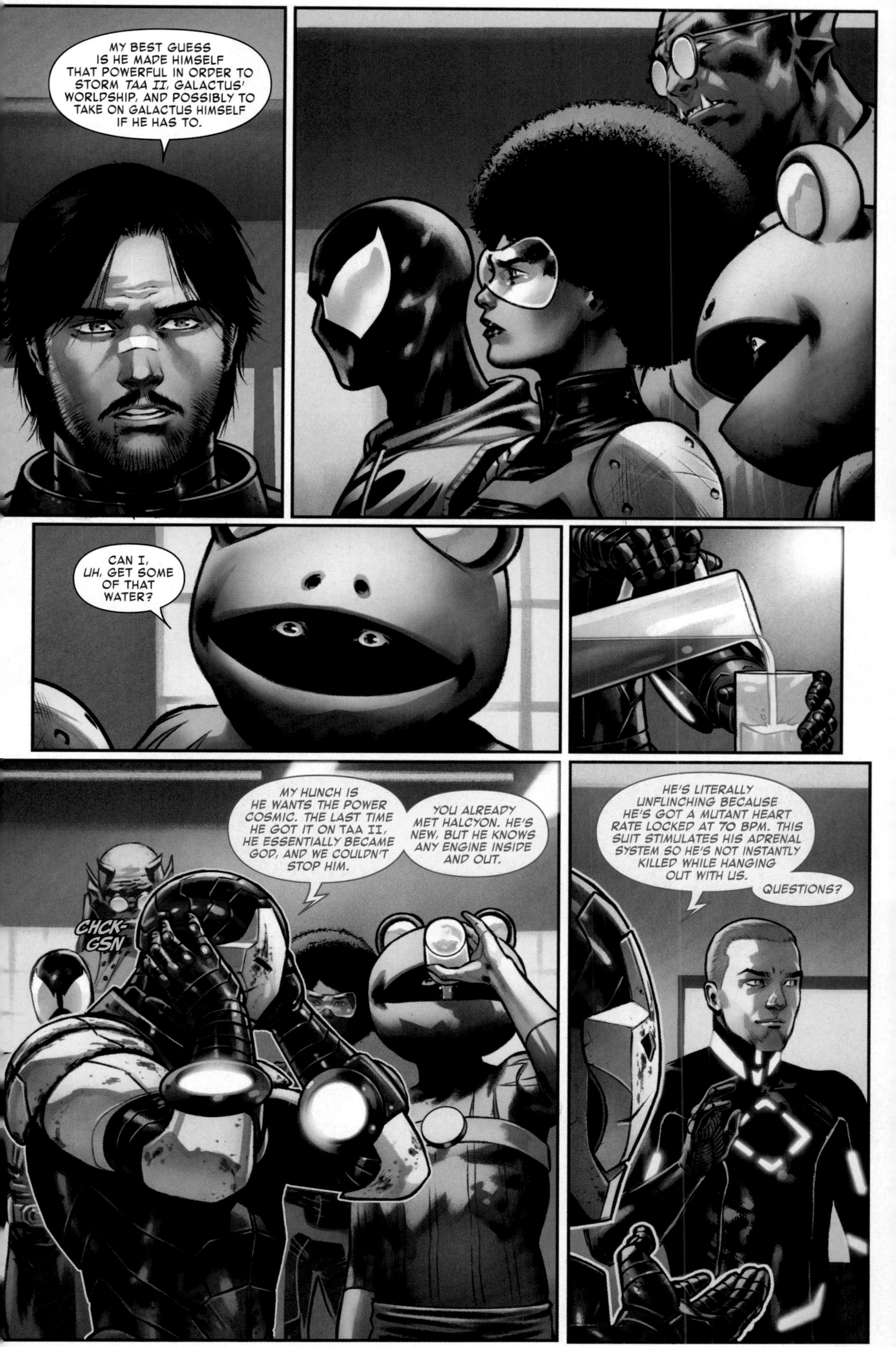
MY BEST GUESS IS HE MADE HIMSELF THAT POWERFUL IN ORDER TO STORM *TAA II*, GALACTUS' WORLDSHIP, AND POSSIBLY TO TAKE ON GALACTUS HIMSELF IF HE HAS TO.
CAN I, UH, GET SOME OF THAT WATER?
MY HUNCH IS HE WANTS THE POWER COSMIC. THE LAST TIME HE GOT IT ON TAA II, HE ESSENTIALLY BECAME GOD, AND WE COULDN'T STOP HIM.
CHCK-GSN
YOU ALREADY MET HALCYON. HE'S NEW, BUT HE KNOWS ANY ENGINE INSIDE AND OUT.
HE'S LITERALLY UNFLINCHING BECAUSE HE'S GOT A MUTANT HEART RATE LOCKED AT 70 BPM. THIS SUIT STIMULATES HIS ADRENAL SYSTEM SO HE'S NOT INSTANTLY KILLED WHILE HANGING OUT WITH US.
QUESTIONS?

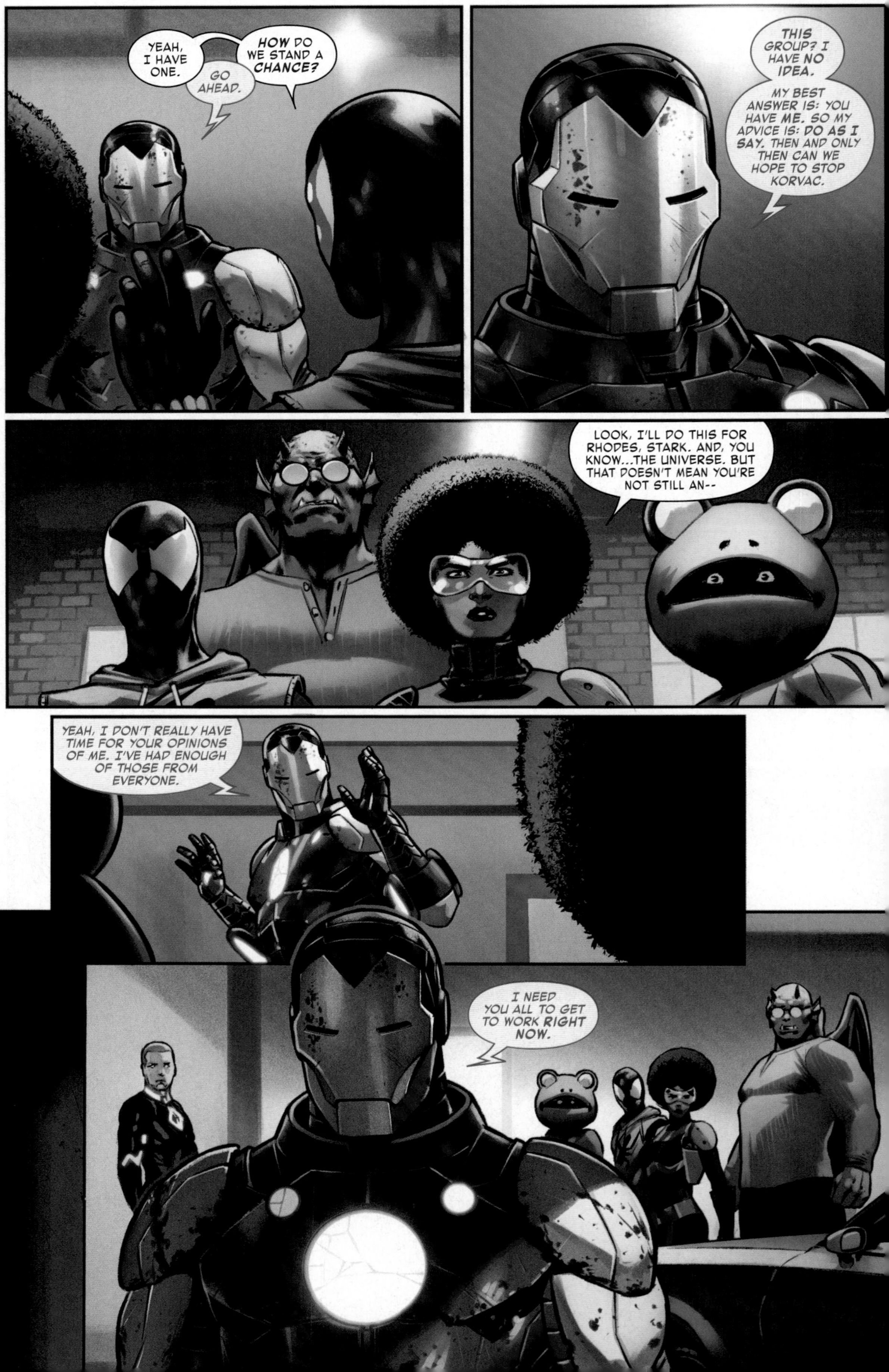
YEAH, I HAVE ONE.
GO AHEAD.
HOW DO WE STAND A CHANCE?
THIS GROUP? I HAVE NO IDEA.
MY BEST ANSWER IS: YOU HAVE ME. SO MY ADVICE IS: DO AS I SAY. THEN AND ONLY THEN CAN WE HOPE TO STOP KORVAC.
LOOK, I'LL DO THIS FOR RHODES, STARK. AND, YOU KNOW...THE UNIVERSE. BUT THAT DOESN'T MEAN YOU'RE NOT STILL AN--
YEAH, I DON'T REALLY HAVE TIME FOR YOUR OPINIONS OF ME. I'VE HAD ENOUGH OF THOSE FROM EVERYONE.
I NEED YOU ALL TO GET TO WORK RIGHT NOW.

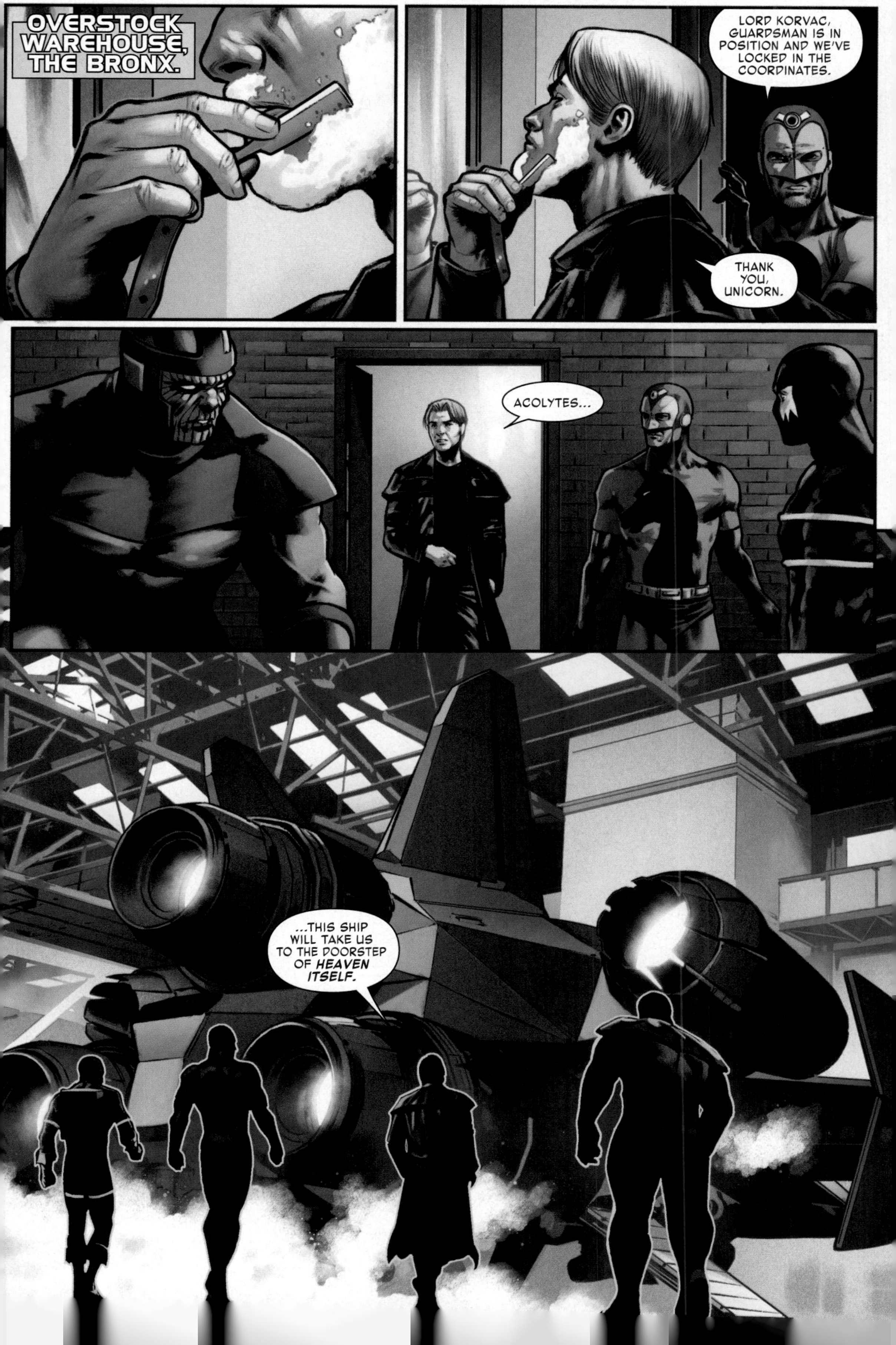
OVERSTOCK WAREHOUSE, THE BRONX.
LORD KORVAC, GUARDSMAN IS IN POSITION AND WE'VE LOCKED IN THE COORDINATES.
THANK YOU, UNICORN.
ACOLYTES...
...THIS SHIP WILL TAKE US TO THE DOORSTEP OF HEAVEN ITSELF.

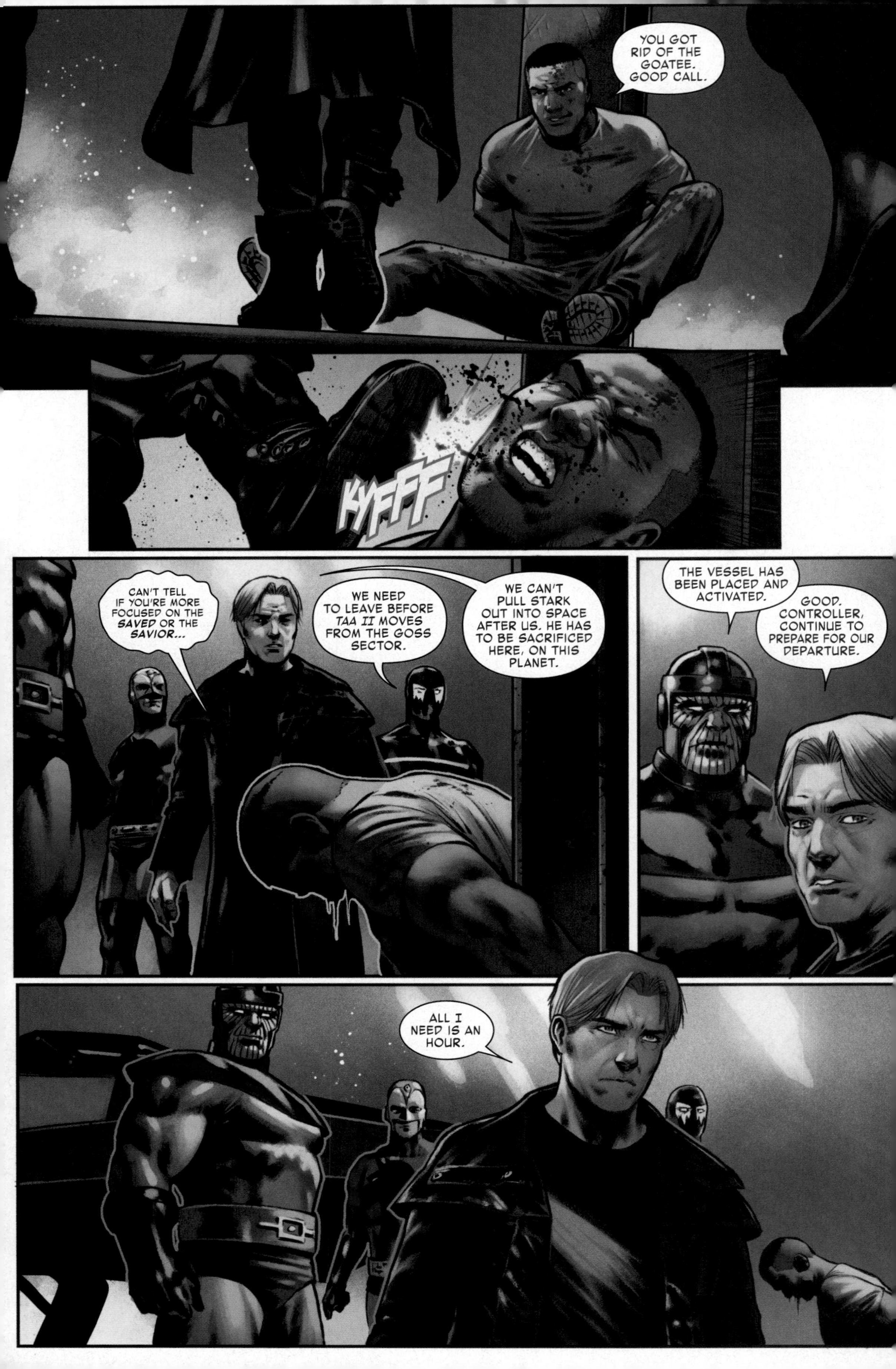
YOU GOT RID OF THE GOATEE. GOOD CALL.
KYFFF
CAN'T TELL IF YOU'RE MORE FOCUSED ON THE *SAVED* OR THE *SAVIOR*...
WE NEED TO LEAVE BEFORE *TAA II* MOVES FROM THE GOSS SECTOR.
WE CAN'T PULL STARK OUT INTO SPACE AFTER US. HE HAS TO BE SACRIFICED HERE, ON THIS PLANET.
THE VESSEL HAS BEEN PLACED AND ACTIVATED.
GOOD. CONTROLLER, CONTINUE TO PREPARE FOR OUR DEPARTURE.
ALL I NEED IS AN HOUR.

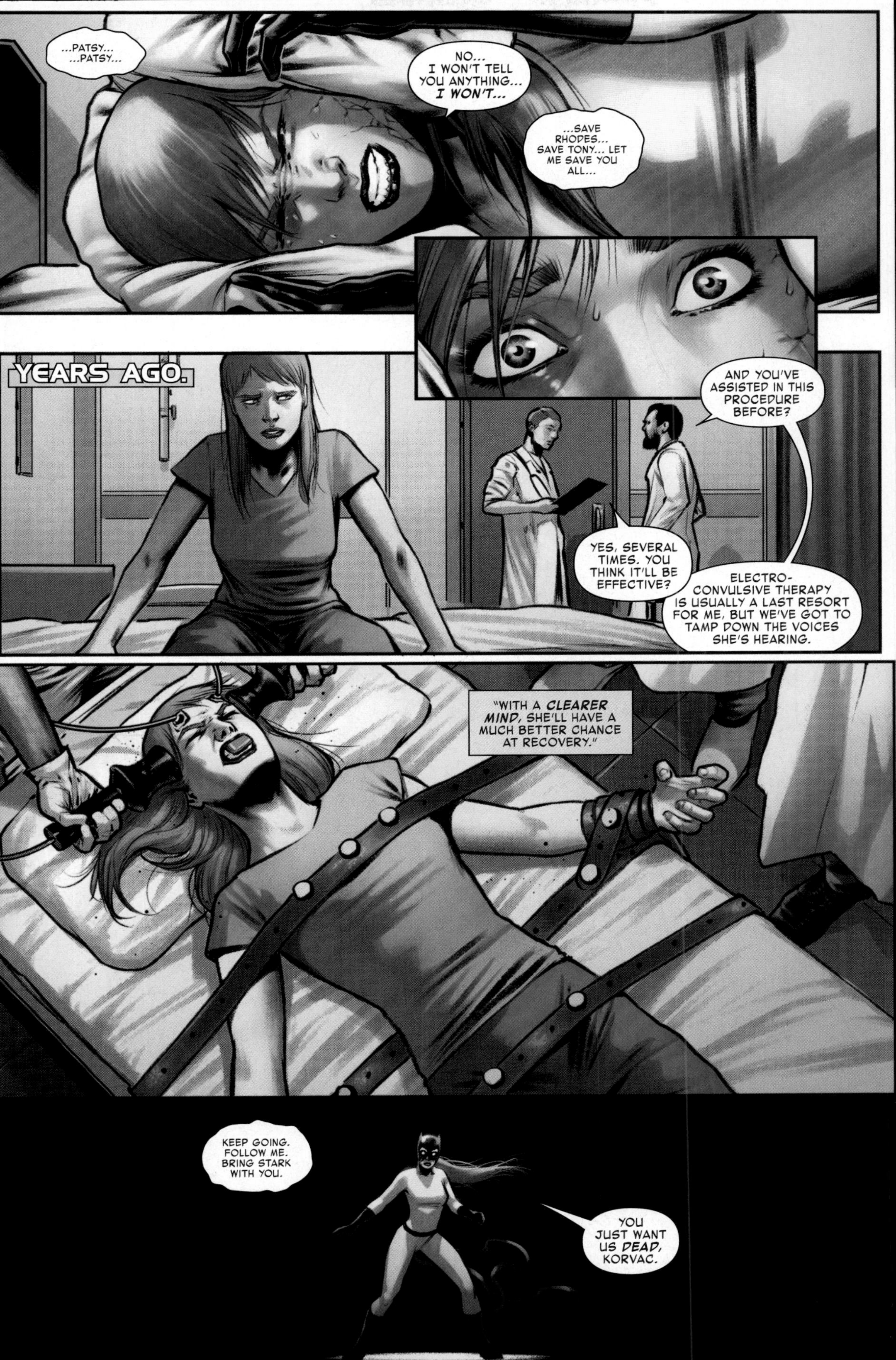

...PATSY... ...PATSY...
NO... I WON'T TELL YOU ANYTHING... *I WON'T...*
...SAVE RHODES... SAVE TONY... LET ME SAVE YOU ALL...
YEARS AGO.
AND YOU'VE ASSISTED IN THIS PROCEDURE BEFORE?
YES, SEVERAL TIMES. YOU THINK IT'LL BE EFFECTIVE?
ELECTRO-CONVULSIVE THERAPY IS USUALLY A LAST RESORT FOR ME, BUT WE'VE GOT TO TAMP DOWN THE VOICES SHE'S HEARING.
"WITH A *CLEARER MIND,* SHE'LL HAVE A MUCH BETTER CHANCE AT RECOVERY."
KEEP GOING. FOLLOW ME. BRING STARK WITH YOU.
YOU JUST WANT US *DEAD,* KORVAC.

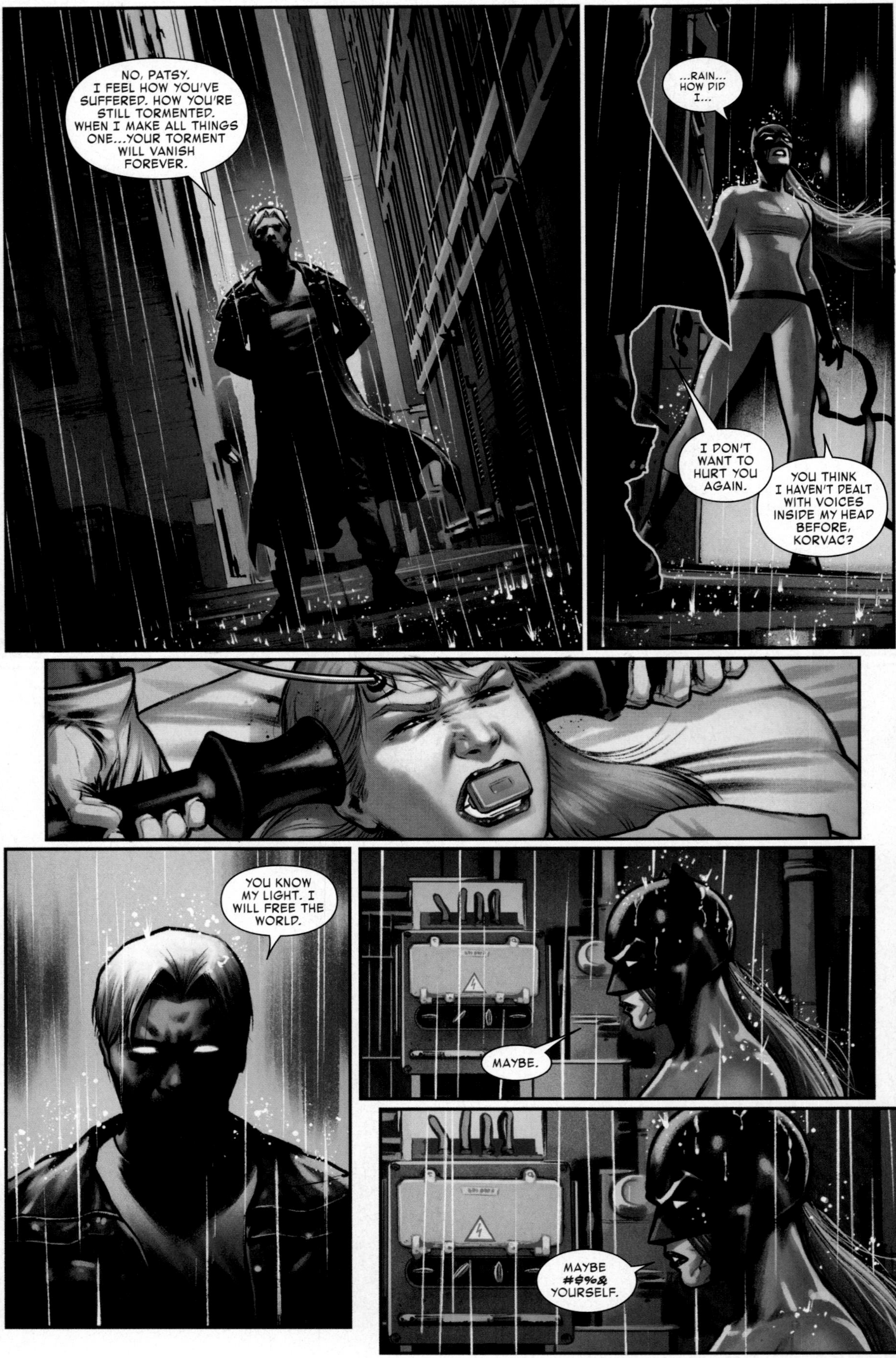
NO, PATSY. I FEEL HOW YOU'VE SUFFERED. HOW YOU'RE STILL TORMENTED. WHEN I MAKE ALL THINGS ONE...YOUR TORMENT WILL VANISH FOREVER.
...RAIN... HOW DID I...
I DON'T WANT TO HURT YOU AGAIN.
YOU THINK I HAVEN'T DEALT WITH VOICES INSIDE MY HEAD BEFORE, KORVAC?
YOU KNOW MY LIGHT. I WILL FREE THE WORLD.
MAYBE.
MAYBE #$%& YOURSELF.

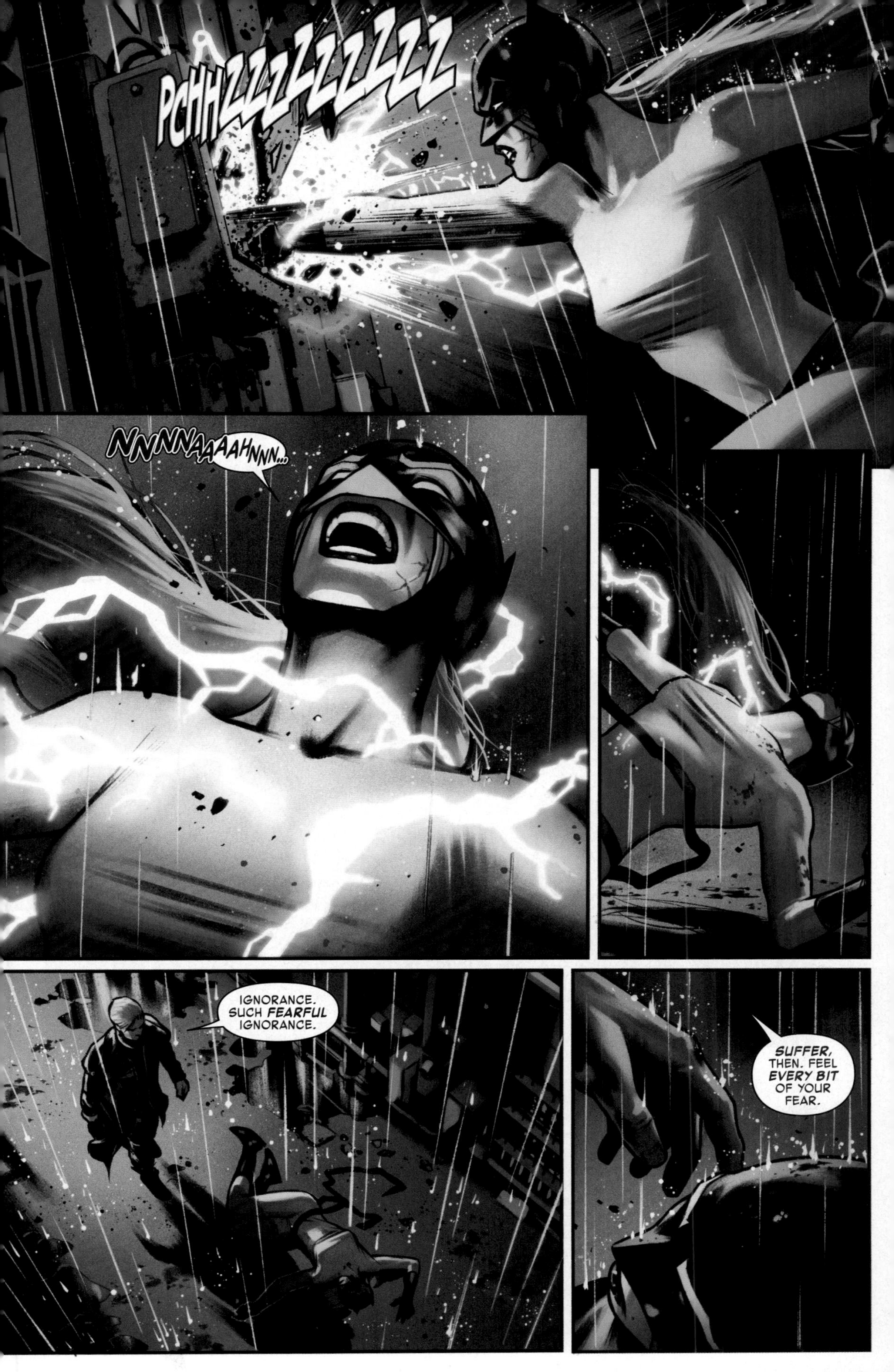

PCHHZZZZZZZZZ
NNNNAAAAHNNN...
IGNORANCE. SUCH FEARFUL IGNORANCE.
SUFFER, THEN. FEEL EVERY BIT OF YOUR FEAR.

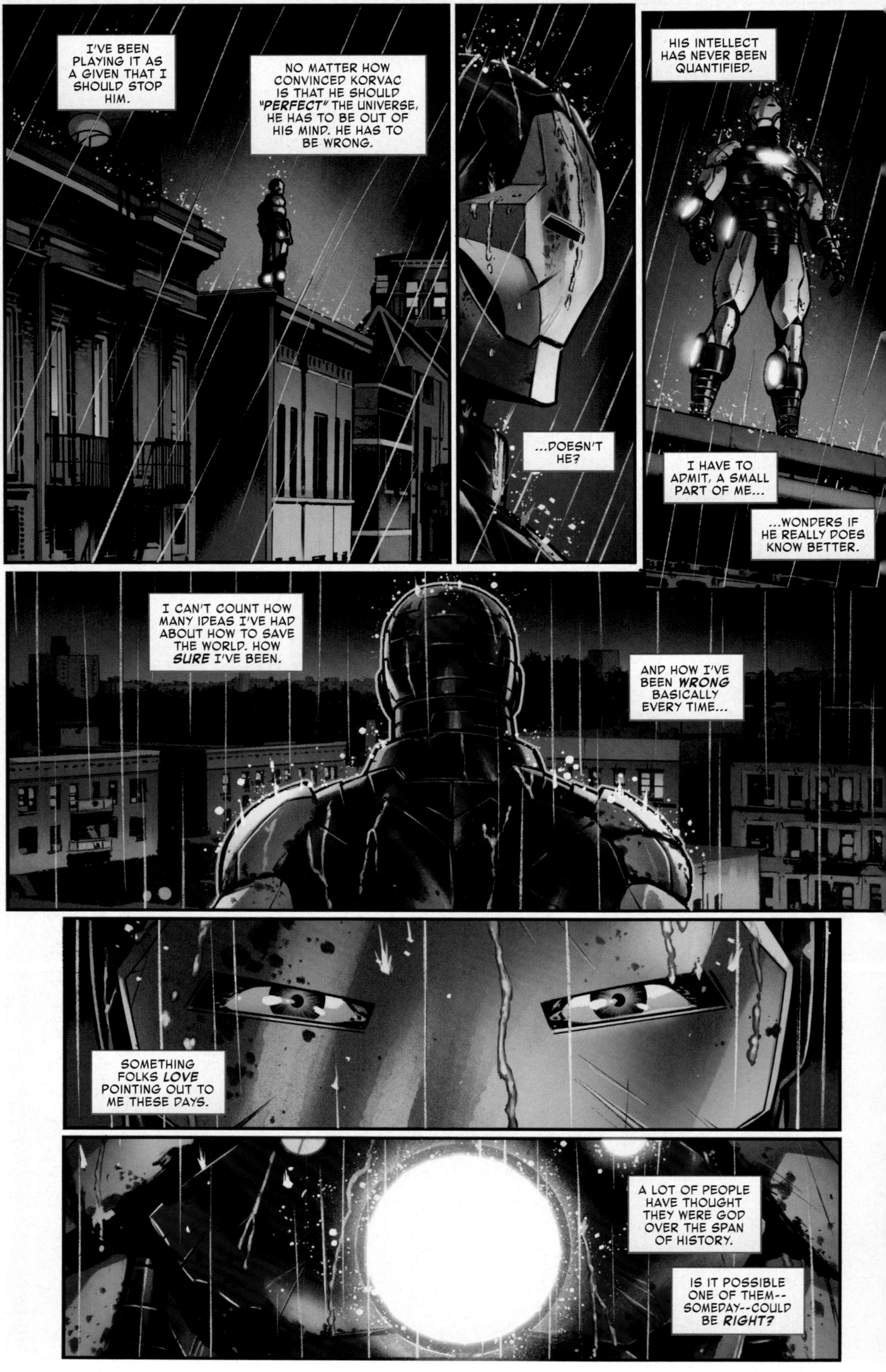
I'VE BEEN PLAYING IT AS A GIVEN THAT I SHOULD STOP HIM.
NO MATTER HOW CONVINCED KORVAC IS THAT HE SHOULD "PERFECT" THE UNIVERSE, HE HAS TO BE OUT OF HIS MIND. HE HAS TO BE WRONG.
...DOESN'T HE?
HIS INTELLECT HAS NEVER BEEN QUANTIFIED.
I HAVE TO ADMIT, A SMALL PART OF ME...
...WONDERS IF HE REALLY DOES KNOW BETTER.
I CAN'T COUNT HOW MANY IDEAS I'VE HAD ABOUT HOW TO SAVE THE WORLD. HOW SURE I'VE BEEN.
AND HOW I'VE BEEN WRONG BASICALLY EVERY TIME...
SOMETHING FOLKS LOVE POINTING OUT TO ME THESE DAYS.
A LOT OF PEOPLE HAVE THOUGHT THEY WERE GOD OVER THE SPAN OF HISTORY.
IS IT POSSIBLE ONE OF THEM--SOMEDAY--COULD BE RIGHT?

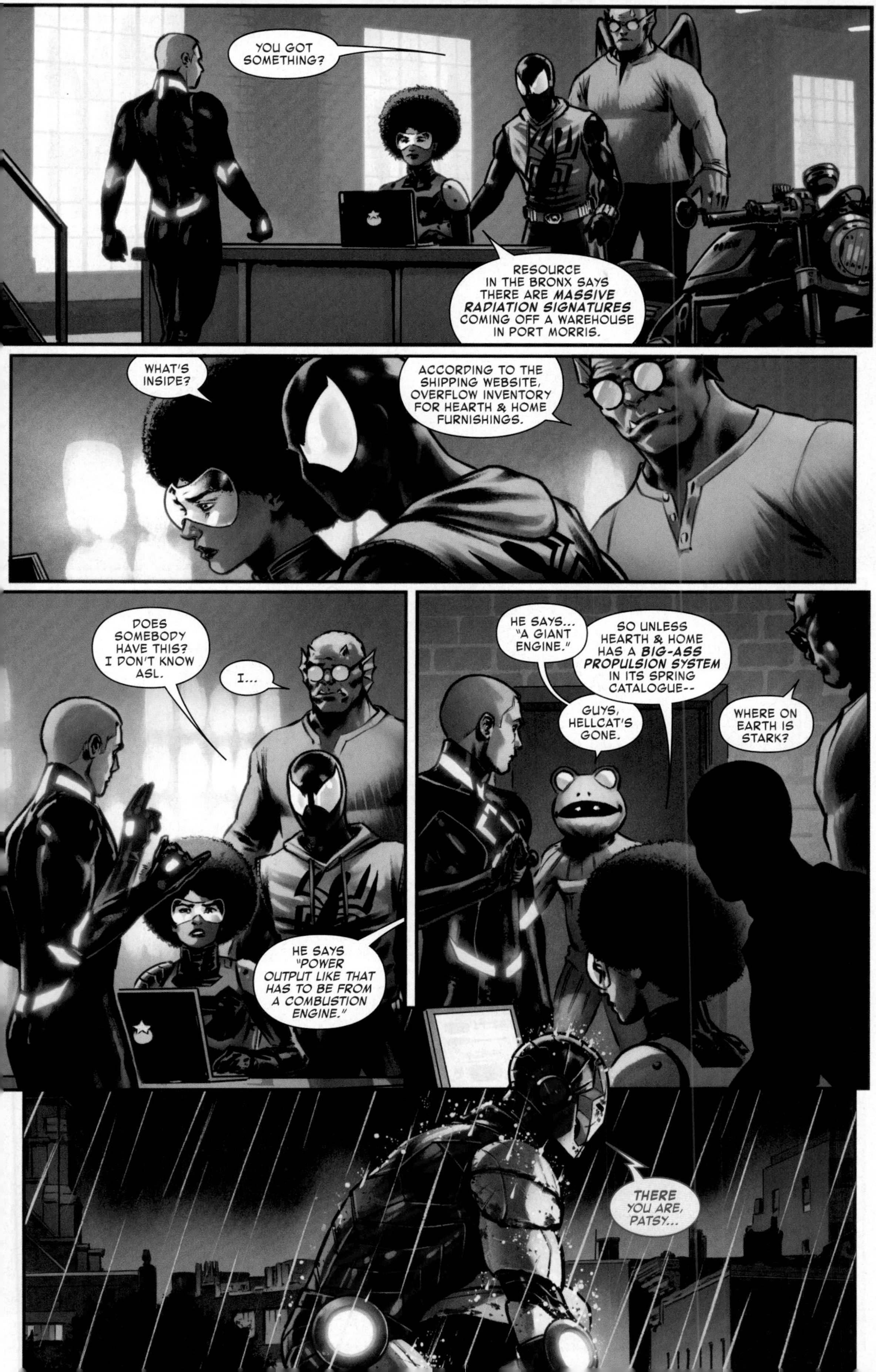
YOU GOT SOMETHING?
RESOURCE IN THE BRONX SAYS THERE ARE MASSIVE RADIATION SIGNATURES COMING OFF A WAREHOUSE IN PORT MORRIS.
WHAT'S INSIDE?
ACCORDING TO THE SHIPPING WEBSITE, OVERFLOW INVENTORY FOR HEARTH & HOME FURNISHINGS.
DOES SOMEBODY HAVE THIS? I DON'T KNOW ASL.
I...
HE SAYS "POWER OUTPUT LIKE THAT HAS TO BE FROM A COMBUSTION ENGINE."
HE SAYS... "A GIANT ENGINE."
SO UNLESS HEARTH & HOME HAS A BIG-ASS PROPULSION SYSTEM IN ITS SPRING CATALOGUE--
GUYS, HELLCAT'S GONE.
WHERE ON EARTH IS STARK?
THERE YOU ARE, PATSY...

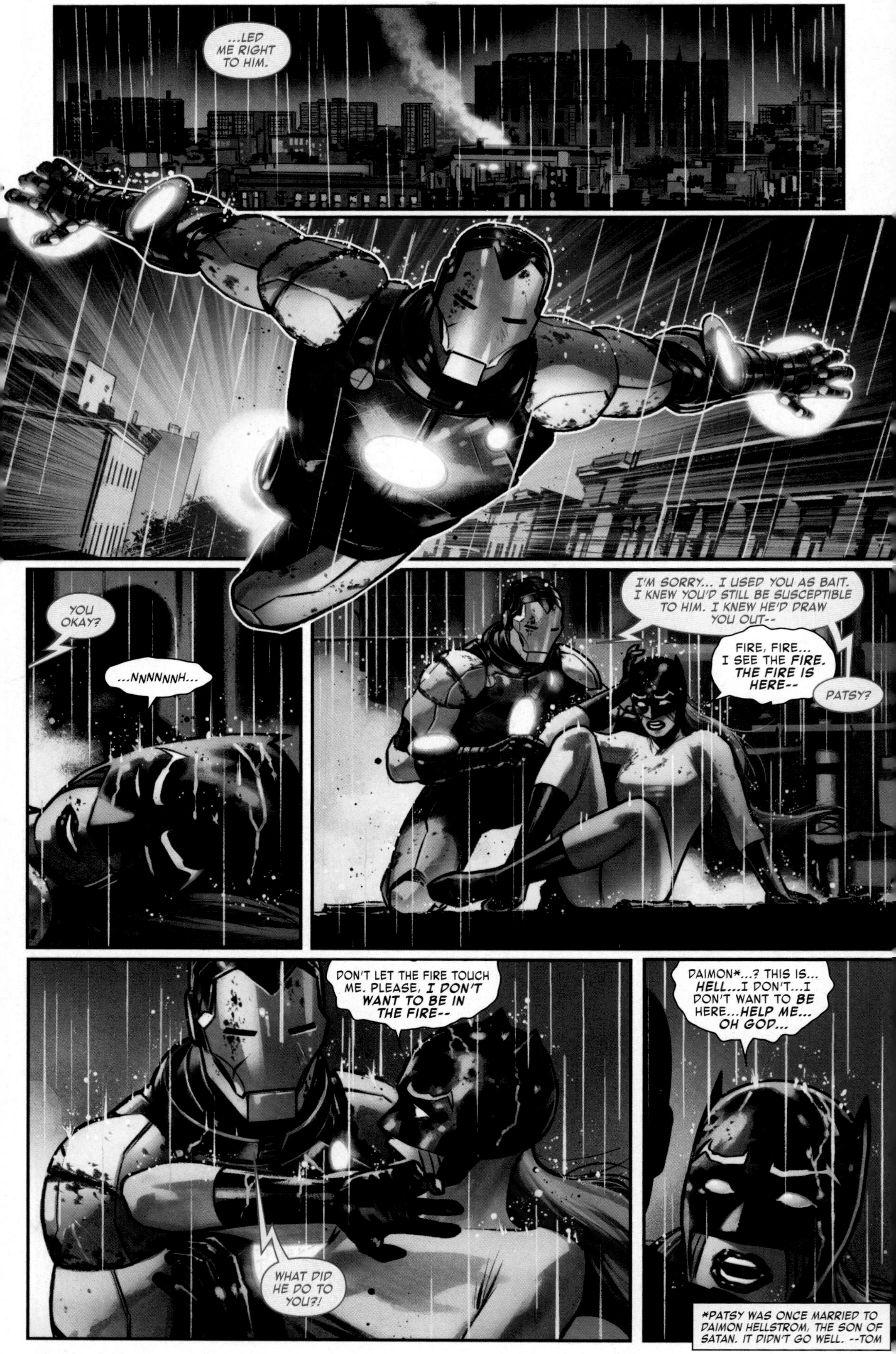
...LED ME RIGHT TO HIM.
YOU OKAY?
...NNNNNNH...
I'M SORRY... I USED YOU AS BAIT. I KNEW YOU'D STILL BE SUSCEPTIBLE TO HIM. I KNEW HE'D DRAW YOU OUT--
FIRE, FIRE... I SEE THE FIRE. THE FIRE IS HERE--
PATSY?
DON'T LET THE FIRE TOUCH ME. PLEASE, I DON'T WANT TO BE IN THE FIRE--
WHAT DID HE DO TO YOU?!
DAIMON*...? THIS IS... HELL...I DON'T...I DON'T WANT TO BE HERE...HELP ME... OH GOD...
*PATSY WAS ONCE MARRIED TO DAIMON HELLSTROM, THE SON OF SATAN. IT DIDN'T GO WELL. --TOM

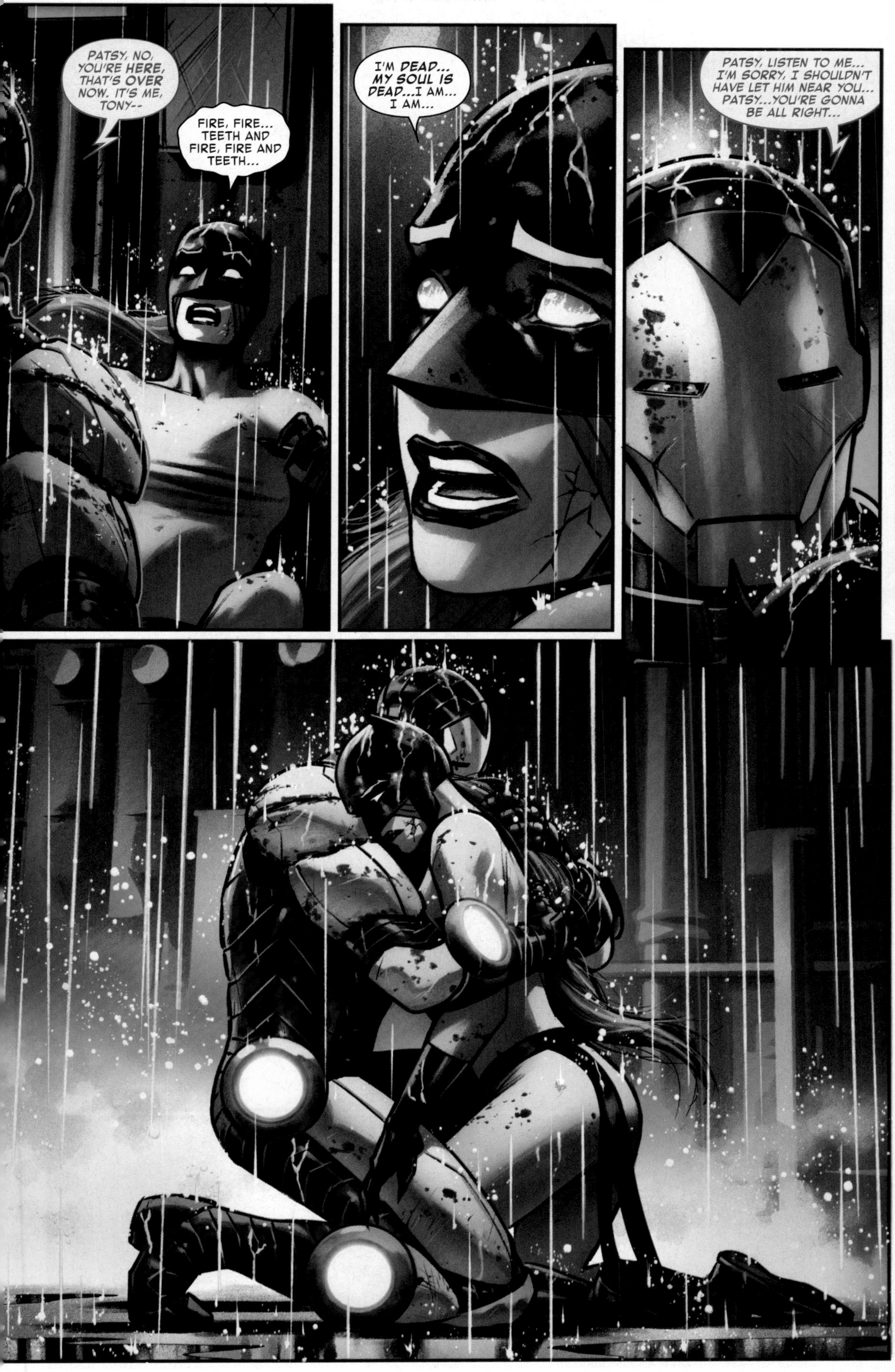
PATSY, NO, YOU'RE HERE, THAT'S OVER NOW. IT'S ME, TONY--
FIRE, FIRE... TEETH AND FIRE, FIRE AND TEETH...
I'M DEAD... MY SOUL IS DEAD...I AM... I AM...
PATSY, LISTEN TO ME... I'M SORRY, I SHOULDN'T HAVE LET HIM NEAR YOU... PATSY...YOU'RE GONNA BE ALL RIGHT...

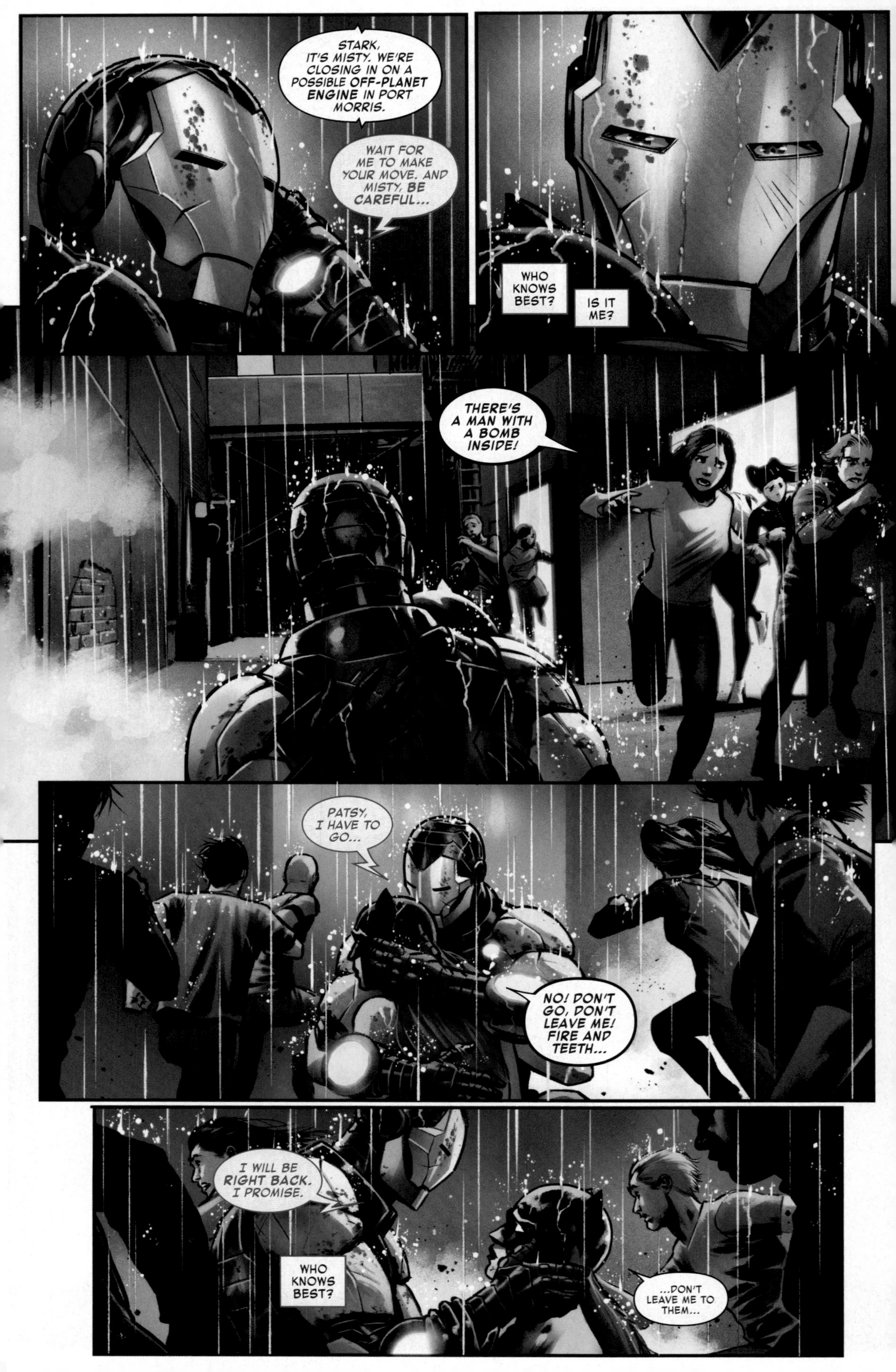
STARK, IT'S MISTY. WE'RE CLOSING IN ON A POSSIBLE OFF-PLANET ENGINE IN PORT MORRIS.
WAIT FOR ME TO MAKE YOUR MOVE. AND MISTY, BE CAREFUL...
WHO KNOWS BEST?
IS IT ME?
THERE'S A MAN WITH A BOMB INSIDE!
PATSY, I HAVE TO GO...
NO! DON'T GO, DON'T LEAVE ME! FIRE AND TEETH...
I WILL BE RIGHT BACK. I PROMISE.
WHO KNOWS BEST?
...DON'T LEAVE ME TO THEM...

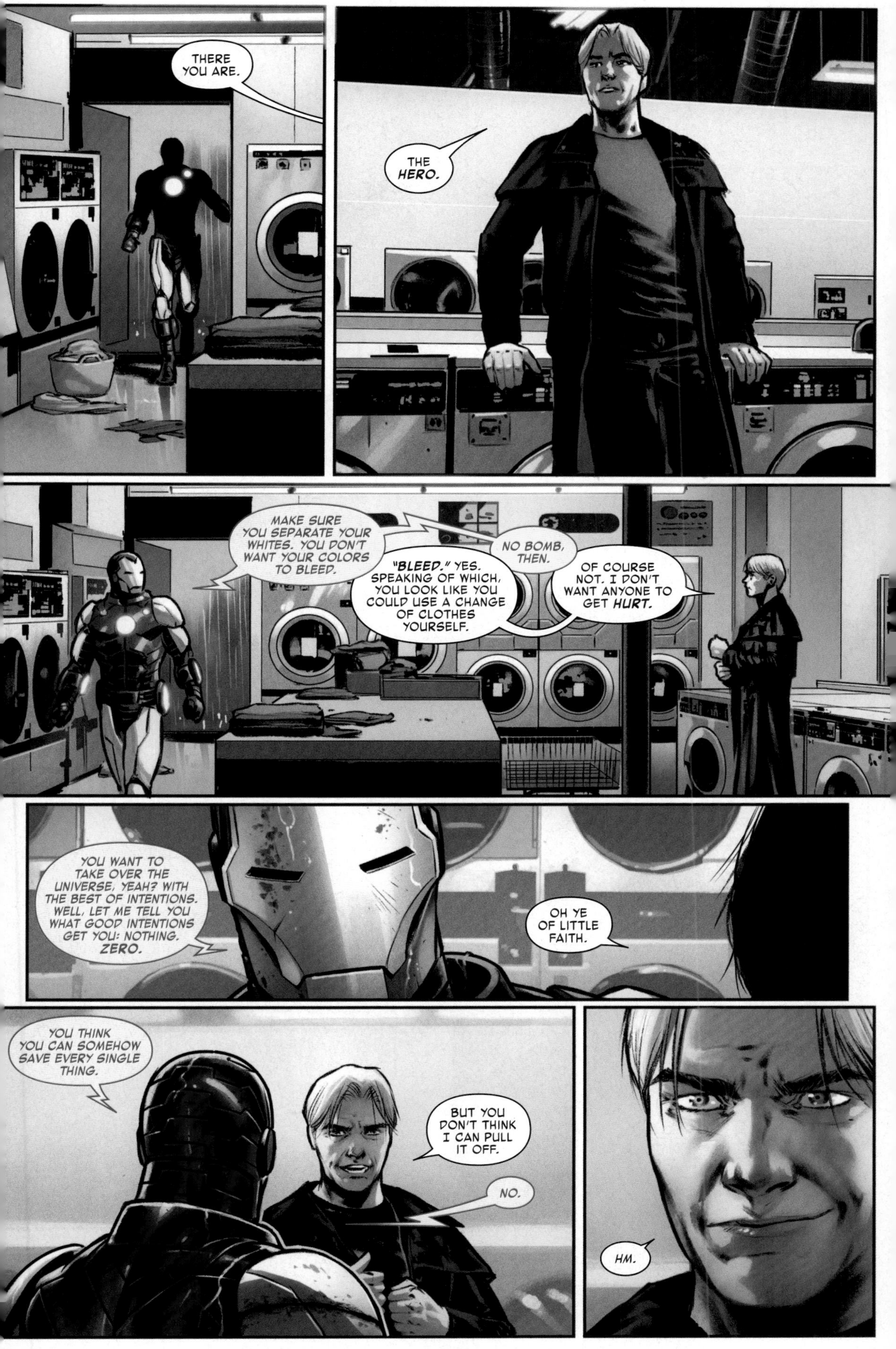
THERE YOU ARE.
THE HERO.
MAKE SURE YOU SEPARATE YOUR WHITES. YOU DON'T WANT YOUR COLORS TO BLEED.
NO BOMB, THEN.
"BLEED." YES. SPEAKING OF WHICH, YOU LOOK LIKE YOU COULD USE A CHANGE OF CLOTHES YOURSELF.
OF COURSE NOT. I DON'T WANT ANYONE TO GET HURT.
YOU WANT TO TAKE OVER THE UNIVERSE, YEAH? WITH THE BEST OF INTENTIONS. WELL, LET ME TELL YOU WHAT GOOD INTENTIONS GET YOU: NOTHING. ZERO.
OH YE OF LITTLE FAITH.
YOU THINK YOU CAN SOMEHOW SAVE EVERY SINGLE THING.
BUT YOU DON'T THINK I CAN PULL IT OFF.
NO.
HM.

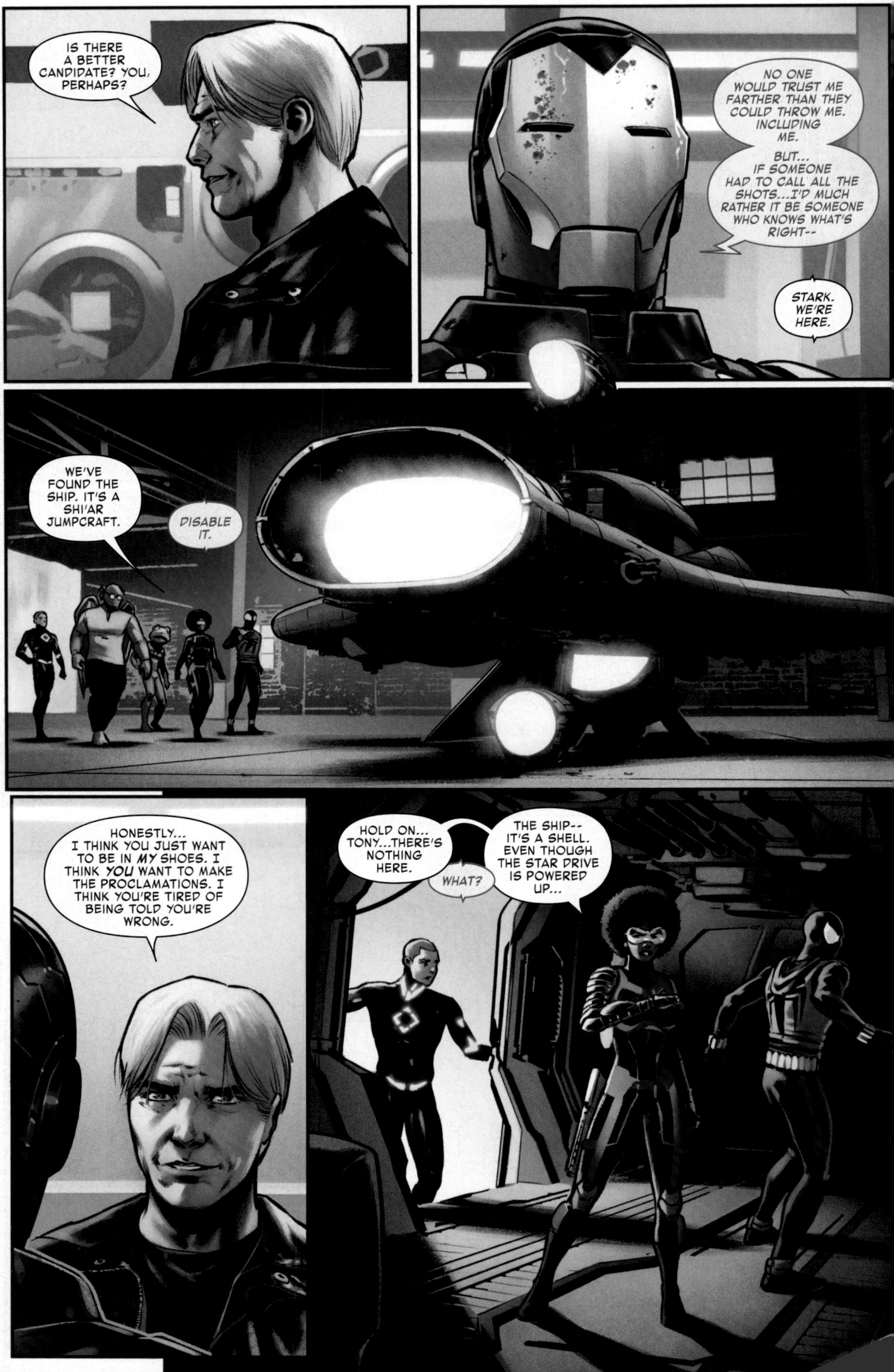
IS THERE A BETTER CANDIDATE? YOU, PERHAPS?
NO ONE WOULD TRUST ME FARTHER THAN THEY COULD THROW ME. INCLUDING ME.
BUT... IF SOMEONE HAD TO CALL ALL THE SHOTS...I'D MUCH RATHER IT BE SOMEONE WHO KNOWS WHAT'S RIGHT--
STARK. WE'RE HERE.
WE'VE FOUND THE SHIP. IT'S A SHI'AR JUMPCRAFT.
DISABLE IT.
HONESTLY... I THINK YOU JUST WANT TO BE IN MY SHOES. I THINK YOU WANT TO MAKE THE PROCLAMATIONS. I THINK YOU'RE TIRED OF BEING TOLD YOU'RE WRONG.
HOLD ON... TONY...THERE'S NOTHING HERE.
THE SHIP-- IT'S A SHELL. EVEN THOUGH THE STAR DRIVE IS POWERED UP...
WHAT?

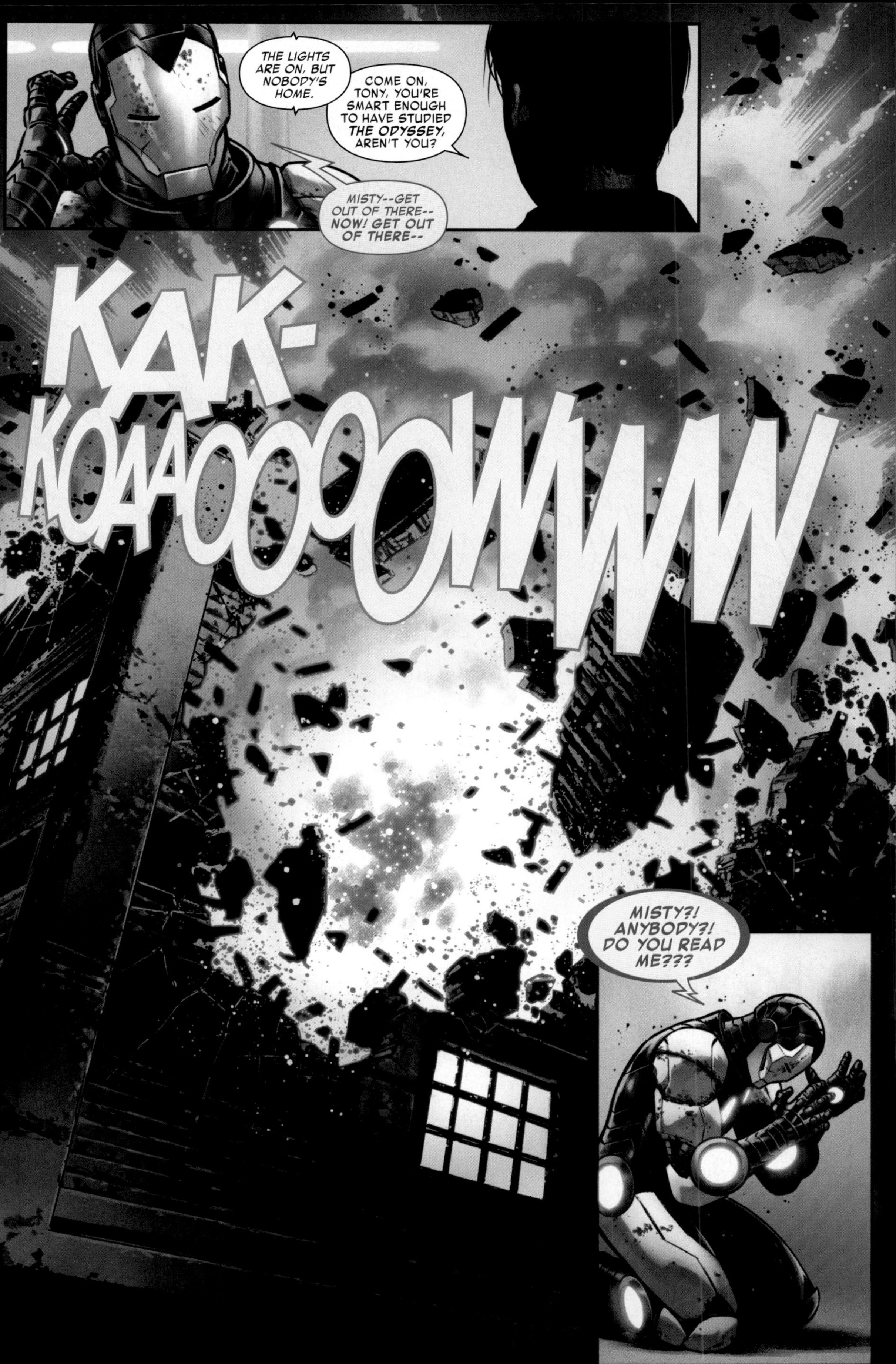
THE LIGHTS ARE ON, BUT NOBODY'S HOME.
COME ON, TONY, YOU'RE SMART ENOUGH TO HAVE STUDIED *THE ODYSSEY*, AREN'T YOU?
MISTY--GET OUT OF THERE-- NOW! GET OUT OF THERE--
KAK-KOAAOOOOWWW
MISTY?! ANYBODY?! DO YOU READ ME???

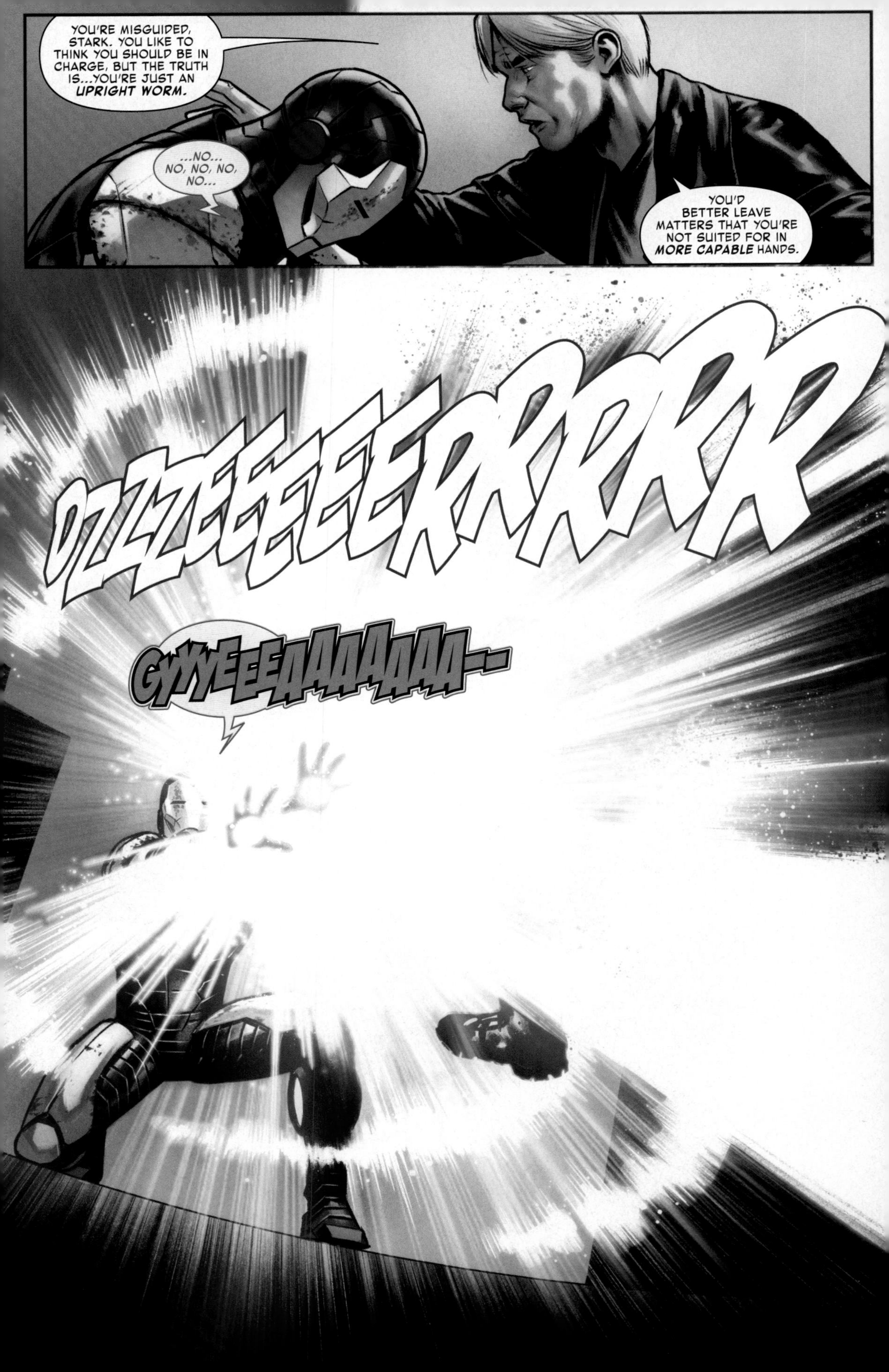
YOU'RE MISGUIDED, STARK. YOU LIKE TO THINK YOU SHOULD BE IN CHARGE, BUT THE TRUTH IS...YOU'RE JUST AN *UPRIGHT WORM.*
...NO... NO, NO, NO, NO...
YOU'D BETTER LEAVE MATTERS THAT YOU'RE NOT SUITED FOR IN *MORE CAPABLE* HANDS.
DZZEEEEERRRRP
GYYEEAAAAAA--

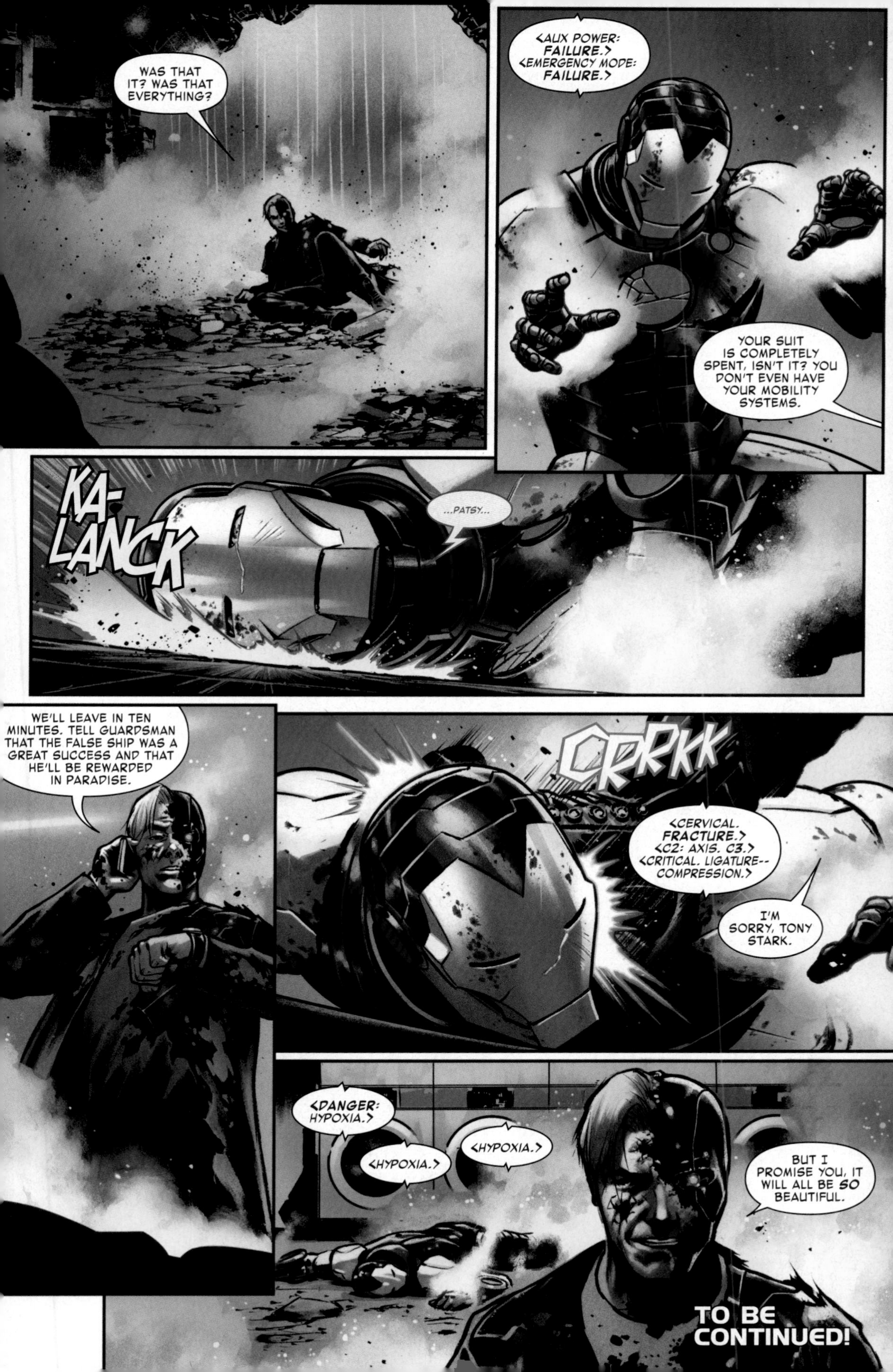
WAS THAT IT? WAS THAT EVERYTHING?
<AUX POWER: FAILURE.> <EMERGENCY MODE: FAILURE.>
YOUR SUIT IS COMPLETELY SPENT, ISN'T IT? YOU DON'T EVEN HAVE YOUR MOBILITY SYSTEMS.
KA-LANCK
...PATSY...
WE'LL LEAVE IN TEN MINUTES. TELL GUARDSMAN THAT THE FALSE SHIP WAS A GREAT SUCCESS AND THAT HE'LL BE REWARDED IN PARADISE.
CRRKK
<CERVICAL. FRACTURE.> <C2: AXIS. C3.> <CRITICAL. LIGATURE-- COMPRESSION.>
I'M SORRY, TONY STARK.
<DANGER: HYPOXIA.>
<HYPOXIA.>
<HYPOXIA.>
BUT I PROMISE YOU, IT WILL ALL BE SO BEAUTIFUL.
TO BE CONTINUED!

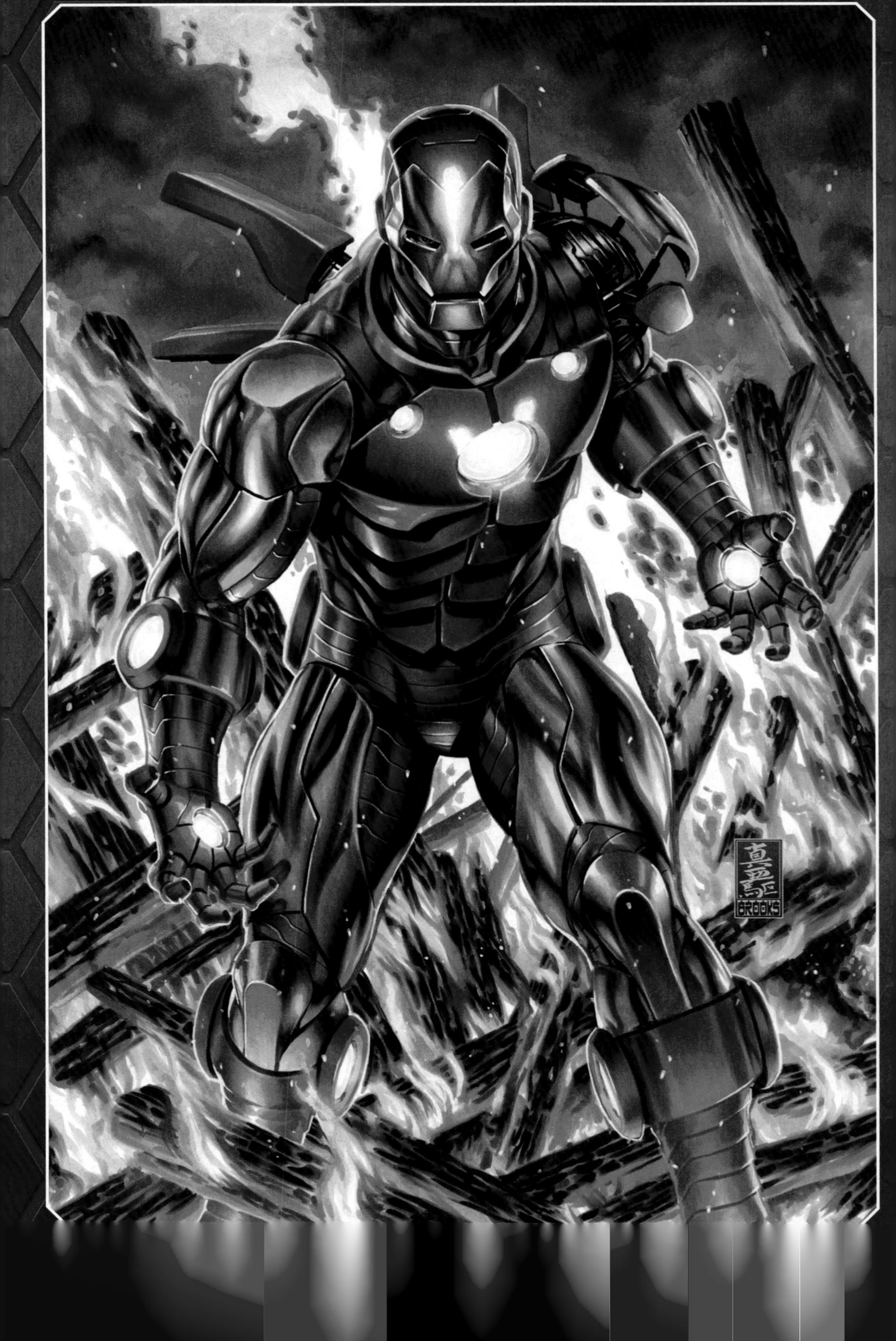
BROOKS

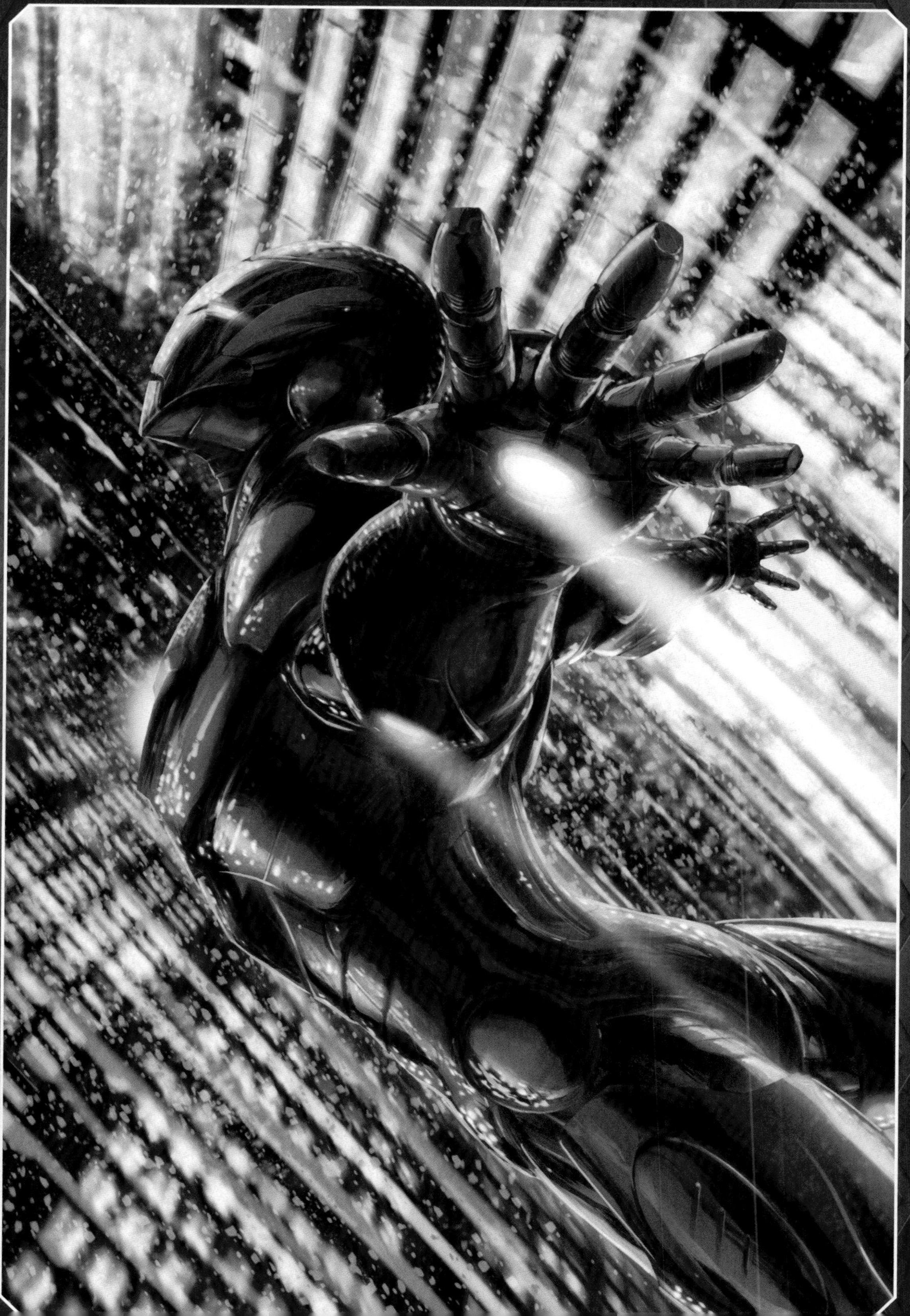

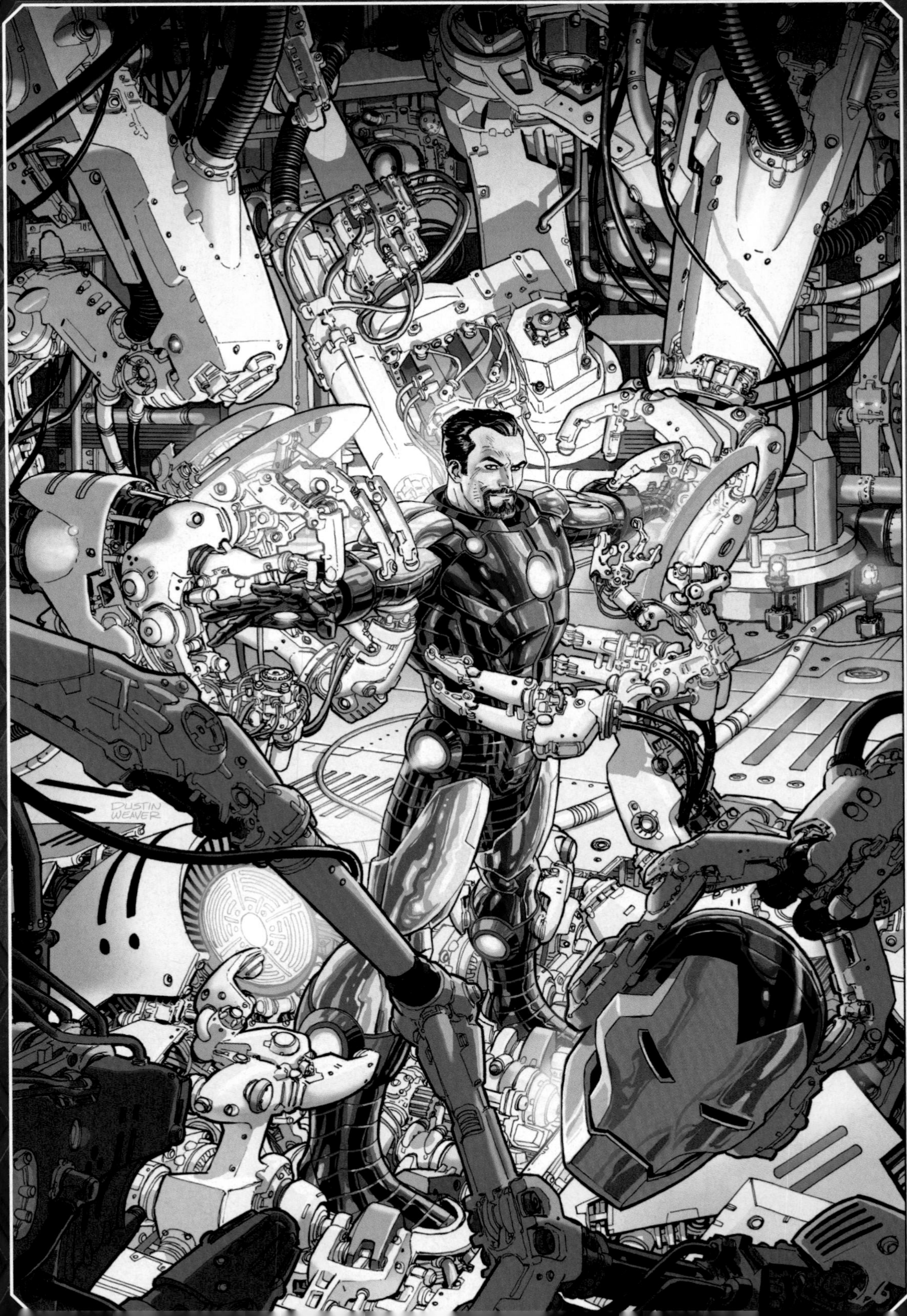
DUSTIN
WEAVER

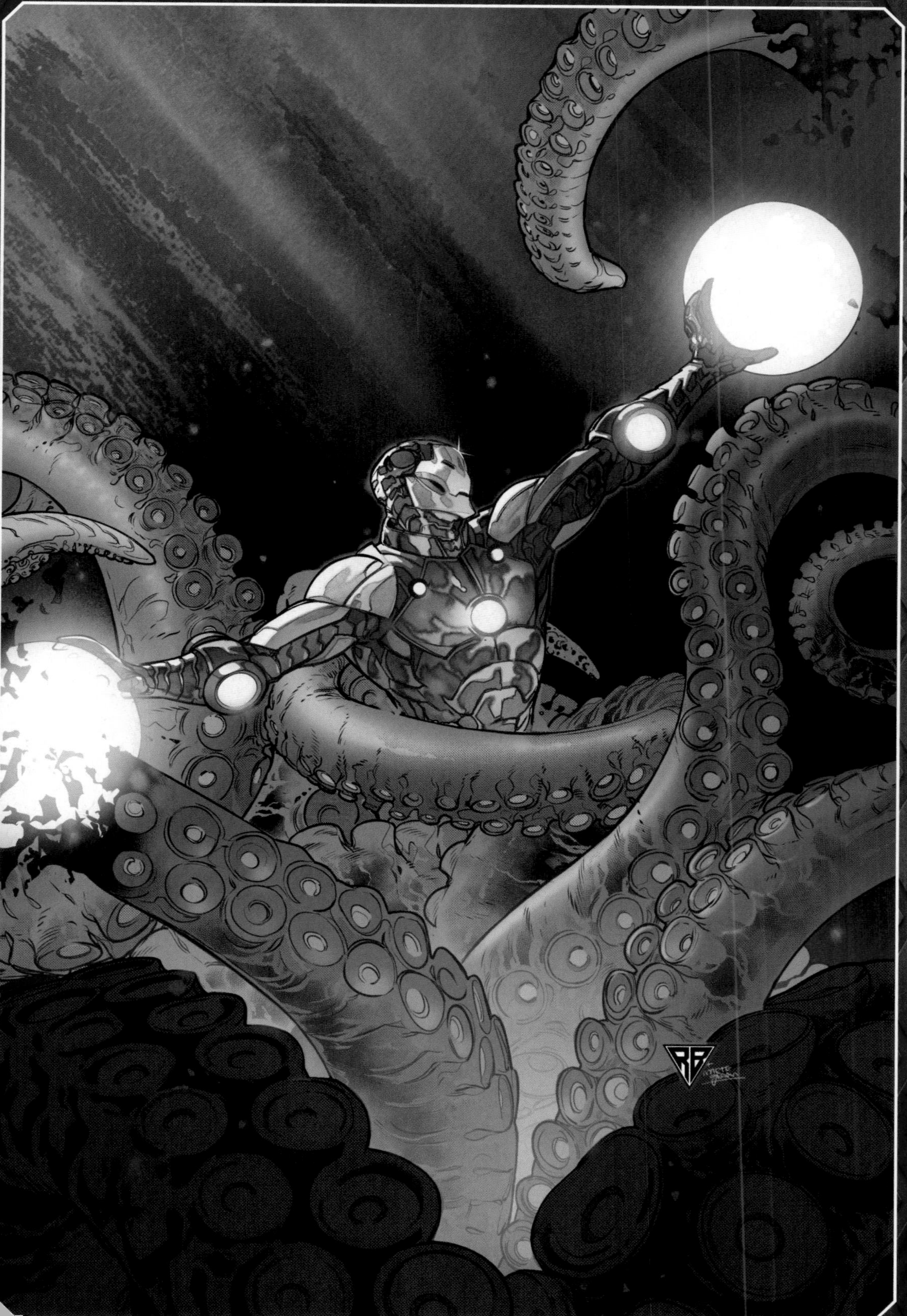

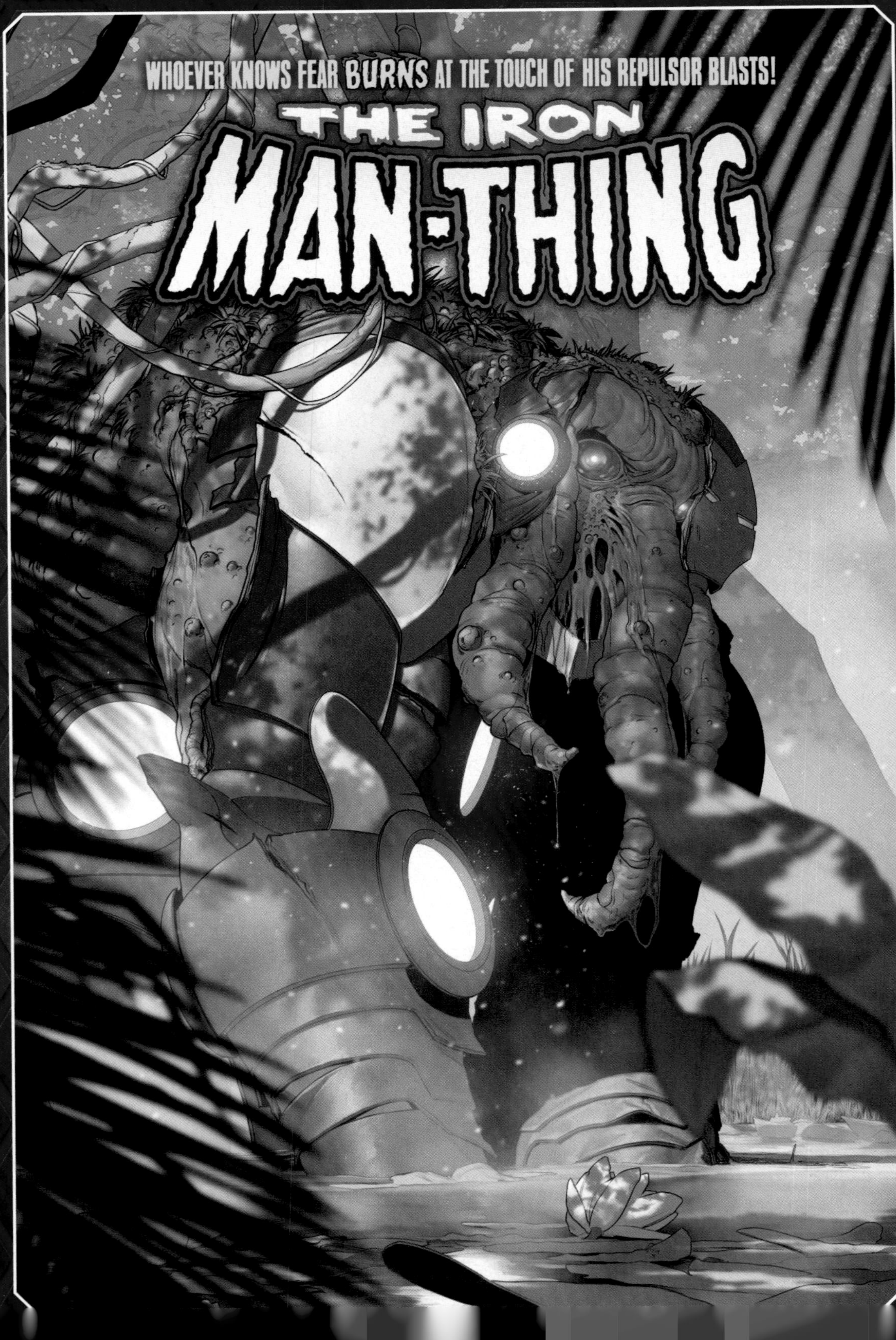
WHOEVER KNOWS FEAR BURNS AT THE TOUCH OF HIS REPULSOR BLASTS!
THE IRON
MAN-THING

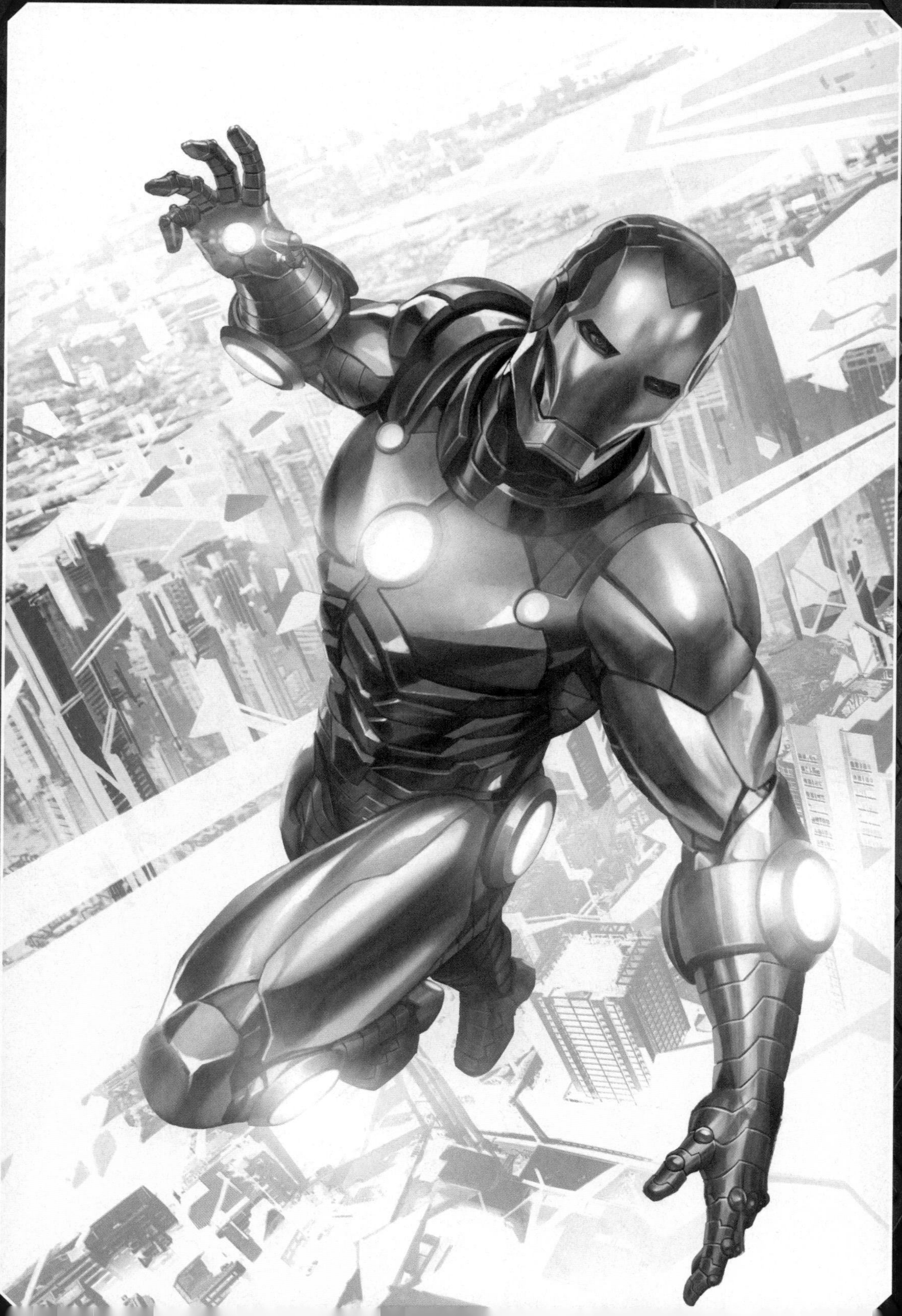

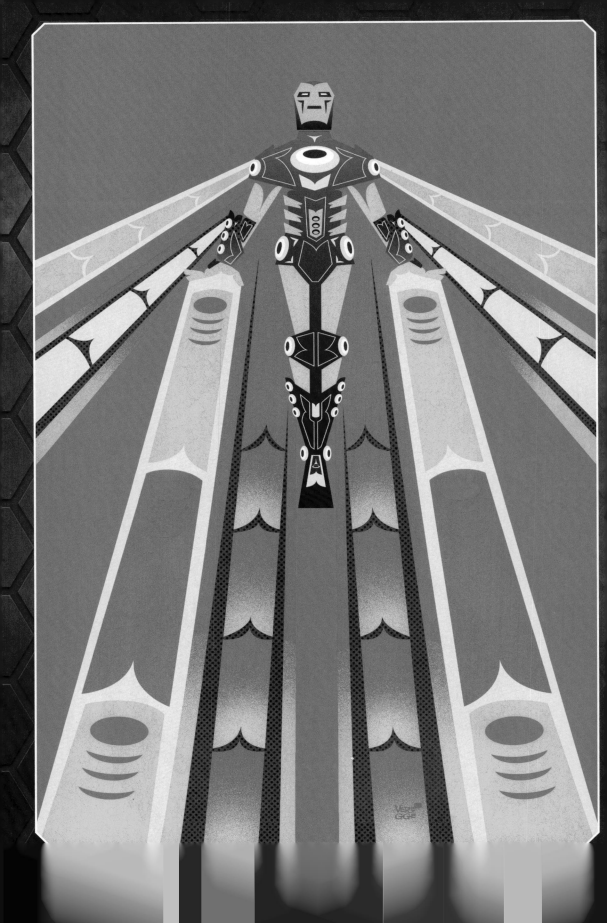

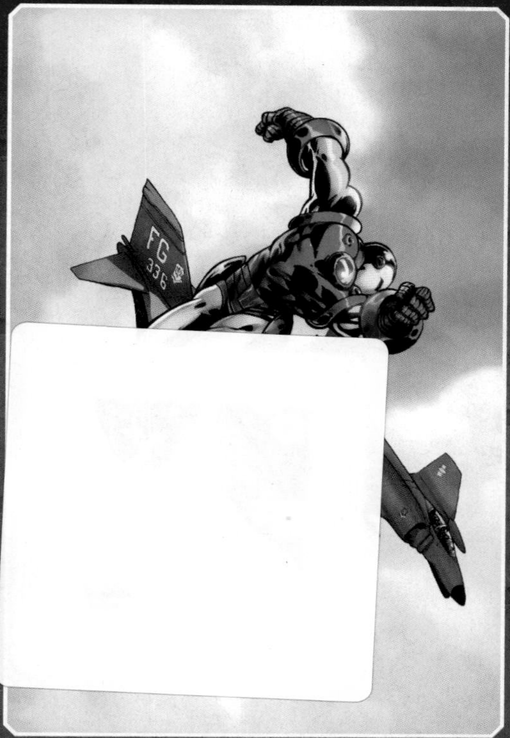

RICK LEONARDI & JASON KEITH
1 VARIANT

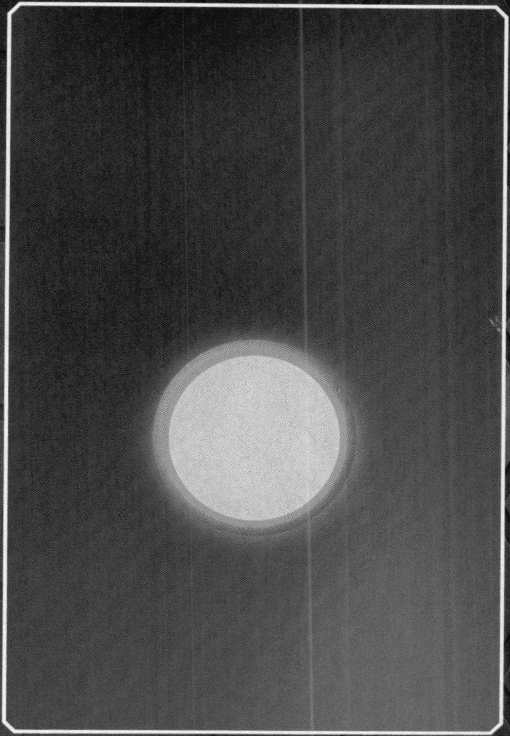

1 RED & GOLD VARIANT

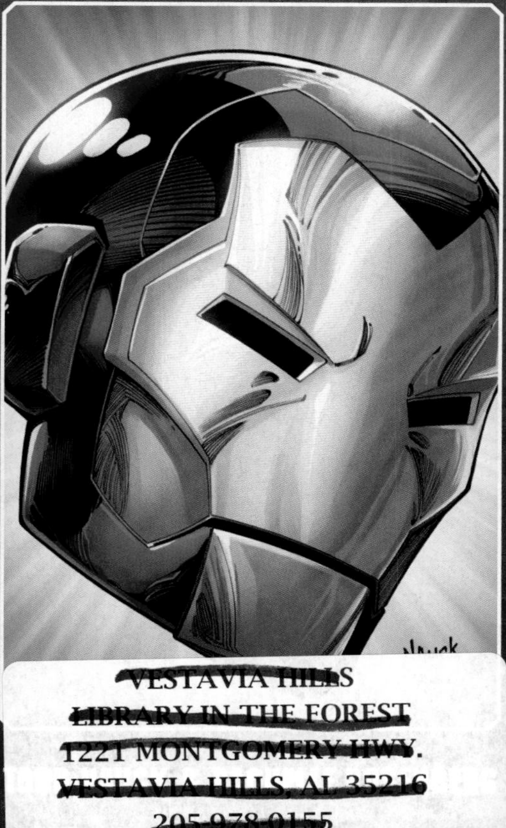

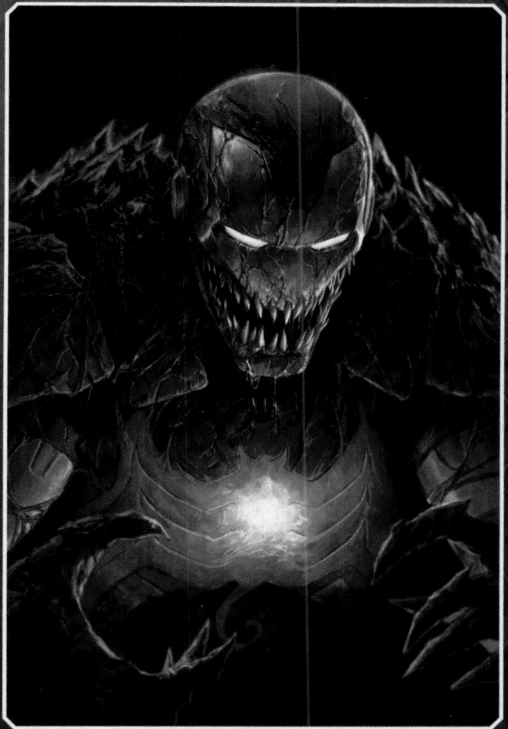

DAVE RAPOZA
4 KNULLIFIED VARIANT

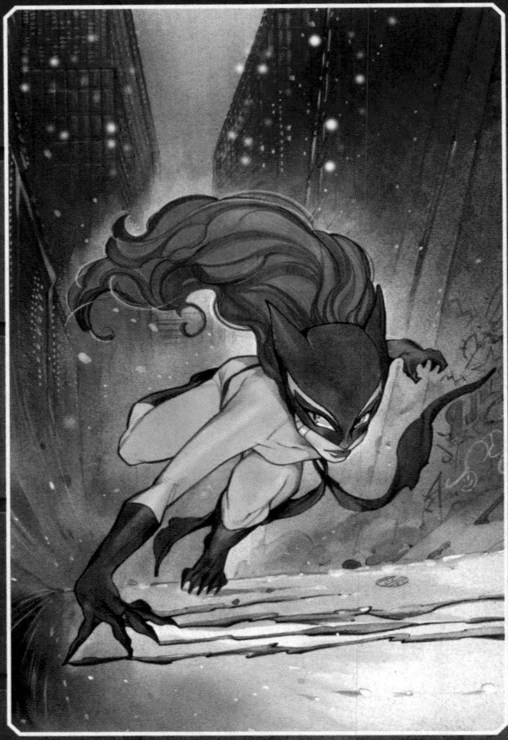

PEACH MOMOKO
4 STORMBREAKERS VARIANT

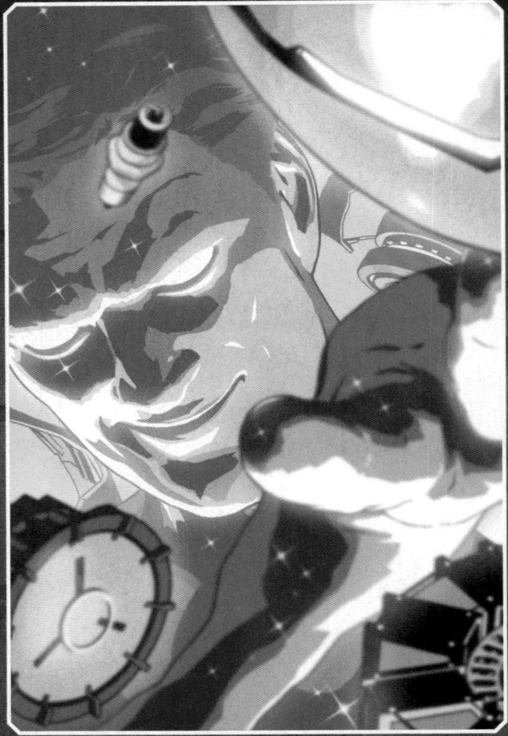

ACO
5 VARIANT

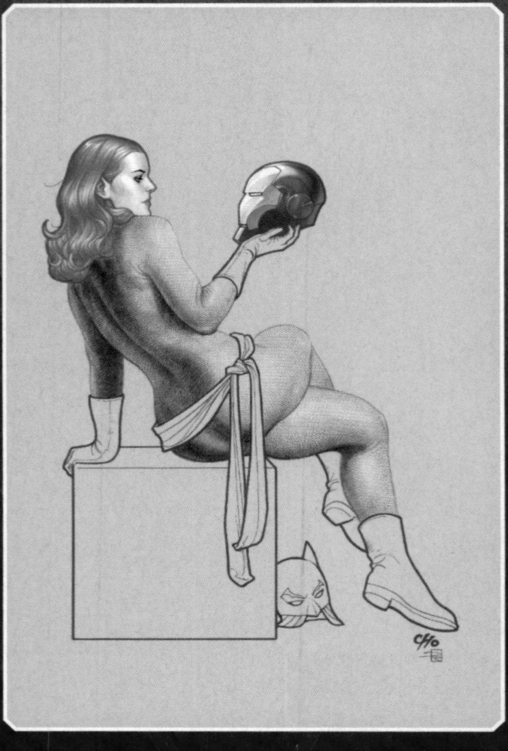

FRANK CHO & SABINE RICH
5 VARIANT